Conversations with Wole Soyinka

Edited by
Biodun Jeyifo

University Press of Mississippi
Jackson

www.upress.state.ms.us

Copyright © 2001 by University Press of Mississippi
Manufactured in the United States of America

09   08   07   06   05   04   03   02   01   4   3   2   1
⊗
Library of Congress Cataloging-in-Publication Data

Soyinka, Wole.
    Conversations with Wole Soyinka / edited by Biodun Jeyifo.
        p. cm.—(Literary conversations series)
    Includes bibliographical references and index.
    ISBN 1-57806-337-X (cloth : alk. paper)—ISBN 1-57806-338-8 (pbk. : alk. paper)
    1. Soyinka, Wole—Interviews.   2. Authors, Nigerian—20th century—Interviews.   3.
Nigeria—In literature.   I. Jeyifo, Biodun, 1946–   II. Title.   III. Series.

    PR9387.9.S6 Z464   2001
    822'.914—dc21
    [B]   00-049526

British Library Cataloging-in-Publication Data available

Books by Wole Soyinka

The House of Banigeji (dramatic fragment) in *Reflections: Nigerian Prose and Verse*. Ed. Frances Ademola. Lagos: African Universities Press, 1962.

The Lion and the Jewel (drama). London: Oxford University Press, 1963.

A Dance of the Forests (drama). London: Oxford University Press, 1963.

Three Plays: The Swamp Dwellers, The Trials of Brother Jero and The Strong Breed. Ibadan: Mbari Publications. Re-published as *Three Short Plays*. London: Oxford University Press, 1969.

Five Plays: A Dance of the Forests, The Lion and the Jewel, The Swamp Dwellers, The Trials of Brother Jero and The Strong Breed. London: Oxford University Press, 1964.

The Interpreters (novel). London: Andre Deutsch, 1965.

The Road (drama). London: Oxford University Press, 1965.

Kongi's Harvest (drama). London: Oxford University Press, 1967.

Idanre and Other Poems. London: Methuen, 1967.

The Forest of a Thousand Daemons: A Hunter's Saga. Translation of Yoruba novel, *Ogboju Ode Ninu Igbo Irunmale* by D. O. Fagunwa. London: Nelson, 1968.

Poems from Prison. London: Rex Collings, 1969.

Before the Blackout (revue sketches). Ibadan: Orisun Editions, 1971.

A Shuttle in the Crypt (poetry). London: Rex Collings/Methuen, 1971.

Madmen and Specialists (drama). London: Methuen, 1971.

The Man Died (prison memoir). London: Rex Collings, 1972.

The Bacchae of Euripides: A Communion Rite (drama). London: Methuen, 1973.

Camwood on the Leaves (radio drama). London: Methuen, 1973.

Collected Plays, Vol. 1. London: Oxford University Press, 1973.

The Jero Plays (*The Trials of Brother Jero* and *Jero's Metamorphosis*). London: Methuen, 1973.

Season of Anomy (novel). London: Rex Collings, 1973.

Collected Plays, Vol. 2. London: Oxford University Press, 1974.

Death and the King's Horseman (drama). London: Methuen, 1975.

Poems of Black Africa (edited anthology). London: Secker and Warburg, 1975.

Myth, Literature and the African World (criticism). Cambridge: Cambridge University Press, 1976.

Ogun Abibiman (poetry). London: Rex Collings, 1976.

Aké: The Years of Childhood (autobiography). London: Rex Collings, 1981.

Opera Wonyosi (drama). London: Rex Collings, 1981.

A Play of Giants (drama). London: Methuen, 1984.

Six Plays. London: Methuen, 1984.

Requiem for a Futurologist (drama). London: Rex Collings, 1985.

Mandela's Earth and Other Poems. New York: Random House, 1988.

Art, Dialogue and Outrage: Essays on Literature and Culture. (Edited by Biodun Jeyifo.) Ibadan: New Horn Press, 1988.

Isara: A Voyage Around "Essay" (memoir). New York: Random House, 1989.

From Zia with Love and A Scourge of Hyacinths (dramas). London: Methuen, 1992.

Ibadan: The "Penkelemes" Years, A Memoir, 1946–1965 (memoir). London: Methuen, 1994.

The Beatification of Area Boy: A Lagosian Kaleidoscope (drama). London: Methuen, 1995.
The Open Sore of a Continent: A Personal Narrative of the Nigerian Crisis (political and philosophical reflection). New York: Oxford University Press, 1996.
The Burden of Memory, the Muse of Forgiveness (political and philosophical reflection, literary criticism). New York: Oxford University Press, 1999.

Contents

Introduction

The citation for Soyinka's 1986 Nobel prize for literature reads: "Who in a wide cultural perspective and with poetic overtones, fashions the drama of existence.'' The "wide cultural perspective" mentioned refers to the fact that Soyinka's writings, especially the dramas for which he is best known, are at once deeply rooted in traditional African expressive and performance forms like myths and rituals, dance and mime, music and masqueradery and are also greatly influenced by such diverse Western dramatic and theatrical models as classical Greek drama, Shakespearian and Jacobean theatre, and modern European and American antirealist and avant-garde forms and techniques.

This dual heritage is one that Soyinka readily admits, but he insists that the roots of his art are in African sources, especially the elaborate body of myths and rituals through which African communities have codified and continue to express a heightened perception of existence and its mysteries, challenges, and possibilities. Indeed, we hear this insistence ringing through clearly and confidently in the first press conference that Soyinka attended in Paris after the announcement of the Nobel award:

> I have not been able to accept the prize on a personal level . . . I accept it as a tribute to the heritage of African literature which is very little known in the West. I regard it as a statement of respect and acknowledgement of the long years and centuries of denigration and ignorance of the heritage which all of us have been trying to build . . . I'm part of the whole literary tradition of Africa. The prize is for all my colleagues who are just as qualified to win it as I. I see myself as part of their collective reality. [*New York Times,* 17 October 1986]

The fact that Soyinka evidently saw the moment of world attention on his own writing as an occasion to focus that attention on the *collective* tradition of modern African literature is completely consistent with the advocacy and solicitude which he has always expressed for the health and vitality of the literary phenomenon in postindependence, postcolonial Africa, from his earliest published critical essay, "The Future of African Writing" through later essays and books like "From a Common Back Cloth: A Reassessment of the

African Literary Image," "The Writer in a Modern African State," and *Myth, Literature and the African World,* to his most recent book of literary criticism and philosophical reflection, *The Burden of Memory, the Muse of Forgiveness.* But it is also the case that though there are different "schools" of writing in modern African literature, Soyinka's writings in a way compositely straddle these "schools," and this makes his corpus peculiarly central to a sense of the wholeness or totality of modern African literature.

Soyinka's greatest creative writings and essays are generally thought to be very complex and often obscure in language, style, and technique. By contrast, writers like Chinua Achebe, Ngugi wa Thiong'o, Ama Ata Aidoo, and Ousmane Sembene are thought to write in language and styles that are more accessible, more representative of common experiences and sensibilities of life in general in contemporary Africa. Moreover, Soyinka draws substantially on myths and ritual beliefs and is deeply interested in the symbolic richness of nonrational, mystical aspects of reality and experience; he constantly seeks out marginal characters and figures from what he calls the "numinous" realm: gods, spirits, demonic or possessed mystics, prophets and sages, and lunatics and fools, whether they are heads of state or village eccentrics. By contrast, writers in the other group draw their characters and situations from the actualities of history and are much closer to what is typical in the broad experience of African peoples. For want of better descriptive terms, we may designate these two schools of writing in contemporary African literature the *modernist* and *realist* schools. And on this point, it is important to note that though realism as a mode of literary representation is generally thought to be an exhausted mode in "highbrow" literary circles in the West, it is still a very powerful and much esteemed mode in many literary cultures and traditions of postcolonial Africa and the developing world where in fact it has been given new forms and shapes and new patterns of social and cultural relevance.

In reality these terms are as useful or helpful as the blurbs on the dust jacket of important works of literature: they are merely rough, oversimplified guides to works that resist oversimplification and labeling. Nothing reveals the inadequacy of these terms than the blurring of lines between the two camps in modern African literature which demonstrate that some writers from these opposing camps have more in common than those from the same camp. For example, there are more similarities between Soyinka and Ngugi in their conception of how to use formal and technical resources like satire, farce, song, folklore, and myth to enhance passionate moral and political commitment than there are between Soyinka and Leopold Sedar Senghor who both abstractly belong in the same "modernist" camp. To read Soyinka's *A Play of Giants,* a ferocious but artfully modulated satire on dictators and dictatorship, is to be reminded more of Ngugi's *Devil on the Cross,* which mixes satire, allegory, biblical symbolism, and traditional African folklore to attack the greed, corruption, and brutalities of the neocolonial African elites than of Senghor's *Nocturnes,* a formalistically distinguished volume of poems mostly concerned with exploring the poet's moods in his idealized search for his roots and identity.

This insistence on caution in applying labels to the great camps or schools of modern African literature is particularly applicable to Soyinka whose total literary output and cultural activities resist any simple schemes of classification, either of forms, themes, or subject matter. This point extends equally to "modernist" writers like Bessie Head, Femi Osofisan, Niyi Osundare, Ben Okri, and the late Dambudzo Marechera, many of whom were profoundly influenced by the protean nature of Soyinka's works. Soyinka indeed remains one of the few all-round artists in contemporary world literature. Though drama is his primary, preferred medium of expression, he is equally at home in all the other literary forms: fictional and nonfiction prose, poetry, criticism, translation. And the range of situations, characters, and human interests and sympathies that we encounter in his works is truly astounding. Some of his earlier and shorter plays, like *The Trials of Brother Jero, The Swamp Dwellers, and The Lion and the Jewel,* have become favorite vehicles of amateur and young theatre groups throughout Africa and parts of the English-speaking Caribbean; moreover, some of them have been performed in Britain and America. These plays appeal to audiences and performers everywhere because, without becoming exotic, they communicate typically African expressions of universal human idiosyncrasies, weaknesses, and perplexities. Many young actors in different parts of the English-speaking world have thrilled to the challenge of playing Brother Jero(boam), the lovable, roguish, priestly charlatan of *The Trials of Brother Jero;* or Lakunle, the schoolteacher of *The Lion and the Jewel,* the ridiculous pretender to city ways and sophistication whose ideas and tactics for "civilizing" his fellow villagers are the source of everyone's irritation and amusement. In all of these plays, as well as in the more sombre and brooding *The Swamp Dwellers* and *The Strong Breed,* we can see Soyinka more or less in the camp of the "realists" of modern African literature, with the sharp, observant eye (and ear) for what is typical and ordinary in contemporary African society that these plays display.

Soyinka's more complex plays offer great challenges to some of the best professional repertory English-language companies in the world. Such plays from Soyinka's corpus are *A Dance of the Forests, The Road, Madmen and Specialists, The Bacchae of Euripides,* and *Death and the King's Horseman.* These plays typically combine a considerable variety of performance styles and modes: trance-like states and behavior in speech and gesture; dance and mime; fragmentary but extended word-play; and dialogue of great poetic beauty and intensity, often shrouded in heavy symbolism and mysticism. And many of these plays revolve around ideas of the enigmatic, imponderable aspects of life. It is perhaps on account of this body of plays that Soyinka's Nobel award citation states in part that he "fashions the drama of existence." It is also on account of these plays and much of Soyinka's mature poetry— composed in times of deep personal stress generated by his responses to dislocating social and political events like the Nigerian civil war—that, though we encounter so much eloquence, elegance, wit, and gaiety in many of his plays and prose works, critics and scholars generally agree that Soyinka's artistic vision tends more to the tragic, the pessimistic, the fatalistic.

This paradox in Soyinka's artistic temperament is most evident in the great themes of his writings. One dominant, recurrent theme is that of the paradoxical union of conflicting, basic drives and impulses, in the individual as well as in culture and society. In exploring the ramifications of this paradox, Soyinka has focused mostly on the opposing forces of creation and destruction, but like Bertolt Brecht, he also explores such opposites in the protagonists of his most ambitious works as selflessness and egotism, courage and quixotic foolhardiness, wisdom and folly. What seems to interest Soyinka in this theme is the thought that there is both a creator and a destroyer in all of us, and that quite often and at great cost, these conflicting drives and impulses become entwined and inextricable. This seems to be the basis of the terrifying mix of altruism and misanthropy, of the conjoining of hatred of hypocrisy and cruelty with violent contempt for ordinary human beings that we see in Soyinka's great creations in dramatic characterization such as Demoke of *A Dance of the Forests,* Professor of *The Road,* the Old Man of *Madmen and Specialists* and Sebe Irawe of *From Zia with Love.*

An associated theme is that of Soyinka's abiding interest in the recovery or recuperation of the life-enhancing values of traditional or indigenous African culture. On its surface, this places Soyinka in the long line of ideological "race-uplift" thinkers, writers, and artists who, from the early nineteenth century, have urged the necessity of a "return to sources" as one of the preconditions for the survival of African peoples before the onslaught of colonialism in particular and, more generally, before the alienating currents and forces of modernity. The great names in this tradition include Edward Wilmot Blyden, J. E. Casely Hayford, Kobina Sekyi, Cheikh Anta Diop, Amadou Hampate Ba, Leopold Sedar Senghor, Amilcar Cabral, Chinua Achebe, Okot p'Bitek, Ayi Kwei Armah, and Soyinka himself. However, there is a distinctiveness to Soyinka's location in this tradition of an *Africanist* modernity. In the peculiarly Soyinkan articulation of this tradition, the master works of traditional African culture in myths and folklore, sculptural arts and artifacts, sacred as well as secular music and ritual festivals, are deemed to encode values and energies which can be accessed for emotional anchor and spiritual revitalization in periods of great individual stress or social calamity. This is definitely Soyinka's explanation of his own obsession with the brooding myths of Ogun, the Yoruba god of war, metallurgy, and creativity. Soyinka contrasts this chosen Muse of his, Ogun, with the god of Obatala, avatar of serenity and purity, presiding spirit of self-control and fortitude in the face of suffering, and this fact is a measure of the tremendous sophistication and nuance that Soyinka has brought to that long tradition of the ideological and intellectual elaboration of a distinctively *Africanist* modernity. Moreover, while like all the other proponents of this Africanist "return to sources" Soyinka places much emphasis on the recuperation of the *positive* values of indigenous African culture, he is nonetheless clearly distinctive in his elaboration of the specific mode in which these positive values may be recuperated and appropriated by the present generation. Specifically, he sees these values both as a storehouse of ideas and expressive material that can deepen artistic expression and as a vital refuge from the horrors and evils of history. These ideas are particularly and extensively explored in two of Soyinka's four volumes of poetry, *Idanre and Other Poems* and *A Shuttle in the Crypt*. It is not difficult to see how this view of the mode of appropriation of traditional culture that Soyinka adumbrates bears a special relevance to cultures that have experienced colonization and external domination.

Inevitably, Soyinka's persistent insistence on this notion makes him seem at times like a cultural conservative, but he has stoutly challenged this view of his "race retrieval project" as he calls it. The fact that Soyinka has been one of the great critics of Negritude in its simplifications and distortions, perhaps gives credence to his rebuttal. But the most telling expression of Soyinka's distance from merely antiquarian interest in precolonial indigenous African culture is to be found in his extension of this interest to the theme of rebirth and renewal after decay or death. For the roots of Soyinka's interest in this theme lie in his deep study, early in his literary and theatrical career, of the rites of "cleansing" and "purification" performed in many traditional African ritual festivals. The idea of rebirth after decay is of course a universal theme which is to be found in virtually all the religions of the world and all the mythological traditions of the world's cultures. And in the notion that therapy requires that a conflicted, traumatized subject must return to the "scene" of the trauma, must in effect undergo a sort of "death" or disintegration of the ego, psychology also presents a variation of this idea.

The exploration of this theme in Soyinka's works is varied, complex, and ambiguous, for it often merges with themes of malevolent, as opposed to voluntary scapegoating. The notion that the destruction of a character, usually a culture hero or an exceptional protagonist, leads to *his* spiritual and moral apotheosis and our symbolic regeneration is a controversial and complicated matter and Soyinka responds fully to this complexity. Such characters from Soyinka's plays like Emman in *The Strong Breed,* the Old Man in *Madmen and Specialists,* Professor in *The Road,* and Olunde and Elesin in *Death and the King's Horseman* show complex, often contradictory expressions of this theme. At one extreme, Professor's absorption in a search for the meaning of death seems entirely narcissistic and quixotic and his destruction at the end of the play seems unregenerative; at the other extreme, Olunde voluntarily submits to the ritual suicide which his father had failed to carry out and he seems in the process to offer a mitigation of the spiritual bleakness produced by his father's failure.

Another theme of Soyinka's writings is the quest for wholeness, the search for connections between all areas of life and reality great and small, seen and unseen, familiar and foreign. This search for wholeness further embraces opposites like youth and age, birth and death, and most important for Soyinka, the connection between the "worlds" (as he expresses it) of living generations and the generations of the dead and the unborn. It is a matter of great interest that as much as the expression of a unique, idiosyncratic *individuality* is a powerful motive force in both Soyinka's writings and his conceptions of artistic integrity, he does appear, in his ruminations on the links between these "worlds," to tilt the balance between our sense of the unique, irreplaceable individuality of each person and the intimations we always have of the connectedness of all things, living and dead and present, past and future toward the latter. It seems that for Soyinka, our objective knowledge of the passage of time and the finitude of individual human life may tell us that the past and the dead are gone forever, but from the recurrent seasons of nature powerful metaphors hint at a level of being and existence in which reality is nonlinear and cyclical—that an unbroken chain exists between all generations, all time, and all cultures. This is indeed one basis of Soyinka's abiding interest in nature—it is a powerful anchor for the quest for wholeness. Soyinka's obsession with this theme probably makes him one of the last great Romantics, for like the nineteenth-century European Romantics and American Transcendentalists, Soyinka has written powerfully against the tendency of modern industrial civilization to cut us off from our links with nature and with those deep parts of ourselves which are rooted in our *natural* condition.

All these themes run parallel to, and sometimes blend with, Soyinka's great political theme: the debunking of hypocrisy and humbug, the relentless exposure of the manipulative abuse and misuse of power, knowledge, and insight, either in religion and matters of the spirit or in the arts of statecraft. Soyinka's trenchant use of satire and parody has been particularly effective in his plays, poems, and short dramatic sketches on this theme; consequently, throughout Africa, powerful political figures and forces have sometimes sought, happily so far in vain, to intimidate, silence, or assassinate him. Many students of Soyinka's works indeed delight in quoting memorable and witty aphorisms and slogans from his works expressing the fundamental dignity and freedom of the human person.

The foregoing profile of the diverse aspects of the forms, themes, and contexts of Soyinka's writings and activities has been extrapolated from his works only through great effort, for as I have observed earlier, Soyinka is a difficult, often daunting writer, even if he is also a rewarding and exhilarating one. Fortunately, it is more of the "reward" and the "exhilaration" that we encounter in his interviews. Indeed, considering Soyinka's reputation as an often willfully obscure writer, it will come as a surprise to many readers of this volume of selected interviews that he is consistently a very accessible, very engaging conversationalist. Perhaps even more surprising is the fact that Soyinka in these interviews is very forthcoming on aspects of his writing that many readers and critics have found baffling or impenetrable. In the light of this readiness to productively engage interlocutors both on specific works and on features of his poetry, prose, and drama that are considered by many to be "obscure," the following comment that Soyinka makes in one of these interviews falls into place as a riposte to his critics, a riposte which the interview mode, if not his literary works themselves, sustains: "I deny absolutely any attempt to mystify or create obscurities. . . . Generally, I never set out to be obscure. But complex subjects sometimes elicit from the writer complex treatments."

Unquestionably, the interview, as a mode of expression, shows Soyinka at his most accessible and illuminating, especially when he is reflecting on very complex issues pertaining to his own writing and the state of culture and society in Africa and the world at large at the present time. This fact both expresses the potential value of this book to students of Soyinka's writings and opens up fertile ground for exploring the other great domain of Soyinka's life and career in which unambiguous clarity has been the guiding principle behind his words and deeds. This is the domain of his political activism, of his long and sustained work as one of the African continent's most vigorous fighters for social justice and most effective campaigners against human rights violations and abuses.

Soyinka has *needed* the interview as a mode of expression, it seems, to make the complexities of his serious writings answerable to the call for clarity and accessibility by many of his readers. Correspondingly, the Nigerian author has needed interviews to enhance the impact of his political activism: the interview has been a form which Soyinka has used to maximum effect in mobilizing international opinion against the African continent's dictators and the climate of fear and repression which they deliberately create to sustain their mediocre and tyrannical rule. The fear or insecurity that Soyinka's exploitation of the interview mode has sometimes instilled in some of these dictators is perhaps the greatest "tribute" to the playwright's effectiveness as a very *canny* fighter for social justice in Nigeria and the African continent. This factor indeed provides a distinctive flavor to many of the interviews collected in this volume, especially those which are explicitly addressed to the political situation in Nigeria or the continent at any particular point in time.

It goes without saying that "politics" is not the only, or indeed a constant, invariable topic in interviews with this author. What is constant throughout the interviews collected in this volume is the sheer range of Soyinka's interests and involvements. Like his chosen Muse, Ogun, whose "oriki," or praise poetry, celebrates him as "Ogun of seven paths," Soyinka wears many hats, and with only one or two exceptions, he wears them smartly. He is a poet and dramatist primarily, but he is also a novelist, memoirist, translator, theorist, and critic. But then, he has also been an actor, theatre director and educator, cineaste, musician, and huntsman. In the specific domain of literature, he writes effectively in all the modes, in their pure forms as well as in their hybridizations—tragedy, comedy, tragicomedy, satire, farce, the mimetic, and the non-mimetic. All of the voices and masks available to this poly-mathic, citizen-of-the-whole-world of arts and letters are on eloquent and engaging display in the interviews in this book.

It is of course true that even one so gifted in many arts of literature and of life, one so favored by Ogun, the patron god of the arts, has his weak points, and so in the media of film and prose fiction, Soyinka has not felt as much in self-possessed control as he exultantly is in drama and poetry. Of prose fiction he says in one of the interviews in this volume: "I'm not really a keen novelist. . . . The first novel happened purely by chance. . . . Then, again, *Season of Anomy* was written at a period when it was not possible for me to function in the theatre. So I don't consider myself a novelist. And the novel form for me is not a very congenial form."

Since we live in an age of ever expanding globalization which fosters the crossing of borders, geopolitical, cultural, and generic, it ought to be noted that the polyglot nature of Soyinka's interests and involvements is nothing like the postmodern celebration of hybridized, decentered identities which tends, in the name of a powerful critique of essentialism, to itself essentialize pluralism and relativism, in some cases evacuating them of ethically grounded investments and affiliations. It is necessary to emphasize this point because in many respects, Soyinka is both very close to and at the same time very distant from the postmodernists. He is, literally and figuratively, the ultimate traveler and nomad; at the same time, his identification with the destiny and fate of his country and continent is so profound that it borders on mystical, autochthonous sentiments. It can thus be said that he is at once the quintessential postmodernist and the nemesis of the postmodernist cele-bration of the fragility, performativity, and portability of identity. To grasp this simultaneous closeness to and distance from this dominant current of contemporary thought and culture, it is perhaps useful to recall here the clas-sical Yoruba myth of the dismemberment of Orisanla, the creator god in the Yoruba *orisa* pantheon, a myth which recalls and runs parallel to myths from other cultures like those of the dismemberment of Osiris or Zagreus. This is a myth whose many versions and fragments recur throughout Soyinka's writ-ings, especially in the two forms in which his genius and talents have found the most capacious and accomplished expression, drama and poetry.

According to this myth, in the beginning, all known (and unknown) facets of knowledge, truth, and consciousness were collected and totalized in the absolute godhead, Orisanla. This mighty divinity had a slave, Atunda. One fateful day, Orisanla was asleep at the foot of a hill. Out of spite, rebelliousness, or god-envy, Atunda rolled a huge rock downhill on the unsuspecting deity, smashing him into innumerable fragments. Thereafter, Orisanla loses his incarnation, vanishes from the pantheon, and becomes a purely abstract ideal or memory of absolutized truth, knowledge, or consciousness. As an abstract ideal or collective unconscious, the Orisanla matrix functions as an invitation to the lesser deities and humankind to reassemble and reconfigure in themselves as much of the shattered and dispersed qualities and attributes of that original unity and totalization.

The implications of brooding, fragmenting violence as a decisive feature of identity formation which this myth suggests has been put to considerable creative use by Soyinka in his writings; I would argue that this conception provides a framework for comprehending the divergent and sometimes contradictory interests and views expressed by our author in the interviews collected in this book. Sometimes in these interviews, Soyinka's involvements and views veer towards the abstract ideals symbolized in the Orisanla matrix such as wholeness, centeredness, nation, and "race" in ways that seem unconscionable from a postmodernist perspective. For instance, Soyinka's notions of a black *racial* identity and heritage, constituted partially by the violence of the historical experience of external conquest and domination but ultimately rooted in an *originary* repletion, is one important manifestation of this Orisanla ideal. But then there is also expressed in some interviews Soyinka's deep identification with Ogun whose gathering into himself of a plenitude of the fragmented and dispersed attributes of Orisanla emphasize not wholeness but contradiction: Ogun, bloodthirsty lover of gore, god of warfare and destruction, but also patron of poetry and the arts and friend and protector of orphans, the weak, the defenseless. At the same time, and above all, there is Atunda, the etymology of whose name connotes *refashioning* or *reinvention* of the self, who stands for a principle of negation and disruption that is available for reactivation by any given combination of the motivations of that primal rebel—a contrary, dissenting spirit, principled and inventive iconoclasm, revolutionary impatience, abhorrence of fixed, stable, and coercive regimes of truth, tradition, or power. No special interpretive talents are required to identify places in these interviews in which this Atunda principle is the source of Soyinka's theoretical or moral acuity.

Most metropolitan, Western versions of postmodernism have written the memory of the abstract ideal of centeredness and wholeness embodied in the

Orisanla matrix out of accounts and explanations of the formation of identities and subjectivities in the modern world, just as their accounts of paradigms that might seem analogous to the Ogun and Atunda archetypes are not sufficiently informed by the ethical and rational choices which underwrite the contradictoriness and disruptiveness embodied in the two archetypes. I suggest that one reason for this is the amnesia of many postmodernist theorists and critics with regard to the role of violence, destructive and fragmenting violence, in the formation of identities. Soyinka's work and vision are burdened, perhaps even *over-burdened,* by the memory of these archetypes and their significance for the identities we are compelled to live through in the modern world.

Brooding myths of violently dismembered gods and contradiction-ridden deities are, alas, not mere metaphors in the hemorrhaging and constantly fragmenting continent that is postcolonial Africa. With some justification, it has been alleged by some critics that while the cluster of myths and myth-fragments around these Orisanla-Atunda-Ogun archetypes and matrices have yielded Soyinka tremendous metaphorical power for exploring individual and collective experience in his trouble-torn country and continent, he has not in his writings sufficiently secularized and demythologized these myths. That criticism can in no way be extended to the interviews collected in this book. The Orisanla, Atunda, and Ogun archetypes stalk many of the views and positions taken by Soyinka in these interviews, but not as named, controlling essences. That is why in the interviews, Soyinka speaks of *racial* burdens but keeps them open to foreign influences and contacts, he speaks proudly of his debts to Yoruba sources and matrices while celebrating other African and non-African traditions, and with revolutionary impatience he savages some critics, many "ideologues," and all dictators for what he perceives as their corruption and abuse of responsibility and vocation. If in the postmodern milieu it has become highly unusual for any writer or intellectual to express such centered, cohering values side by side with allegiances and filiations riven by contradictions, it is important to bear in mind that Soyinka in these interviews simultaneously speaks *from* a separate earth and *to* our common Earth.

It remains for me to add that the interviews are republished in this volume in the chronological order in which they were conducted. Soyinka is a much interviewed writer and activist; thus, it was not easy to choose from the great number of interviews in print. For instance, this writer alone has interviewed

Soyinka at least three times, but only one of these appears in the present volume. I have generally been guided in my choice of items by the searching nature of a particular interlocutor's questions to Soyinka, primarily because this never fails to provoke a lively and equally searching response from our author. Another consideration has been the relative obscurity or unavailability of an item, especially where such an item clarifies much that has been considered obscure or esoteric in Soyinka's writings; it seemed to me that such items ought to find a more accessible forum in this volume. Finally, I confess to a certain *aesthetic* imperative in my selection of some particular interviews, interviews in which Soyinka's extemporizations take on the eloquence, wit and provocation of some of the protagonists of his plays like Professor of *The Road,* the Old Man of *Madmen and Specialists* and Alaba in *Requieum for a Futurologist.* I can only hope that these considerations will carry over into the reader's experience of the materials collected in this volume.

B. J.

Chronology

1934 Born 13 July, at Abeokuta, western Nigeria, the second child of Samuel Ayodele and Grace Eniola Soyinka.

1944–45 Attends Abeokuta Grammar School.

1946–50 Attends Government College, elite high school where he begins writing and wins prizes for his poems.

1950–52 On graduating from high school works in Lagos as an inventory clerk at a government pharmaceutical store. Has stories read on national radio.

1952–54 Attends University College, Ibadan.

1954–60 Five-year sojourn in the U.K. Attends the University of Leeds, obtaining the B.A. English Honors degree in 1957. Begins writing two plays, *The Swamp Dwellers* and *The Lion and the Jewel.* Works for some time as a playreader at The Royal Court Theatre in London. In 1958 directs the Nigeria Drama Group in *The Swamp Dwellers* and has an evening of his work comprising poems, songs and a play. *The Invention* performed at The Royal Court.

1957 Independence of Ghana, inaugurating the postcolonial era in Africa.

1960 Returns to Nigeria, the year of the country's independence from Britain. Receives a two-year Rockefeller research grant to study drama in West Africa. Completes *Camwood on the Leaves,* a radio play, and *The Trials of Brother Jero,* a stage play. Forms a theatre group, The 1960 Masks, and produces *A Dance of the Forests* which raises questions about the country's future for Nigeria's independence celebrations.

1962 Appointed a lecturer in English at the University of Ife but resigns in protest when the authorities of the university align the institution with the unpopular government of Samuel Ladoke Akintola. General social and political unrest in Western Nigeria.

1964   General strike of Nigeria's trade unions, effective countrywide.
           Soyinka is very actively involved around the Lagos-Ibadan area.
           Produces *The Lion and the Jewel* in a season of plays in English
           and Yoruba. Forms a new theatre group, The Orisun Theatre Com-
           pany.

1965   Produces satirical revue, *Before the Blackout* as political turmoil
           escalates in Western Nigeria. Premieres a major new play, *Kon-
           gi's Harvest,* in August in Lagos. Later in the year in London for
           the Commonwealth Arts Festival another major play, *The Road,*
           is staged and Soyinka reads from his long poem, "Idanre." Ap-
           pointed senior lecturer at the University of Lagos. Publishes *The
           Interpreters,* a novel. Turbulent election in western Nigeria and
           disputed victory of S. L. Akintola after widespread rigging of the
           elections. A gunman holds up the radio station of the Nigerian
           Broadcasting Service at Ibadan and forces the station to broadcast
           a recorded speech disputing Akintola's victory. Soyinka is later
           charged for the action, but is acquitted on a legal technicality.

1966   First military coup in Nigeria, 15 January, topples the federal
           government of Tafawa Balewa. Second counter-coup in July after
           May pogroms against Ibos in Northern Nigeria. The country
           slides irreversibly into civil war.

1967–70   Nigerian civil war pitching federal forces against Biafran seces-
           sionists.

1967   Publishes *Kongi's Harvest* and *Idanre and Other Poems.* With
           Tom Stoppard, receives the John Whiting Drama Award in Lon-
           don. Off-Broadway productions of *The Trials of Brother Jero* and
           The Strong Breed at Greenwich Mews Theater, New York. Ap-
           pointed Head of the School of Drama, University of Ibadan, but
           unable to take up the position because of arrest in August by the
           federal government for activities to stop the war. He is incarcer-
           ated without trial for most of the duration of the war and spends
           most of his time in prison in solitary confinement. Smuggles some
           protest poems out of prison; later writes a book of his prison
           experience, *The Man Died,* published in 1972.

1968   Receives Jock Campbell–New Statesman Literary Award, Lon-
           don. Publication of *Forest of a Thousand Daemons,* Soyinka's
           translation of D. O. Fagunwa's classic Yoruba hunter's saga, *Og-
           boju Ode Ninu Igbo Irunmale. Kongi's Harvest* produced by
           Negro Ensemble Company at St. Mark's Theater, New York.

1969   *Three Short Plays* (new edition of *Three Plays*) and *Poems from Prison* published. Released from detention in October and takes up post of head of Department of Theatre Arts, University of Ibadan.

1970   Directs *Madmen and Specialists* at the Eugene O'Neill Theater Center, Waterford, Connecticut. Plays the role of Kongi, the dictator, in Calpenny Films production of his play, *Kongi's Harvest.* Inauguration of Orisun Acting Editions with Soyinka as literary editor.

1971–75 Years of self-imposed exile from Nigeria, traveling around the world and ultimately settling in Accra, Ghana, where in 1974 he assumes editorship of the journal, *Transition,* which he re-names *Ch'Indaba.*

1971   *Before the Blackout,* the first title in the Orisun Acting Editions, published. Directs *Madmen and Specialists* at Ibadan. The play is published later in the year. Plays the role of Lumumba in Joan Littlewood's Paris production of *Murderous Angels,* Conor Cruise O'Brien's play on the Congo crisis.

1972   *A Shuttle in the Crypt* and *The Man Died* published. Resigns as head of the Department of Theatre Arts at the University of Ibadan. Directs extracts from *A Dance of the Forests* in Paris.

1973   Appointed Visiting Professor of English at University of Sheffield and overseas fellow at Churchill College, Cambridge University. Publication of *Collected Plays, Vol. 1, Camwood on the Leaves,* and *The Bacchae of Euripides,* which is given an unimaginative production by the National Theatre at Old Vic, London. Publication of second novel, *Season of Anomy.*

1974   *Collected Plays, Vol. 2,* published. Teams up with the South African poet, Dennis Brutus, to form Union of Writers of the African Peoples and is elected its first Secretary-General.

1975   Yakubu Gowon overthrown in a military coup. General Murtala Mohammed becomes head of state. Soyinka returns to Nigeria and is given appointment of professor of Comparative Literature by the University of Ife. *Death and the King's Horseman* published. Edits *Poems of Black Africa.*

1976   Murtala Mohammed assassinated, General Olusegun Obasanjo becomes head of state. *Myth, Literature and the African World* and *Ogun Abibiman* published. Governmental corruption and social inequality intensify in the wake of an oil-boom economy. Soyinka is fiercely outspoken in his social criticism and faces intimidation by agents of the military regime. First stage production of *Death and the King's Horseman* at the University of Ife in December.

1977   Administrator of FESTAC (International Festival of Negro Arts and Culture), Lagos. Completes and directs *Opera Wonyosi,* a composite adaptation of John Gay's *Beggars' Opera* and Brecht's *Threepenny Opera* which savages several African military and civilian despots and the values they are entrenching across the borders of African countries. Soyinka is prevented from staging this play in Lagos and he forms a group called Guerrilla Theatre Unit out of the professional company of the University of Ife Theatre. Writes short, biting, and highly popular skits attacking governmental hypocrisy, corruption, and sadistic policies. These skits are performed by the new group in open-air markets, streets, community centers, and school playing fields.

1979   Joins the People's Redemption Party, a social-democratic party whose leadership is made up of the most prominent progressive politicians of the North and the South and trade union and academic leftists. When the party fragments into conservative and radical factions, Soyinka goes with the latter and becomes its Deputy Director of Research. Directs *The Biko Inquest,* an edited version of the court proceedings of an inquest of the death of Steve Biko in police custody. In the fall he directs *Death and the King's Horseman* at the Goodman Theater, Chicago. Upon successful run at the Goodman, production is transferred to the Kennedy Center in Washington, D.C. where it is also well received. Shehu Shagari wins federal elections and Nigeria returns to civilian rule.

1981   Appointed Visiting Professor, Yale University. *Opera Wonyosi* and *Aké,* the first part of Soyinka's autobiography, published. Produces satirical revue, "Rice Unlimited," with the Guerrilla Theatre Unit.

1982   *Aké* launched at Ake, Abeokuta in January. Soyinka uses the occasion to lambast the policies of the Shagari government and its "achievements": the plundering of the country's wealth; the massacre of unarmed farmers and peasants at Bakolori in the North; the subversion of the Kaduna and Kano state governments controlled by the People's Redemption Party (PRP); the destruction of the offices of *The Triumph* newspaper owned by the PRP; the storming of an elected legislature by the paramilitary detachment of the Nigerian Police Force controlled by Shagari's government; the deaths of students, athletes, members of the National Youth Corps, and ordinary citizens at the hands of the police at the innumerable check-points set up by the government to intimidate and cower an increasingly restive populace. Late in the year *Die Still, Dr. Godspeak!,* a play on the influence of the quackery of parapsychologists and metaphysicians in Nigeria, broadcast on the African Service of the BBC World Service.

1983   Production of *Requiem for a Futurologist,* stage version of *Die Still, Dr. Godspeak!* Soyinka uses countrywide tour of the production to spread ideas contained in the "Priority Projects," a satirical revue attacking corruption, mismanagement, and hypocrisy of the country's political rulers. On the eve of the national elections in August, Soyinka releases the songs from this revue in a record album titled *Unlimited Liability Company;* the album takes the country by storm and is a huge success. Shagari wins the elections which are marked by massive vote rigging, use of the armed services of the state to intimidate opposition parties and their supporters, and widespread outbreak of violent protests and demonstrations. Soyinka flies to London and uses the BBC World Service and the international press to condemn the corruption of the just concluded elections. He predicts revolution or a coup. On the last day of the year, Shagari is overthrown in a coup which brings general Mohammadu Buhari to power.

1984   *Blues for a Prodigal,* Soyinka's film on the elections of 1983 released. In May an unsuccessful production of *The Road* opens at the Goodman Theater in Chicago, and in December Yale Repertory Theatre produces *A Play of Giants. Six Plays* and *A Play of Giants* published.

1986   Nobel Prize for Literature and the second highest of Nigeria's national honors, the CFR (Commander of the Federal Republic).

1987   *Death and the King's Horseman* produced at Lincoln Center, New York City.

1988   Publication of *Art, Dialogue and Outrage,* a major collection of Soyinka's essays on literature and culture. *Mandela's Earth* published.

1989   *Isara: A Voyage Around "Essay,"* a fictional account of the au-
            thor's father and his friends published.

1991   *A Scourge of Hyacinths,* a new radio play, broadcast on BBC
            Radio 4.

1992   *From Zia, with Love,* a stage version of *A Scourge of Hyacinths,*
            is premiered in Sienna, Italy. The play uses a satirical and farcical
            exploration of the inner workings of the international traffic in
            drugs to attack the corruption and hypocrisy of the Nigerian mili-
            tary rulers.

1994   Publication of *Ibadan: The "Penklemes" Years—A Memoir,*
            1946–1965, the third part of the author's memoirs.

1995   12 June, the victory of Moshood Kashimawo Abiola at the federal
            elections to return Nigeria to civilian rule canceled by the military
            dictatorship of Ibrahim Babangida. Massive protests in Lagos,
            Ibadan, and other Nigerian cities met with brutal force by the
            army. Attempt by Soyinka to organize a long protest march from
            the South to the nation's capital in Abuja in the North is aborted
            by the regime. The country is plunged into constitutional and po-
            litical crisis as Babangida is forced from office and hands power
            over to a lame-duck civilian-led caretaker government headed by
            Ernest Shonekan, a crony of the generals. In August Shonekan is
            removed from office and General Sani Abacha replaces him as
            head of stage. *The Beatification of Area Boy,* a new play on the
            revolt of the underclasses of the Lagos slums, is given its world
            premiere at the West Yorkshire Playhouse, Leeds, and is pub-
            lished.

1996   Soyinka forced into exile in the face of threats to his life from the
            Abacha regime which escalates repression, intimidation, and po-
            litically motivated assassination beyond anything previously seen
            in the country. Publication of *Open Sore of a Continent: A Per-
            sonal Narrative of the Nigeria Crisis.*

1997   Soyinka and eleven other pro-democracy members of the internal
            and external opposition to the Abacha regime are charged with
            treason and placed on trial *in absentia.* Meanwhile, in association
            with other members of the external opposition, Soyinka launches
            Radio Kudirat, which transmits broadcasts to Nigeria in English
            and the country's main indigenous languages challenging the le-

gitimacy of the Abacha regime and exposing its isolation in the international community.

1998   Early March, Sani Abacha dies unexpectedly and is succeeded by General Abdulsalami Abubakar. Two weeks later, on the eve of his release from prison, Moshood K. Abiola dies mysteriously. In September, Soyinka returns to Nigeria, ending his two-year exile.

1999   In February, Olusegun Obasanjo wins federal presidential elections and becomes civilian head of state in October. Publication of *The Burden of Memory, the Muse of Forgiveness.*

Conversations with Wole Soyinka

Wole Soyinka: In Person

University of Washington / 1973

From *In Person: Achebe, Awoonor, and Soyinka at the University of Washington.* Karen L. Morell, ed Seattle: University of Washington, 1975, 89–130. Reprinted with permission.

KCTS/9 Television Studio, 19 April 1973, Art France, director. The discussion followed a scene from *The Trials of Brother Jero,* presented by students of the University of Washington School of Drama.

Televised Discussion

Soyinka: How do you feel about the role of Jero? An expression was used and I wonder if you would like to discuss it. When your professor was talking about the play she emphasized what you might call the more corrupt aspect of Brother Jero, who is of course a very corrupt character, but I wonder whether you find any slightly more fascinating aspects of him. He is a rogue, yes, but how do you react to him? Do you think he is just bad through and through or does he have any redeeming qualities? I am very curious to know how you react to him generally.

Participant: Well, I feel like he is a rogue but he's sincere to a certain point. He is conceited, though he says he isn't, and that has something to do with it also. But I feel when he started off, when he says he first came into calling, came into his own, he might have been sincere then, when he helped Noah, but then he helped his old master only to help himself. There are times when I think that he might be sincere; then it all changes.

Soyinka: How do you react to him, Chume? After all, he torments you most.

Participant: I look at Brother Jero kind of like you said; you can see some justification in the character, but then again the way he abuses people! I, Chume, am so gullible and so naive I accept what he says, and it is very interesting to see how the other characters are played, like myself and other villagers, how they readily accept him as the chosen prophet and don't question too much. It's really curious.

1

Soyinka: I have a feeling that you are taking him a little too seriously. Does anyone have a lighter view of Jero?

Participant: In the first place, he is a man who survives, and he doesn't seem to have excuses for failure. Everybody else has a tendency to find lots of reasons for failing. No matter what happens, he adapts. He doesn't seem to say, "Who am I," or "My life is sad," or "All these misfortunes have stopped me." He'll give his little spiel, but then he runs back on and lives, and he is a very live person.

Even in a shallow way, he's still alive, he bubbles.

Soyinka: What of this society he represents? Do you find him a creature of this society, a representative of that society? What feeling do you get about a society which has produced and nourished and maybe deserves Brother Jero?

Participant: I would say that such a society is based around the fact that they need certain crutches. In other words, they are using Jero for a crutch. Chume definitely uses Jero for a crutch because the game Jero is running down, you could see thorough it if you wanted to, but he doesn't want to really. He wants to see Jero as something of a prophet so he can feel that there is such a thing. In other words, he wants to make his life somewhat easier or more bearable one might say.

Soyinka: I must stop asking you question; perhaps you have questions to ask me.

Participant: I was wondering—there is one part in the play where he says "strange dissatisfied people. I know because I keep them dissatisfied." Well, it seems like somebody should be able to see through him and see what he is doing, and I'm still at a loss by that. I don't really follow that. It seems like the whole population is just made up of dummies.

Soyinka: He is obviously more intelligent than the people around him for a start, and it's just that he's using his genius in a rather warped manner. When you say that people don't see through him, I think it is simply because he is a warped genius.

Participant: But isn't he a lot worse than that? I can see how if the play just ended with him beating his wife you could say that he is a harmful, fun rogue, but he does some pretty rotten things at the end, doesn't he?

Soyinka: When he has Chume certified, this is the survivalist instinct again in Jero. Now, don't misunderstand me. All I am saying is this: you see I am trying to find, discover whether you find in him a certain dimension. In fact, when I was talking about a different dimension, I wasn't talking about social justification; I wasn't talking about any excuses at all. I was thinking about you as theater people, whether you find him a likable, theatrical character. This is really what I am trying to discover. In other words, do you really enjoy playing Jero?

Participants: Yes, definitely. Jero is the type of character that is a very stimulating force, and he is very vibrant and very sure of himself. He doesn't make any mistakes; he knows he has his game together. And you know it is the type of play that is very interesting to watch.

Participant: He reminds me of a lot of renowned preachers—well, maybe not renowned—but am I allowed to call any names? Well, anyway, there are a lot of preachers who go on the pretense that they are really into God and that this is the way, and they will do this for you if you pay. I know a lot of preachers are like that and he kind of typifies that to me.

Participant: Jero's really a pretty good businessman because he has the young ladies at his disposal that he can visit on the beach. He has everybody believing that he lives on the beach and he seems like he might even have all the traders trained so that he can get his supplies when he needs them and not be expected to pay back, until he runs into Amope. So I think that he can also be considered the typical businessman of today that rips off a lot of people. He has a nice setup, everyone respects him, he provides entertainment and enjoyment for the people when they have their spiritual times at night. So I think there is a need for a person like him because I think that people are so weak, they are all followers. They need a leader like him to lead them. So he's usually someone that rips them off.

Soyinka: I noticed that you got very much into the part of Amope. You seemed to fall, you find no difficulty at all in. . . . [laughter]

Participant: Are you trying to say that I'm a natural—I was type cast!

Soyinka: No, I was wondering whether you really . . . because it was even more than merely being shrewish. You seemed to have found a very beautiful natural rhythm for that role. A few more gestures and I could really have mistaken you for a real market tough who goes around collecting debts. Did you have any model for this or did you bring it out of yourself?

Participant: Naturally I didn't bring it out of myself! But actually, I think that a lot of black women are like this in America by way of force because the black man has been ripped off so much that he's had a hard time maintaining himself until the last few years. He hasn't even been given the tools; he's just been told to go out, do his thing and pull himself up, while the wife has always had to maintain the homefront. She feels like she has to protect him from making his own mistakes, not letting him live his own life, and I see this a lot in a lot of black American women, although it is changing. What do you think of Amope? Does she reflect some idea that you have of women?

Soyinka: That is taken straight from women I know in my society. My own mother, for instance, was a terror. Not by nature, but she was a trader, and I know that even she, who was a rather gentle person, when she got fed up and she wanted to collect her debts from her customers—it is no joke— suddenly she was transformed. I think most of our, what you might call, petty trader character is very strong in a lot of our women. They are not quite as downtrodden as some people will have the world believe in these days of women's revolution. They know how to handle themselves.

Penthouse Theater

University of Washington, 20 April 1973. Discussion with faculty and students, School of Drama.

Participant: Would you tell us about your experiences with your theater companies?

Soyinka: I'll give you a brief history. I returned to Nigeria for the first time in four and a half years—in 1960. My last year and a half in England, when I should have been working for my higher degree, I spent out of preference in the theater in London. I was just sitting in on rehearsals, being a playreader for the Royal Court Theater, and twice doing experimental productions of my own, both at the Royal Court Theater and at the Annual Student's Drama Festival for which I got together a company and we worked up a little production. Don't ask me what play it was I experimented with at the Royal Court Theater; I've done my best to bury it. [laughter] Oh, there was a third one which there is simply no script of. It was a kind of semi-political improvisation around the Hola Camp theme. This was in Kenya when some British people beat to death certain so-called Mau-Mau prisoners and we did some kind of living theater improvisation around it.

Anyway, with this background the first thing I wanted to do when I got back to Nigeria was to get my own company together. There were many ways in which this could be done. I could move towards trying to establish a full professional theater from the very beginning, but there were many factors which militated against this: lack of money, and then there was the training problem because this was in January, 1960, and I wanted the company to be ready—say, in October, 1960—when we would stage a production for the Independence Celebration. I very badly wanted to do this because we could obtain money for that if we managed to swing the other. So I rejected what was really my main intention, my real ambition, which was to start a company from scratch: young, semiprofessional people, and go through the process of training and so on. We had to make do instead with those who'd had enormous acting experience. This meant both on the radio, on the stage, and it meant I wanted those who could use already the English language because I wrote in English, those who could use it and be very articulate and be comfortable in it. In other words, I was reducing the handicap of the training process. And that is how the 1960 Masks was born.

It consisted mainly of the middle class civil servant types, you know, who had senior service jobs, were very comfortable, had their cars and their houses, were used to being home with their families over the weekend. But I needed them, and somehow I could break their habit of always rushing home every weekend to their families because weekends were the only continuous period we could rehearse. Now I selected the very best people I could find in Ibadan and Lagos—separated by a hundred miles. Those of you who know anything about Lagos and Nigeria might know what the roads are like and would understand what it is to travel backwards and forwards between those two cities. And very often we'd do preliminary rehearsals in a jolting landrover while going to meet the other group. We would rehearse in Lagos this week; the next weekend would be in Ibadan.

Now, I had the advantage of being on a kind of fellowship; I am very fond of these research fellowships. [laughter] They give you time to move around, very little teaching to do, and this was my very first one. I had it two years so I had plenty of time, and I commuted between these two places rehearsing groups individually wherever it was convenient and bringing people together over the weekend. We would start rehearsals, let us say, on Saturday morning. All the members in turn would house and give hospitality to the rest of the company. We'd rehearse all day Saturday, go to the nightclub all night, drink, dance, do a bit of rehearsing also in the nightclubs. It was a way I have of slipping in the quiet rehearsal. "Oh, by the way, you know when we were doing this thing this afternoon, what I'd like you to do is . . . have another beer." [laughter] And then on Sunday we'd begin work at eight and carry on continuously until about seven in the evening, with maybe just a small break with a big meal, however, prepared by all the families. They were very happy; some of them were housewives who had given up all hope of finding any real artistic fulfillment since they got married and had children. And it was a kind of community theater but with a very strong sense of professionalism. Finally when we were ready to produce a play the result was quite satisfactory.

But this was not the theater I wanted, and from the beginning they understood that they were there to encourage a new younger group of fully professional actors and actresses. And from the beginning they never took any money at all. What little money we had went to three or four people whom we began training right underneath the major productions, increasing their number as time went on. They understood this really was to become the theatrical company, and they were very generous, they really loved what they were doing. So that by 1962 or 1963 we were able to bring out the first fully professional theater still attached by an umbilical cord to the 1960 Masks, and what happened was that this young group performed their first play while the 1960 Masks organized, did all the advertising, the selling, handled the administrative section, and left the rest entirely to me and this new young group. And that was the Orisun Theater Company. That company also had its advantages, and this also was one of the reasons why I was determined to bring this company out, because they had less at stake. In other words, there was a limit to what I could get the 1960 Masks to do. They had their jobs; I could not jeopardize this. For instance, I wanted to stage some very caustic political sketches. With the Orisun Theater they did anything and everything, and so it was the Orisun Theater whom I used for the two sketches *The New Republican* and *Before the Blackout,* and one or two other pieces we did on television and radio. They understood that theater obviously meant risks. And that is the Orisun Theater.

When I went to prison for political troubles, the theater fell to pieces. There was an assistant of mine who was very, very keen to keep this group going at all costs. Formerly I had been able to raise something for them one way or the other, begging, borrowing, stealing, or whatever. This became a real problem when I wasn't around, and he took a regular slot on television and actually began producing a one act play every fortnight for television. Now this was absolutely insane. They just were not equipped for that sort of speed. Also, as a result of the war and the upheaval the group had become broken up; in fact, even before I went to prison. There was the massacre and the political things. Many people, Igbo members, had fled back to the East, others had left, and everything was really in pieces. It was just a matter of keeping a small core of the group going. When I was away he tried to resuscitate the entire thing with his absolutely, you know, incredible program that's really a strain, trying to produce with this company a regular play every fortnight. So naturally, standards fell to pieces. When I came out, and I saw their first performance on television, the first thing that I did was to call up, break that contract with television and disband the group. Then since I was now going into the Theater Department fully and I had some facilities there, I took the core out of the group again and joined them with the new student company which I was forming and so built a new semi-professional troup attached to the University, the Theater Arts Company; it was that group which I brought to the States in 1970 to the Eugene O'Neill Theater Center to do *Madmen and Specialists*. That's about the story of my theatrical company activities in Nigeria.

Participant: Did you produce anything besides Nigerian plays?

Soyinka: Yes, we did a West Indian play, a play by a Sierra Leonian, one by a South African. We did some adaptations. I tried as much as possible to not do my own plays; but we did do a few.

Participant: Were they all in English?

Soyinka: I did them all mostly in English, English except the songs; I have a facility for writing songs in Yoruba.

Participant: Is it lack of common language that led you to use English?

Soyinka: We have about four main languages and about thirty-something other languages in Nigeria. So English, some kind of English, is mostly used. English is the common language—not always the Queen's English but what you call broken English or pidgin English. The result is that literally every man in the street can understand some form of English.

Participant: What different methods have you used to train actors?

Soyinka: I had many different methods. My own interest in actor training is, if I boil it down to the essence, is what I call the principle of empathy; in other words, just trying to make one human being lose his ego and relate completely: physically, rhythmically, even mimetically, but, most important of all, intellectually, with the other human being, the character. Achieving this is what constitutes the routine exercises of my training methods. But I also believe in exploiting external agencies. For instance, we have in Nigeria several companies, what you call folk theater companies. I've spoken about these multi-media troupes: current news, dance, rhythm, music, improvisation, everything is integrated to produce a very lively and rather straightforward, gutsy form of theater. There is one man, Duro Ladipo, and he has a

very remarkable training method: when he gets his new actors he would sit
them down and go "Habhaa," and they were to imitate that. And then "Bboo-
hohoo," and he goes on like that all day if necessary. [laughter] He throws
himself on the floor and shakes, and they must do the same. Now from time
to time I send my actors to experience a bit of Ladipo for a weekend or so.
You know, it's very good for their souls. [laughter]

And then take the Goethe Institute, the French Cultural Center, and the
British Council. From time to time they have actors coming through or some
dancers, sometimes it's a ballerina, a mime-specialist, maybe a Shakespear-
ean actor. And whenever they come through I make sure that I expose my
actors to the experiences of these various forms. It never does them any harm.
To force a twenty-year old with set bones to do a pirouette is very good for
him. I mean, he'll never use it on stage, but the training, suddenly trying to
balance on his toes and making all of those ridiculous gestures, I think it does
two things: number one, it makes him use unexpected muscles, and secondly,
it makes him lose whatever inhibitions he still has which I am not aware of.
The whole purpose for me is a continuous process of training which is to
make the body and the mind as malleable, as flexible, and as ready to accept
any experience as possible. So the training process never stops. And then a
very good training process also is to go out with them all night and keep
them active until early in the morning. It brings all of us together.

All of the methods to me are involved in making an actor. Also it ends up
leaving the personality exactly what he is without exaggerating one single
aspect of a new awareness of his body. In other words, his body is so ready
to accommodate and to jettison that he remains his own unique personality;
he doesn't get actors' hang-ups, actors' self-consciousness. They also do
everything—the painting, the sets, the billboards—we design them together;
we have to use a needle and thread; they know we must use it. And they learn
to cope with suddenly blacking out on stage. I put them through all sorts of
things, "What would you do if this happened: this man is not giving your
line?" It's really an ongoing course of the theatrical experience.

Participant: What physical facilities are available for your plays?

Soyinka: We don't have real theater structure; we have halls which we
designate theaters. In fact, the sort of halls which we had mostly were built
by the British Council; in other words, the first cultural civilizers who came
to our coast. And they built these little Masonic Halls where there's a platform and everything opens squarely onto the audience. And because their
libraries were about the only place you could find playscripts, the only kind

of play known to the theater-mad person in Nigeria and in West Africa was a bit of Bernard Shaw and bit of Priestley.

Most of my actors in fact at the beginning came from the amateur acting companies who used these halls; they never forgave me for picking off their best actors. One, who's the finest actor I've ever had, came from the Ibadan Operatic Society. The expatriates would get together to play Gilbert and Sullivan. I just went to look at them one day and saw this incredible actor, and I said, "Why are you wasting yourself in this project?" It took a slow process to convince him that there was more to life outside the Ibadan Operatic Society. So there has always been this tradition of the amateur provincial company playing on the proscenium stage, unable to even imagine any other form of theater beyond that which goes across a square framework.

Then, however, there is a far more interesting form of theater, the one I've described: the folk opera or theater which is developed out of the normal, secular masquerade, the traditional secular masquerade of our society, and moved into contemporary themes—both social realism or satire and political satire—and then moved also into the epical theater, the reenactment of legends and so on. That was very exciting theater and itinerant. They moved from place to place in rickety old lorries with all their things in them. My theater has attempted to combine this form of theater, the folk opera, with a lot more dialogue, a diversity of themes, etc., and is in English: in other words, one which appeals equally to, let us say, intellectual preoccupation in the theater as well as the visual excitement on stage.

Participant: Did you ever use white people in your company?

Soyinka: We usually brought in from time to time, whenever we needed it, white people who were interested.

Participant: Were they ever written into the plays?

Soyinka: No, we didn't have specific parts as such except during the satirical reviews when, you know, we needed a white fellow or two. [laughter] We had lots of volunteers, and we used to have some white people who were very interested in the stage who we depended upon backstage and who even came forward occasionally; this was certainly true from the university community. There was once an Indian doctor who was a passionate theater buff, and he was willing to do anything. He became more or less the medical officer for the company.

Participant: What is your attitude towards negritude now?

Soyinka: Well, I can tell you straightaway, I'm not a negritudinist; in fact, I am counted among the antinegritudinists. Our attitude has simply been that negritude is a historical phenomenon. It had to happen in the period that it had to happen. It was essential to the people who formulated this philosophy of renewed consciousness in their black identity, but as with most movements which begin on the cafe sidewalks, it is largely artificial, rhetorical. It is also exaggerated because the people who needed this reclamation were the aliens; they had no relationship to the bulk of their country's people. In other words, the African people have never lost their negritude, never. Now the situation in Africa is very different from what it was in the States. Here, negritude, or the black personality, black consciousness, was not merely a historical phenomenon; it had to be a sudden sharp revolutionary activity. It wasn't mere rhetoric, mere conceptualization of what existed; it was a real process of rediscovery. But for the Francophone intellectuals in Africa, it was an exaggeration. It is not surprising that it was taken up by such intellectuals as Jean Paul Sartre because for them it was yet another branch of European philosophy. Negritude gave birth to magazines like *Black Orpheus,* the title of which takes its reference point from European mythology; and *Black Orpheus* was born during that strident period of negritude. It's a title which I find very embarrassing even though it was a very good magazine and brought out a hell of a lot of literature, not merely of Africa but of black America, the Caribbean, and Latin America. But the whole mentality at that time was relating the African personality to European points of reference. Negritude has not really affected my life.

Participant: If you are embarrassed by the title *Black Orpheus,* why are you doing a play of Euripides?

Soyinka: Oh, that's two different things. I acknowledge the myths. For instance, I have subtitled the play *The Bacchae of Euripides: A Communion Rite.* I simply come to it as a writer. This is a play which first of all has always fascinated me. I consider it one of the first of the classics. It is also a very uneven and, in many ways, rather a crude play. I come to it as a craftsman.

Do not misunderstand me; I do not say that there is no meeting point, no correlation, possible between European culture and African, no. I merely say that the reference point must not be taken, necessarily, for preoccupations and institutions supposedly African, the reference points should not be from European culture.

Participant: Do you like to work with established groups of actors?

Soyinka: In directing I prefer to work constantly with a company. It doesn't mean necessarily the same company all the time. I don't like to just come upon a group of people and do one production. I like to work together with them and let a production grow out of this relationship.

Participant: Have you had any difficulties in bringing together people of different nationalities in the same theater group?

Soyinka: There has been no problem at all. I wouldn't do it consciously, but if I'm trying to build a new company and the ones who immediately strike me as having real talent and dedication in themselves happen to come one from India, Brazil, etc., then I'd bring them into the group, and there would have to be a process which would evolve naturally during exercises and rehearsals. But to set out consciously to find a kind of amalgamated style for a group like that, a hybrid group like that, would be a mistake; I wouldn't attempt it, but I have no doubt something would evolve. Peter Brook is working on this principle for, what shall I call them, an International Theater, an International Theater of Expression, or a Universal Theater of Expression. In his company they have a black from Senegal, a Japanese, Americans, French, the whole lot, and his rationality is that theater really began not with words, and, therefore, it should be possible for a variegated group of humanity to go back to the roots of theater. And he has created one fabulous thing after another. He has a poet working for him, Ted Hughes, who invented a new language, and it was in this language that *Orghast* was written or produced by all of them in Persepolis. And they played this among the ruins. I wish I'd seen it. But this to me is a very self-conscious way of creating new difficulties for oneself, and it simply doesn't appeal to me.

Participant: Do you like directing your own plays?

Soyinka: I like to.

Participant: Can you edit them as the need arises?

Soyinka: Oh yes, I'm good at slashing my own plays.

Participant: Have you assisted when others have directed your work?

Soyinka: Yes, that has not been a very happy experience, in fact. When I am directing someone else's play I can't stand them around, so it's not surprising that I can't stand to be around anybody directing my play, and I tend to keep out. The closest I've worked with any director was on *The Road* when it was done in England in 1965 and even there I came in as little as possible—only when the director required some help, then I'd go in and assist him on that specific point. If he wanted to discuss things with me, then he would come outside rehearsals. But I think playwrights are a bloody nuisance when you're directing.

Participant: What has been your experience with television?

Soyinka: I've written plays specifically for television in Nigeria. I've never directed a television play, although each production that my group has performed in the studio I have had to literally set, set all of the shots, then give it to the technicians to work out what it means in terms of camera. This is for the simple reason that if you don't, all they understand is "close-up, two-shots, wide angle . . ." and they just vary it, 123, 321, 421, and after a few experiences like that I insisted on setting things.

Participant: Is there a national theater in Nigeria?

Soyinka: No, there isn't one; the argument goes back and forth as to whether there should be.

Participant: What are your feelings about it?

Soyinka: I'm not that interested in national theater. I'm against the principle of it. What I think should happen is that there should be a national repertory of works. In other words, suppose some company somewhere, no matter whose, does a really first class production, someone like Duro Ladipo's *Oba Koso,* which is the first sort of piece I would like to see in the national repertory. Something like a library collection. I'd like to see the state, having recognized the value of this production, ensure that it is kept in repertory. The machinery for this can be worked out in detail; it can be in the form of a little subsidy to that company to be used for maintaining that production in some form so that we could have it ready as needed within maybe a month; it's not very difficult to work out. But it is in these terms that I envisage a national theater of plays. But I would not serve on the other; it would just become another bureaucratic arm of the government, and then it would be a political ally of the government.

Participant: What about national theater in general?

Soyinka: I had a chance to study the national theater situation in other countries, including England, for whom I'm doing this adaptation. I can understand, say, the National Shakespeare Theater which has both sentimental values for the British but which also celebrates true genius. Shakespeare is dead so there can be no political infighting over his worth. That kind of institution I understand; so there should be a Brechtian theater or a theater devoted to Molière in France. But national theater reduces, from what I have seen, people of genius and talent to squabbling children and political fools. That seems to be a disease that transcends any cultural bonds.

Participant: Has the government ever accepted your theatrical work?

Soyinka: Oh, the government's never accepted me. But it hasn't got much choice. It was during the hot political arena in 1963, 1964, and 1965, the civilian period where elections were being rigged, and people were disappearing, and all opponents of the government could be taxed out of existence, their cocoa farms just taken away like that, when armies of thugs literally reigned as roving pirates. One of the things which we had to do, which I made sure that my actors knew about was—you see, not only had several theater groups been banned and performances banned, but some of them broken up physically—you never knew whether they were police or just thugs. Every member of my company knew how to use a fire extinguisher, and not just to put out fires. That was one of the many tactics which had to be learned by the Orisun Theater. We had a very strong security check on the approach of any destructive elements. Curiously enough throughout, not once was a performance ever successfully interrupted. A few of the senior members had to keep a low profile during this, you know the parent group, and we made sure that Orisun Theater became very, very distinct from the 1960 Masks. There were, you know, situations.

Recently when I directed again *Kongi's Harvest* with the University Theater Company—and this is ironic because I directed it at the request of the University, for the University's twenty-first birthday ceremonies, to which everybody came, the military governors, the commissioners, all the embassies, you know, it was one of these almost semi-state occasions—I had reinterpreted *Kongi's Harvest* with a military image on top at a very direct reference point, and the program itself made the message very, very, plain. But there was very little that could be done. The play went forward, and in fact these people were struggling for seats for they hadn't seen the play yet. After that there was flak, but it was too late.

Participant: Are there special schools for children's theater?

Soyinka: There are special schools for the theater, and then there is the children's traditional theater. I believe theater should be part of school. There could be theater, for instance, if you were in a situation where not all children go to school, and you want to expose that community to some form of theater, then you can go into that community and establish a theater program there. I don't believe very much in what we were doing, which was bringing the children into the drama department and running weekend theater. We did it, and I continued it simply because they seemed to be having some fun, but I really didn't believe in it. Community theater, yes, but generally children make their own plays and in our society especially are used to making their own plays; they even carve their own masks and imitate the elderly things which they see, go around, and tour the locality all on their own initiative, and I would rather this sort of instinctive playmaking among children is subtly encouraged rather than being institutionalized.

Participant: You must not have children who are television addicts.

Soyinka: Well, it's creeping in, but it's not yet very serious. The situation isn't so bad that if you chased them away from the screen they'd shout back at you; no, we haven't got to that stage yet. [laughter]

Class Discussion

Kane Hall, 20 April 1974

I'll read some straightforward lyrical verses which I wrote while I was sort of a guest of my government for some time. I selected this one because it begins with an imagery which has always appealed to me tremendously. As some of you may have heard before, I have a phobia of pop musicians. Now this will qualify that statement and indicate that I distinguish between that which I call pop—deliberately commercial and tawdry music—and that which springs from a genuine poetic feeling. I found myself borrowing a phrase, a kind of metaphor, a plaint of loss, anguished dissociation. Literally the whole of a series which I called "prisonettes" stemmed from the recollection of this phrase, the haunting quality of it, when I was, as I said, in that place. It also acknowledges a debt since I'm so critical of your society. It's called "Flowers for My Land."

> From a distant
> Shore they cry, Where
> Are all the flowers gone?
> I cannot tell
> The gardens here are furrowed still and bare.
>
> Death alike
> We sow. Each novel horror
> Whets inhuman appetites
> I do not
> Dare to think these bones will bloom tomorrow

Garlands
Of scavengers weigh
Heavy on human breasts
Such
Are flowers that fill the garden of decay

Seeking:
Voices of rain in sunshine
Blue kites on ivory-cloud
Towers
Smell of passing hands on mountain flowers

I saw:
Four steel kites, riders
On shrouded towers
Do you think
Their arms are spread to scatter mountain flowers

Seeking: Truth
Seeds split and browse
In ordure, corruption. From
Beds of worms
Ivory towers uphold the charnel-house

I know
Of flowers unseen, and they
Distil beatific dawns
But tares
Withhold possession of our mangled lawns

Visions pall
Realities invade
Our innermost sanctuaries
Oil erupts
Upon the altar, casts an evil shade

Hooded hands
Knock upon our doors
We say, let them have place
And offer
Ours in hope to make a common cause

It cannot be!
Hands of slag, fingers
Of spike, they press to full
Possession.
Creepers, climbers thrive beneath their rule

Slogans
Louder than empty barrels
And more barren, a rattle
In cups of beggary
Monkeys in livery dance to barrel organs

Break who can
The yet encroaching ring
Their hands are tainted, their breath
Withers all
They feed their thoughts upon the bounty of death

I traced
A dew-lane on the sun-
flower leaf; a hailstone
Burning, blew
A trap-door on my lane for falling through

These buds
That burst upon our prayers
Diffuse an equal essence
Will for ill
As others their atomic efflorescence

Alienates
Of heart from land, outcasts
Of toadstool blooms, the coral
Is a grim
Historic flower, a now and future moral

Come, let us
With that mangled kind
Make pact, no less
Against the lesser
Leagues of death, and mutilators of the mind.

Take Justice
In your hands who can
Or dare. Insensate sword
Of Power
Outherods Herod and the law's outlawed.

Sun-beacons
On every darkened shore
Orphans of the world
Ignite! Draw
Your fuel of pain from earth's sated core.

That will do, I think, to start with. Now, comments, talk; don't feel that you have to ask questions, you can just make comments.

Participant: Do your brothers in Africa feel that way? Are their souls that crushed?

Soyinka: Well, since it came from an experience which was not personal, the feeling, the rapport with that experience was personally felt and corresponded to some extent to *where* I was when I was writing it, but the experience from which it came certainly affected millions of people, millions. So whether they articulated this or not, and it has been articulated by many in songs, is less important.

It just occurred to me maybe I should balance that by reading something else. Yes, I just realized it was a very heavy poem. I was thinking more in the terms of borrowed imagery than the actual theme. Let me read to you "And What of It If Thus He Died." This was again born of the same reality. It represents a very different mood, a very different condition of mind, and I was thinking this time of Victor Banjo who was the military leader of the Third Movement which tried to break away from the secessionist principle and at the same time repudiate the Central Government in Lagos which was, whether you liked it or not, founded on a certain genocidal event. And Victor Banjo was one of the leaders of the Third Movement which tried to find a more ideological basis for reconstructing the entire society and obliterating the tribalistic lines which formed the original context of that war. The movement lost; a number of the leaders were executed by Biafra, including Victor Banjo himself and others on the Biafran side. In other words, this Third Movement got caught between the two because it set out to repudiate the two aspects. While it accepted the moral justification of Biafran secession, it felt that this was the wrong political action, but at the same time it could not accept or condone the moral basis, that is, the non-moral basis or the non-ideological basis of the government in Lagos. So this was the third force, and Victor Banjo lost his life with a number of others. When I came out—I think I first drafted it shortly after the event of the death of Victor Banjo, and I thought I'd rewrite it a little bit to make it less localized.

And What of It If Thus He Died?

    for Victor Banjo
    And for George Jackson
    And All, All, All

Not that he loved sunrise less
But truly, as love's caress
Whose craving must to spring devices lead.

Nor deaf nor blind lived he
To beauty's promise, to laughter
In light hours, but these he sought
To seal and to perpetuate
Upon the face of dearth.

Knowledge was not a golden plate
For feasts at the board of privilege
But a trowel laid to deep foundations
In sighted fingers of a master mason.

They said unto him, Be still
While winds of terror tore out shutters
Of his neighbour's home.

Beyond their walls to insulate
He felt his eyelids shrivel
In fires of rapine. The wrongs of day
And cries of night burnt red fissures
In chambers of his mind.

And so he set upon the quest
Seeking that whose plenitude
Would answer calls of hate and terror.

He looked with longing
To the lay of ocean pastures
Sought to harness their unbidden depths,

To measure the wind for symmetry
And on the wheel of earth to place
A compass for bewildered minds

He wondered in a treasure-house
Of inward prizes, strove to bring
Fleeting messages of time
To tall expressions, to granite arches
Spanned across landslides of the past

Even in the blind spoliation, amidst
Even the harrying of flames, he wished
To regulate the turn of hours

He lit the torch to a summons
Of the great procession—and, what of it?
What of it if thus he died
Burnt offering on the altar of fears?

Participant: What are you referring to by "the great procession"?

Soyinka: That's any procession. It means perhaps, to use the common parlance, "revolution," any movement towards change, any action which tries to move away from stagnation and retrogression. It's "great procession," with the emphasis on the great; it's a mass procession.

Participant: You seem to wear three caps: the poet playwright, and novelist. Is there any conflict between the three? And which do you prefer?

Soyinka: Yes, well there were more than three caps. One which you omitted to mention is that first and foremost I wear the cap of a human being. And, therefore, the other caps are really very minor: you know, rain covers, sun shields, and things like that. In other words, I don't distinguish between these various forms of expression. It so happens that I don't think I deliberately set out to seek which formats belong to particular events, or particular statements. In a dire political confrontation—let us say I'm working at the time intimately with an acting company—then I write political sketches, you know social commentaries, because this operates on two levels, not merely as a statement but as a physical, human confrontation with what one might call the retrogressive forces. In a situation where I want to make a very direct and immediate statement related to a situation which might disappear or be forgotten or be allowed to be forgotten, allowed to slide and become calcified by default, if I'm in that sort of situation, then I know I must find a medium which speaks very directly, very immediately and also represents a human confrontation. So, in such a situation I think I'm conscious of what form I'm using, but otherwise I don't think I work out a form in advance. I think the theme, the occasion, sort of brings out the form it operates through. I don't find any contradiction, or any stress, any strain between one form or another.

Participant: Are you a compulsive writer?

Soyinka: Oh, definitely not, I don't feel compelled. In fact, I'm basically a very lazy person. I'd rather nothing ever hit me. I'd sooner be doing many other things most of the time. [laughter] I've read about writers who must write so many pages a day, and I envy them. But I can't.

Participant: You seemed to object in your lecture to Brecht's concept of the theater. Would you comment on that further?

Soyinka: I'm glad you asked that because it seems there was a misunderstanding there. I did not raise any objections at all to Brecht's idea of revolutionary theater. No, I was very anxious to relate drama and theater to the actual practice of theater, to the resources of the people, whether it's mental or material resources, and to the political situation. I was trying to point out that very often what we consider poor proletarian theater is not proletarian theater, and I pointed out an example of the fact that some of Brecht's plays, for instance, are rehearsed for about a year-and-a-half. The Berliner Ensemble rehearses until every single action, motion, every single gesture is worked out to a level of breathtaking perfection. It's really incredible to watch this, and it's beautiful to see, but I'm suggesting that the logistics of organizing this particular thing is not exactly proletarian theater, even though the theme of the theater, the subject, the attitude, the didacticism, the message which is delivered is very strongly socialist. Nevertheless, it is not proletarian theater: not with the Berliner Ensemble anyway.

Participant: Which of your plays do you consider the most proletarian of the ones which have been performed in Nigeria?

Soyinka: Of my plays? Oh, I think I shouldn't really be the one to answer that question because it is a very difficult question, operating as I have done much of the time in an academic atmosphere. Then the purpose of a production is more than merely communicating to or entering into a rapport with the audience. There are so many other purposes involved. It becomes a teaching vehicle. I could be emphasizing for my students and for maybe a special theater workshop certain themes. Therefore, the purposes of that particular production go beyond even the direct confrontation with an audience. So I cannot speak in terms of a play, and that's why I keep pointing out the fact that in these discussions I am trying to get beyond the mere ideas in the plays to what actually happens. And that includes the sweat, the mechanics, the organization, the gritty details, because theater to be part of a people has got to include all these other details. It isn't merely the text.

Participant: Do you have any desire to take your plays to the rural people in Nigeria?

Soyinka: First of all, my plays have been done in this sort of atmosphere. I toured with a very small improvisational company into the hinterlands of the country and we used whatever has been available at the time. With *Brother Jero,* the political sketches I spoke of, and *The Lion and the Jewel,* I went through the same experience. Even though it was in English, it didn't matter at all because of the way it was done. In fact, I think that it had a

greater success in the rural areas than on the formal stages where we sometimes got trapped. I remember a bad experience in one of those. It was mainly
my fault as I was trying to use every single thing which happened, which
evolved in the theater, and it wasn't such a good production. So it depends
entirely on the play, the circumstances, environment, and things like that. In
any case, for tours like that, one would always choose the sort of play which
would lend itself to improvisational treatment such as short sketches which
are very topical and relate immediately to the people, and what you might
call the eternal comedies, like *The Lion and the Jewel,* which existed thousands of years ago and will exist in a thousand years' time. These obviously
are natural choices for situations like that.

Participant: When you write do you have any particular audience in
mind?

Soyinka: Well, again I make this distinction about the political sketches
because this relates to a particular moment, a time, a people, some villains,
some allies, some converts whom one is aiming at. I'm very direct and very
conscious of events. Each performance changes from day to day. Every single
sketch never is the same, it's interlaced with what has happened in the last
twenty-four hours. But otherwise, when I'm writing I'm not aware that I think
of a particular audience. I think that like most writers I have this basic creative arrogance and believe that there must be a thousand people around that
are on the same wave length and who will not make a publisher go bankrupt
by putting the stuff into print. I think it is that sort of feeling which gives the
writers the nerve to write.

Participant: How familiar are you and other West Africans with Malgreb
writing?

Soyinka: Not very much. In fact, the process is just beginning. There has
been this most annoying historical situation in which most of the Malgreb
area has been French speaking. But the communication is beginning. It began
in fact, curiously enough, with the cinema. You know the cinema was the
first to penetrate, even before the theater and the poetry. And you now have
black African Theater being translated into and published in Arabic magazines and vice versa. Then Arabic into French, French into English, etc.—a
tortuous process which, however, is beginning to end the long mutual isolation.

Participant: What is the function of the albino in your works?

Soyinka: Do you know the play *The Road?* In *The Road* a certain essence
of human consciousness—in Yoruba metaphysics I define it as the area of

transition—happens to be something which preoccupied me. Yoruba meta-physics holds the view of there being three major areas of existence. What you might call the traditional Yoruba sensibility is constantly in touch with and aware of these three. It's the world of the unborn, the world of the dead, and the world of the living. There is a mutual correspondence between these three areas. But I believe there is also a fourth which is not often articulated but which I recognize as implicit. It is not made obviously concrete by the rituals, by the philosophy that is articulated by the Ifa priests. This is the fourth area—the area of transition. It is the chthonic realm, the area of the really dark forces, the really dark spirits, and it also is the area of stress of the human will. So many physical symbols keep cropping up as an expression of this area of transition. Now one of them for me is the albino. He is a kind of twilight creature, the albino, and I entered into a feeling with the albino personality very early, from childhood, maybe as a result of knowing and having a rapport with them. There's this feeling of them not being quite of this world; they can't see very much in daylight, they see better in the dark-ness; they're very fragile; you feel that if you hold them they'll dissolve in your hands. And I think it is this which creeps into *The Interpreters,* as you have rightly observed. It's a kind of spillover of this feeling for the numinous area of transition.

Participant: How does the albino relate to the idiot in the mythology? Aren't there certain beings like albinos and idiots which are also certain deities?

Soyinka: Yes, they are, indeed. In most traditional culture the half-wit is not really considered a sick person. There's always the feeling that he has a certain area of awareness, of consciousness which is closed to the normal human being. The *abiku* is another one. This is the myth of infant mortality. We believe that the same child who dies is reborn in the same mother, keeps coming back, and therefore, because it constantly passes through this area of transition, through the unborn to the living world, from the living world to the dead, and makes this journey over and over again, that he acquires a certain honing of his psychic essence. The idiot also happens to be in Yoruba mythology a creation of the god Obatala, that is, the god of creation. And the myth is that he was like most of these deities, you know, pretty strong on the drink, and he got drunk while molding forms, human forms. He made some imperfect ones, thereby creating the cripple, the albino, the half-wit. There-fore, these are respected in society because it's understood that they are evi-dence of the moment of weakness of a god. But they also, for me especially in my own private mythology and also for lots of Yoruba people, they represent this area of transition since they have to breach or cross this gulf over and over again, more than other people.

Participant: Is the cripple as important as the others in Yoruba mythology? I'm wondering about your use of the cripple in *Madmen and Specialists*.

Soyinka: Yes, but in this instance I would say that there is less mythology. It is far more physical, almost a medical and political fact. The cripple here represents the mental cripple, the war cripple, the really dissociated personality in modern contemporary terms. The aspect of mythology in the play is a different one. It is merely part of the ritualistic consciousness which always wants to earth, the earthing principles of society, of human relationship to eternal ones, as represented by the creative earth mothers. I think that is the aspect of mythology.

Participant: Is there really any evidence that these abnormal people are more gifted?

Soyinka: Oh, there's no question of that. They come out with sudden remarkable statements which actually can be understood even in modern medical terms, if on wants to use that frame of reference. I remember a study of the autistic child I was looking at not so long ago. For the first time in decades the problem of trying to penetrate the internal world of the autistic child was taken seriously by medical science. In this study they referred to this child who used to sit for hours just looking at a wall. Finally it was possible to penetrate into him and ask, "Why do you sit there, looking at the wall all of the time?" And he said, "I'm watching the wallpaper dancing, making patterns, moving out and going back in." He used to sit for hours apparently, and he was supposed to be ill, but in actual fact he was studying the wall. He said with great intensity, "They make patterns, they dance beautifully, and they come out, and they settle in, and they turn themselves inside out." So that the Yoruba curative wise man, you know the medicine man, recognizes also that there is a certain internal world. He does not articulate it in those terms; he has probably never, for all I know, tried to find out from the child. Perhaps he has; we don't know as there are no case histories in the European sense that we can look up, but the fact is that he understands intuitively that the child has a certain world which contains its own complete logic. And as long as it is not harmful to the larger community, he must be allowed to exist in this world.

Participant: Do children ever function as oracles?

Soyinka: Yes, there are several like that. Children who from very early

childhood display these gifts, this strange awareness and who are close to the
so-called normal people, they go off in very different directions. They can be
marked and selected from childhood to become apprentices of the oracle, the
priest, acolytes in a shrine. It can be discovered that because of certain things
they say, certain things they do, certain attachments they have to symbols, to
artifacts—fetishes if you like, which are associated with certain deities—it
can be recognized that they are attached, that they are claimed by that deity,
in which case they are brought up in the process of learning all of the lore,
the myths, principles, and worship of the deity. On the other hand, in modern
times since the advent of Christianity, you can find the same signs in a child,
but if it comes, let us say, from a family who is beginning to lean towards
the Fundamentalist church, and you find a child of about three endowed with
mantic powers, it is claimed that that child is a prophet. Before you know
where you are, he is hollering like mad, you know, and prophesying, but this
time in purely Christian terms. I think you know the phenomenon here. So it
depends entirely in which frame of reference the child is in. I believe that the
phenomenon does not belong to any particular society. It is only the mythological frame of references, the metaphysical beliefs of that particular community which decides which way the child goes.

Participant: Is mythology in West Africa comparable?

Soyinka: Yes. The thing to remember is that most of these are basically
nature myths. They have to do with the cycle of birth, renewal, death, purgation, passage, trial, journey, all of the various patterns which we recognize,
even in European mythology; very basic human cycles of existence. For instance, there is the earth goddess of the Igbo, Ala, which has for its symbol
three sort of mounds, and even though there is no real earth goddess we
Yorubas have Ile, which is the earth god. But there isn't a fully corresponding
goddess to Ala for the Yoruba. There is one, and though it isn't the same
thing it embodies the same principles of procreation, fertility. There is Ikenga
again, which is more a cult than a deity among the Igbo, the cult of pure
strength, force. We don't have that in Yoruba. On the other hand, we have the
deity Ogun which is the principle of war, brute force, and at the same time
creativity. This god is a cycle, the complete cycle of destruction and creativity. These things sort of overlap in many ways, but they have not the same
precise significances.

Participant: I wonder what you've found retained of the Yoruba traditions
in the Americas?

Soyinka: I attended a few *bembes* in Cuba—in Brazil the name is *candom-*

ble. Of course, there are enormous changes, the syncretic process has been going on now for hundreds of years and the Roman Catholic saints have been completely merged. But I can tell you that in the case of Ogun the far more potent force of African deity is what predominates. So in the *bembe* of Saint Anthony, the symbols of Ogun are more evident. At first I was flabbergasted to find the liturgy so well preserved. Even though the priest in this particular case did not know the meaning of the words, he had the pronunciation and transcription. But the basic liturgy was there and recognizable. Ogun's praise songs, the rhythm also, the drum, the actual pattern of the drumming was the Ogun rhythm. I found it so exciting that we all ended up dancing. It is also more tinselly; you find Ogun decorated with silver foil paper, and one cannot help that. But there's no question at all of the force of the Yoruba religions. Oya and Oshun are the other shrines which I went to in Cuba but without seeing the ceremony. Shango was another very strong one in Cuba. It really was an incredible survival, and I understand it is even more so in Brazil.

Participant: Is there a traditional Yoruba theater which is an extension of storytelling?

Soyinka: I object to this idea of linking traditional theater with the expansion of storytelling. Storytelling is one form of activity, theater is different and stems from very different roots and occupies or utilizes very different forms. It must be admitted, however, that both forms do merge. But there is traditional theater, both secular and sacred. They take many forms. Also there is what you might call a repertory of legendary theater, such as the histories of the Rivers people. One example from the Rivers State is reenacted every two years. It is a very elaborate one, and it occupies five continuous days of play enactment. This is legendary theater; it merely recounts and reenacts the legend of a hero of that area who was transformed into a deity, a water deity, and there are many like that all over the country.

Participant: What do you think of writers like Pinter and the absurdist school of dramatists?

Soyinka: I know their plays very well. I even know some of them directly, but I find no subjective attachment to them. I admire their craftsmanship very often.

Participant: Do you think you are hard on black Americans? I'm thinking about the American Joe, Joe Golder, in *The Interpreters.*

Soyinka: No, I don't think so. I wouldn't agree that I was hard. Although in the beginning there was some kind of shall we say a searchlight bearing on him as a character, I think after his disaster, catastrophe, tragedy, whatever you like (and I remember this because I was conscious of it), I found myself in very great sympathy with his predicament. And, again I haven't read this book for ages, I think when he was singing his Negro spiritual I acknowledged in the writing the fact of a great anguish inside of him which is, I think, the greatest sympathy one can express for any other human being. But he is representative of a certain type of unthinking superficiality, and he represented actually the kind of black American who used to come to Africa at one time. That's changed completely now, but it was true up to even 1963 and 1964. One doctor was different from the Joe Golder type—I want to give you an example of what we used to put up with in those days. This doctor came to Nigeria and gave interviews in which he said that he didn't understand what fuss people were making about the Negro problem in America; he was a doctor, and he'd made it, and there was opportunity for black people who, you know, who worked hard, and who just didn't whine and so on. I remember getting a friend of mine on the television in Ibadan to invite him for an interview. And I think the State Department must have warned him in advance because he chickened out at the last moment. We were waiting there just to have a chat with him about these statements. I think they had to put on *I Love Lucy* instead that night. [laughter]

Really, Africa was flooded by all types of black Americans. Some of them had a genuine desire to relate to Africa, but they became literally like white colonialists. If we didn't dance in a raffia they felt that we were not being African. It was a natural, understandable, historical thing, but it was not easy on those of us who were waiting to welcome brothers from the Diaspora. But as I said, that's a very old picture and that book was written ages ago.

Participant: Have you been involved with any films?

Soyinka: No, that is, I hope that I have not made any movie which is widely distributed. I have been involved in one or two cinema disasters, and I just hope they are not widely distributed! [laughter]

Participant: Do you find the film a more difficult art form than others and would you comment on the state of film producing in Africa?

Soyinka: It is more difficult in this sense: it's a far more complicated art which depends very much on the proficiency of a number of people on the technical level. African cinema has suffered from the same kind of colonial imposition as other art forms. Although I must qualify this; it is really not so much an imposition as an acceptance by Africans. The French cinema school, that is, the Franco-phone cinema school, was the first to start in Africa, and unfortunately it did not concern itself with producing really good faithful pictures which stem from the imagination of the creators. It was more concerned with trying to establish itself as French. In other words, it became or wanted to be a part of the French culture, and it therefore tried to establish in Francophone Africa a kind of French New Wave cinema. It became preoccupied with problems of style and imitativeness instead of getting along with the real business.

By contrast, the Anglophones, when they came into the field, wanted very much to capture what Hollywood had been jettisoning. It is very strange, the contrast between the two. I have sat through hours as a member of the film jury both in Dakar and Tunisia just going through film upon film which either was in the worst Hollywood taste or was a cheap unimaginative pastiche of the French New Wave, such as *Last Year at Marienbad* or *Hiroshima Mon Amour*, but without the kind of historical accumulation which worked on these creators to use that particular form and to make that particular statement. So it was just idiotic. And, unfortunately, the action was no better in the Anglophone simply because the producers attach themselves to some American principle of film producing in which the producer could lift the entire footage and say "O.K., I'm going to get a new editor," or "I don't like the way you are shooting this; I want Americans to be able to understand this film." So by the time he is finished he's gone through about five editors. Stockholm, America, London, back again to America—you know that kind of thing. Simply because the producer and the producing company in West Africa had got themselves enthralled to the monied interests. So there have been difficulties both on the technological level, the commercial details, the amateurishness of some of the techniques, but also some genuine problems. But I don't think the cinema form is alien to the African creative instinct. If we can learn from past mistakes maybe in the next five years we will see an attempt from Africa to obliterate Shaft and Company. [laughter, applause]

Participant: What are the revolutionary qualities of drama? How does the revolution work within one person, especially in black American theater?

Soyinka: First of all I believe implicitly that any work of art which opens out the horizons of the human mind, the human intellect is by its very nature a force for change, a medium for change. In the black community here, theater can be used and has been used as a re-educating process. It has been used as a form of purgation, it has been used cathartically; it has been used to make the black man in this society work out his historical experience and literally purge himself at the altar of self-realization. This is one use to which it can be put. The other use, the other revolutionary use, may be far less overt, far less didactic, and less self-conscious. It has to do very simply with opening up the sensibilities of the black man not merely towards very profound and fundamental truths of his origin that are in Africa, in suddenly opening him, as in the example which I quoted in my speech—the introduction of Oshun worship into a production in Harlem—to new experiences. This worship was put there not for its own sake, not as a piece of exotica but simply as a means of making the audience question an identity which was taken for so long for granted, suddenly opening the audience up to a new existence, a new scale of values, a new self-submission, a communal rapport. By making the audience or a member of the audience go through this process, a reawakening has begun in the individual which in turn affects his attitude to the external social realities. This for me is a revolutionary purpose. Finally and most importantly, theater is revolutionary when it awakens the individual in the audience, in the black community in this case, who for so long has tended to express his frustrated creativity in certain self-destructive ways, when it opens up to him the very possibility of participating creatively himself in this larger communal process. In other words, and this has been proven time and time again, new people who never believed that they even possessed the gift of self-expression become creative and this in turn activates other energies within the individual. I believe the creative process is the most energizing. And that is why it is so intimately related to the process of revolution within society.

Participant: Can satire by used for revolutionary purposes?

Soyinka: Satire is necessarily negative in impulse. It sets out to demolish, to destroy. Satire in itself is useless; satire has to be coupled—again I must qualify this. The very fact of arousing people to a negative concept, a negative attitude toward an existing situation, can and should breed in a politicized society the need to effect positive changes or to think of the possibility of creating something in turn. But I think those who use satire in the theater generally recognize the fact that it is not the entire demand which is made of them; it's not the entire story, but first of all you have to arouse in the people a certain, well to put it crudely, a certain nausea towards a particular situation, to arouse them at all to accept the possibility of a positive alternative when it is offered to them. But first you must break their habit of thought, their habit of acceptance. You must be able to indicate to them first of all that the monster whom they thought could never be laughed at is you know very laughable, and maybe that's not so negative after all. But satire is not aiming for Utopia, nor does it see a Utopia which makes it intolerant of the present.

Maybe it does, but it doesn't have to state that. In fact, if satire begins to postulate a Utopia within the satire it probably ends up sounding ridiculous.

Participant: Do you see anything but negative forces at work today in Africa?

Soyinka: Well, before I deal with that, I am very grateful for that question because it gives me the opportunity to also say something positive. I will tell you what to expect in retrogressions in a moment. Let me tell you what political retrogression is not. Take what is happening in Ghana today. You had the phenomenon of an Nkrumah who, in spite of criticisms I have myself made of him—of his carelessness in developing a personality cult, for instance—still remains for me the number one Africanist. I do not say this because he is dead—I noticed recently since he died many of the people who were trampling him down are now beginning to eulogize him. But anyway, you have this situation of Nkrumah who with all of his faults was a number one Africanist and had certain direct and expressed visions. Then you had the phenomenon of Busia who came into power and proceeded to destroy every single Pan-Africanist concept whose foundations Nkrumah had laid, who proposed and really worked hard at obtaining a backward direction for the OAU, that is, dialogue with South Africa, who completely negated the principle of a single African brotherhood by expelling over a million West Africans from Ghana in the most brutish, most inhuman way which set forth waves and waves of refugees for the first time on that coast, and who finally got what was coming to him. This was a clear case of retrogression. Now a new government has come in which we are still watching very closely but which for me has already begun by trying to reverse Busia's process. The new Acheampong government seems to be imbued with certain—at the moment imprecise—socialist-communalist fervor. They have turned the whole external policy of Ghana the right way around and are progressing towards what we hope is the ultimate goal of most African leaders, that of a single African community. Now for me that's a progressive thing. Busia was very distinctively retrogressive. There are many examples which can be cited on the continent. Banda, of course, we don't even have to talk about, but if you want another example of retrogression it's him.

Participant: Several organizations and conferences are suggesting the need for a single African language. What is your opinion?

Soyinka: Yes, I believe it is inevitable for those who are serious about an African revolution (and when I use that term I mean a complete reexamination of principles which we have taken for granted for a very long time: the principle of dependence on outside countries—on the former colonial masters, the principle of the division of Africa into entities some of which are French oriented, others which are British oriented, others American in a far more subtle way in spite of America's claims that it has no colonies in Africa). But the reexamination of this entire concept must force a serious search for a new concrete identity, not a term or a slogan but one which is realized by every single member of the African masses in very concrete terms. One of these terms, one of the ways in which this sense of the new identity or thinking can take place obviously is, among others, the idea of a single language, the possibility of one person from West Africa being able to speak to a South African in a single language, the automatic understanding which will take place, the proliferation of ideas which will transcend all problems of linguistic translations and by which the African masses themselves will test all the various political ideologies which exist there. At that moment they will be able to decide whether they believe in Ujamaa, in Nyerere's socialism, or whether they prefer Mobutu's so-called African authenticity. They will be able to actually see which is the mere rhetoric and which is the reality tested against the real evidence, the concrete evidence.

Now the difficulties are not to be underestimated. In speaking for instance to some of the liberation fighters in Africa, you'll find that some of them are most strongly against the idea for simple strategic reasons. It's a question of an overall sense of priority; they are right on the front line; they believe that they must not diffuse their energies, their efforts by creating at the moment even the possibility of internal suspicions (of cultural domination, tribal domination, etc., through the fear of losing your own language. Which nobody suggests by the way). You know, all of our languages should stay. But the front-line liberation fighters are cautious, and quite rightly so. Their priorities are different, and it is as it should be. But the fact is that all over the continent, at the moment people who are interested in creating political diversions within the small entities which are so-called nations, these nations are now calling for national languages. In other words they're about to perpetuate the principle of artificial geographical boundaries which were set there by the colonial powers, by creating linguistic boundaries in these narrow, small, and artificial entities. Now it is obviously more logical to defuse the bomb, to expand the problem, not to create a claustrophobic conflict within very narrow boundaries. If you have a large concept of a continental language you spike the guns of these so-called politicians who know very well what they are doing because all they really want is to create internal chaos. They know that there are many tribes in these various nations who will reach for their guns sooner than accept a language of the other tribe who is enclosed with them. When you think of Nigeria, for instance, after the Civil War, think of somebody trying to suggest that one of the Nigerian languages become the national language. Yet the idea is constantly mooted, and it is solely for the purpose of creating utter chaos. So, logically, it is far more realistic to think in terms of a continental language as a psychological weapon of liberation. That it is difficult I do not deny, that it is desirable I think is obvious. Whether we'll do it in the next five, ten, twenty years is immaterial as long as we agree that this is the goal, and we start working toward it.

Participant: Do you have any language in mind?

Soyinka: I will not make that mistake of starting the controversy. Let's just say that I have certain ideas, but we mustn't begin by awakening suspicions. I'll only tell you it is not any language from my own country, that's all I'm willing to tell you. [laughter] Thank you very much. [applause]

Interview with Wole Soyinka
John Agetua / 1974

From *When the Man Died.* John Agetua, ed. Benin City: Bendell
Newspaper Corporation, 1975, 31–46. Reprinted with permission.

Agetua: Wole, could you tell us how you got into this business of writing?

Soyinka: As far as I can recall I've always scribbled something . . . . But
first of all, I was deeply interested in literature, that is reading fiction, poetry,
biography and so on. I suppose that sooner or later, I had to try my hand at
it. I did the usual entertainment pieces at school; I tried the then N.B.C. for
two short stories which were used and even a radio-play. I realised myself
that I was beginning to write seriously only after I had left Nigeria. Then I
realised that writing was going to be more than a hobby.

Agetua: Is it true that some writers are at their best when they are in love?

Soyinka: Well, I can only answer personally. And the answer for me is no.
I don't see what being in love has to do with writing well and producing
much except maybe writing more love lyrics.

Agetua: Do you think that certain occupations and pre-occupations are
more conducive to creative writing than others? In other words does the work
you do or the company you keep affect your writing?

Soyinka: It affects the theme inevitably for the simple reason that one's
immediate external environment impinges on his preoccupations and centres
of interest. But I don't think that any particular form of employment is conducive to writing. Experience comes from any activity of the human mind.

Agetua: Would you suggest newspaper work for the young writer?

Soyinka: Not particularly except that for the more verbose ones it might
teach them to be more economical.

Agetua: Do you think that the intellectual stimulus of the company of
other writers is of any value to an author?

Soyinka: For some writers, yes. And to all, to a small or larger extent,
even when it is not intentional some kind of spark, some ideas can pass
between one and another. Two people in a similar profession tend occasionally to swap ideas and intended useful lines of thought. I personally find that

I work more in solitude. I find the company of other writers pretty trying if, that is if such writers insist on talking about their work because I don't really like talking about my work; I don't like talking about the processes of writing. But I do acknowledge that there are some writers who seem to thrive on this continuing exchange of ideas.

Agetua: Have you ever felt that weight of loneliness which is the lot of the writer?

Soyinka: You know I think that there is too much angst put into this loneliness of the writer. All human beings are to a larger or smaller extent alone ultimately and I wouldn't like to put writers in a solitude category.

Agetua: In Ibadan, in the '60s there was quite a community of writers. Did you have any sense of group feeling with other writers?

Soyinka: Oh yes, very much. We certainly enjoyed being together and organising cultural events and also creating a place which was congenial to young up-and-coming writers and artists. But we didn't shop talk much. We mostly met or did things and tried to create the right environment for all those who were interested in writing. We didn't form a school though each person was a very strong individual and worked as an individual.

Agetua: But I hear, Okigbo had a habit of discussing his work with J. P. and others.

Soyinka: O yes, I remember that Okigbo was really fond of discussing the progress of his work. He used to have a lot of discussions with J. P. Clark and they talked about the work in progress. With me also, but generally I listened to him read his lines and I think it was only rarely I would offer any suggestion because I really find it very, very difficult to try and intrude into the creative process of another writer. In fact this creates difficulty for me when young writers come to me for help and advice. Unless the work is so bad that it cannot arouse my interest in any way then I say flat: "Please go and start all over again." But if it is worthwhile and I can recognise the actual organic process of bringing out this matter then I find myself very, very reluctant to offer any suggestion. I must confess that I find it impossible to enter into a dialogue with a writer over a work in progress.

Agetua: What would you say makes the writer different from other people?

Soyinka: Nothing at all. Except that he uses the idiom of words while others use the idiom maybe of bricks, or wood or metal.

Agetua: If you are agreeable, Wole, lets talk about your technique. How do you name your character?

Soyinka: You'd find that when it comes to technique my answers are really going to be brief because I really don't like discussing the processes of writing. . . . Well . . . I don't name my characters, they mostly name themselves. Occasionally I do name them.

Agetua: Do the titles come to you while you are in the process of writing?

Soyinka: At all phases at the beginning, sometimes I change the title when the work is actually in print.

Agetua: Does the theme or character change as you go along?

Soyinka: Occasionally but very rarely. The theme doesn't change. The actual manipulation, the intended manipulations of the characters could. The character doesn't really change.

Agetua: Do you ever use maps or charts to guide you in your writing?

Soyinka: No. Never.

Agetua: How do you go about revising?

Soyinka: Oh, one just revises. One continues revising.

Agetua: Where do you think your style of writing came from? Was it a gradual accumulation out of your character or does it have any literary antecedents?

Soyinka: From theme, from character and from a sense of rhythm in my head. I do not try to imitate any stylist.

Agetua: Your work includes a great range of experience as well as of form. What do you think is the greatest quality a poet can have?

Soyinka: That's a difficult question. Sensibility, I suppose would be the word.

Agetua: Do you plan the shape of your stanzas?

Soyinka: No, the theme dictates it.

Agetua: Are you aware that there has been general tendency in your work to move from a narrower to a wider audience?

Soyinka: This is a familiar question and I would just say again that I'm not usually conscious of the dimension of the audience for whom I'm writing except of course in my political sketches and of course in my recent book, *The Man Died* which is very pointedly political and which was geared towards re-educating the minds of Nigerians by relating things which they thought they knew about and shaping their ways of looking at so-called public leaders and figures. In a book like that, there was a very conscious orientation and the same thing for my former political sketches. These were written for specific events directed at specific abuses, but other-wise, I write under the conviction that there must be a number of people on that wavelength for whom whatever I write must have a meaning.

Agetua: Some critics say your works are difficult. For example, the opening sentence in *The Interpreters* "Metal on concrete jars my drink lobes," would put any average reader off. Is there any conscious effort on your part to blur meaning?

Soyinka: No. I have to concede, since I also consider myself as a critic, I tend towards what's called the elliptical style of writing. That's not deliberate, it's just a deliberate quirk about which I cannot do much. But I deny absolutely any attempt to mystify or to create obscurities. Certainly, if I thought that the first sentence of any work I wrote is going to put anybody off I'd change it immediately. Where I become concerned is where educational institutions do not sufficiently examine the works which they set for their students. Let's face it. Take any single writer, there are works of his which are a little bit more difficult, more obscure than others. No single writer writes evenly from start to finish. Fagunwa's novel in Yoruba, *A Forest of a Thousand Daemons,* is a head cracker for indigenous Yoruba speakers. I know what problems we used to have in school. Generally, I certainly never set out to be obscure. But complex subjects sometimes elicit from the writer complex treatments.

Agetua: Some critics talk a lot about Greek, American poetry with reference to your work. You'd read a lot in the classics?

Soyinka: I've read widely in the world's literature, European, Asiatic, American, there are Buddhist's reference points and mythologies in my poetry too. In other words, I cannot cut off and will not attempt to cut off what is my experience and what is afterall, the world's experience. There is a great deal of intercommunication in the world. A lot of people tend to forget that. As long as I find the means of expression, a form of communication which does not alienate my immediate readership and I do not deliberately cram my work with foreign references to a point where the work is indigestible—these are faults which should never be permitted by any serious writer. I believe that in expanding the horizons and the curiosity also of my readership, I think I'm contributing to both their intellectual and general uni-versal conceptualization even of their immediate experiences. The actual form, the medium, the metaphor, which one uses is ultimately unimportant because this is merely the framework upon which one poses certain themes. As I said as long as the actual metaphor itself does not become an obstacle to the appreciation of the entire message, I don't think a poet should worry unduly about the eclectic appearance or structure of his work. We must not think that traditionalism means raffia skirts; in other words it's no longer possible for a purist literature for the simple reason that even our most tradi-tional literature has never been purist.

Agetua: In *The Interpreters*—you criticised the elite for not having the moral courage to cope with the social problems to which he returned from Europe. What can the intellectual of today be given the sad lack of valid political forces in our midst? Does he have a duty, on each and every circum-stance to express his feeling and opinion publicly and to everyone whatever?

Soyinka: I think so but I would qualify that. I believe that all the people cannot speak all the time, they certainly should not all speak at once. This is unnatural. I believe also that one must not make the demand that every single voice be raised. What we need really is an element of integrity. In other words, I would sooner have 99% of the intelligensia silent rather than have 99% vocal of whom about 90% are purely hypocritical. There exists of course those I'd prefer to call intellectuals of the establishment; their position is clear, no matter what the status quo is, they consider it their intellectual responsibility to find reasons to justify this. They exhort the people to accept indignities, to accept situations that obviously are detrimental to their health—to their social health. Not only that. By lending the veneer of intellec-tual approval to the status quo they enable the most moronic set of rulers to claim that they also have intellectual support on their side. I don't know whose crime is worse; the establishment intellectual or the intellectual who trots out ideological dogma, and, whose very conduct in society is ostenta-tiously contrary to the very ideology he preaches. Such people betray genuine mass movements, time and time again. I remember the Morgan strike, I re-member the revolt against Akintola and his regime in the West and I know the part played by this sort of intellectual at the time. They are never abashed even when they are finally defeated. They are right again on the soap-box. Eventually, I think, it is not to the intelligensia that we must look for salvation in the society. One responsibility which the genuine ones in this group can assume is the real political education of the masses—not education merely as to their immediate right; social, economic and judicial rights, but educate them about their own potential in society.

Agetua: But what of the artist? Don't you think he should just carry on his work as best he can in view of the current political situation?

Soyinka: What I said just now goes for the artist. But again let us not impose these duties: let us say that only those who feel sufficiently degraded by the actualities of the society and who feel that they cannot really function with any sense of self-respect, knowing very well that even their own individual potential is being operated at about one-tenth its strength, its possibilities, because of the restrictive and reactionary environment in which they are compelled to work. Only those who feel this sufficiently should be permitted to work in the manner which I have just described.

Agetua: There has been a controversy over the literary value of *The Man Died*. Some critics maintain that it is a flawed work because passages of great beauty alternate with passages that are too subjective to be artistic. The chief weakness of the book lies in your failure to maintain an artistic distance between yourself and the events described. What's your reaction to this?

Soyinka: First of all, I think the received ideas about what constitutes the correct literary style for any particular experience have got to be shattered. I'd like to say that several of such critics are still very much enslaved by the received traditions of European literary style. What they would like perhaps is something in the Dostoyevsky's experience, or they would like a straight-forward ideological re-working of a particular experience including a kind of textbook pronouncement for projection for the future. In other words, there are ideas which are brought to bear about a situation and there is no prepared-ness in the minds of most people for a complete radical and deliberate depar-ture from what should be the normal expectations. The fact of this disturbance in the minds of many readers is for me a testimony of the success of what I set out to do. Squalor, sordidness, ugliness exist side by side with the most transcendental phases of human subjectivity. Villainy, and general treachery exist simultaneously and are conceived by the run of humanity. The juxtaposition of what you call beautiful passages with languages of sheer deliberate brutality, was a deliberate tool. I tried several ways of narrating this experience and making certain indictments. As I said in the Preface, I even thought one time of separating the two things. And then I thought a book if necessary should be a hammer, hand grenade which you detonate under a stagnant way of looking at the world. And so those critics are not used to this particular form of juxtaposition. I would like to suggest that in another five to ten years with the reality of African politics, as the sensibilities of those who actually participate in the process of creating change in society grow this sort of style, which I insist is very deliberate, will become commonplace. In other words, writers should not feel that they are obliged to create a mono-stylistic narrative. I believe that one can obtain a dual readership, those who would like only to read the winnowed passages of an excruciating experience, distilled into a aesthetic format, they are compelled whether they like it or not, to come sharply and rudely across this very brutal narrative suddenly. They would not like it, but at the same time it is a therapy. I believe it will shatter their whole way of viewing man and society. Society acquiesces very easily; for instance, a power-drunk official taking up his machine gun and mowing down a number of innocent suspects or maybe challengers to his position and returning afterwards to hold a polite conversation with some diplomat elsewhere. Society doesn't think that the gloved, beautifully be-ribboned leader who has just waved so graciously to the people, who has just wiped with a laced handkerchief the drops of champagne from his lips, has just before that moment given the order for the quiet liquidation of a number of innocent trade-unionists. This kind of juxtaposition of ugliness and a kind of superficial aesthetic beauty—these are the realities of life—we haven't begun actually using words to punch holes inside people.

But let's do our best to use words and style when we have the opportunity—to arrest the ears of normally complacent people, we must make sure we explode something inside them which is a parallel of the sordidness which they ignore outside.

So I've been very gratified by the shock reaction because it was actually my intention to create feelings of revulsion, of disappointment, of bewilderment because I know very well they will have a therapeutic effect and will completely revolutionize the ways of their thinking, of perceiving and therefore of participating in whatever sort of programme is envisaged for society.

Agetua: Some writers are painfully sensitive to criticism. Have you been much affected by your critics?

Soyinka: No. Not very much. In fact, I find it difficult to read—both the positive and negative criticism of my work. I didn't read much of the foreign criticism of *The Man Died,* but I made sure I read nearly everything that was written by Nigerian critics for this book is meant for the Nigerian readership.

And so I read these very carefully and as I told you earlier, I was very gratified by the extreme reactions, the confusion even which it created in the minds of the people. I think there was only one criticism which distressed me very much and that was the script written by Adamu Ciroma where he accused me of being a Yoruba jingoist and hating Northerners! And that really hurt me because first of all it isn't true and because it is a very dangerous thing to say. Because let's face it; how many people will read *The Man Died* and judge for themselves? But a lot more would read *The New Nigerian*. It was a political statement which should only be made by someone who's absolutely certain and can prove what he said. I would have thought it was obvious from the book that in fact I left Kaduna prisons in a state of mutual respect between me and my warders and in fact, I depended on their humanity and understanding—and I owed my very survival to their understanding. I think I dropped enough hints on that but I didn't make it all the more obvious because I was requested—and now—I think I'm no longer bound by that promise since it has led to this grievous and dangerous idea that I don't like Northerners. I'm no longer bound by my promise which was that I would not publicly thank them because that might get them into trouble because they went beyond their belief in their anxiety to ease the rigours of solitary confinement for a year and nine months. So, now I would like to use this medium to say that I now deliberately break that promise. I want to say as publicly as possible that I owed my very survival to the humanity of prison officers who were Northerners. And that I can never forget.

I hinted this in the "An Acknowledgement" which was a kind of preface to *The Man Died.* Perhaps another reason why Adamu Ciroma says this is that I'm very frank about what I consider the immediate effects which led to the Biafran seccession and which for me represented a crime against the entire Nigerian people.

Agetua: In your most recent works there co-exists philosophical pessimism and a certain confidence—not optimism; confidence in the spirit rather than in man, in nature rather than in the universe, in action rather than in results. Do you think that this attitude—which is essentially that of the rebel—can be adopted by the majority or is it condemned to remain the priveledge of a few wise men?

Soyinka: Another word for it as used by a certain critic is ambivalence. For me the word I prefer to use is the reality of nature. You must know of course about my fascination with the symbolic figure of my society—Ogun.

He represents this duality of man; the creative, destructive aspect. And I think this is the reality of society, the reality of man, and that one would be foolish not to recognise this. I cannot sentimentalize revolution. I recognise the fact that it very often represents loss. But at the same time I affirm that it is necessary to accept the confrontations which society creates, to anticipate them and try to plan a programme in advance before them. The realism which pervades some of my work and which has been branded pessimistic is nothing but a very square, sharp look. I have depicted scenes of devastation, I have depicted the depression in the minds even of those who are committed to these changes and who are actively engaged in these changes simply because it would be starry-eyed to do otherwise. I think one should not promise what is not there. Only one thing can be guaranteed and that is the principle of accepting the challenges of life, of society in the same way as nature does. Those who are expecting a one-dimensional statement from me as a writer are looking for a cheap injection of optimism in their nervous system. What I'm saying is that we must all accept the negative potential of action and then transcend this. And this is why I use Ogun as a representative symbol because it represents the Promethean reality of our existence.

Agetua: In a paper on your most recent novel, *Season of Anomy,* Dr. Dan Izevbaye said that having experimented with the theme of Prometheus and got dissatisfied with it you've now taken up the theme of Orpheus. Is that correct?

Soyinka: It is not true to say that I've got dissatisfied with Prometheus—on the contrary. These various explications of human conduct, of man's relationship both with society and with the universe are not mutually exclusive. In a paper which I did some years ago I described for instance our own Ogun, the Yoruba diety, in terms of a combination of the Promethean, the Appolonian and the Dionysian instinct. This is not because it is impossible to explicate Ogun except in terms of foreign deities. It all came about because I was trying to explain these qualities in relation to the literature of other societies. Prometheus is a metaphor just as Orpheus. It might interest you to know that a magazine like *Black Orpheus* used to upset me a lot because of the name. I felt it was wrong and retrogressive to name a magazine devoted to African Literature, art, to relate it to a European point in mythology. And one of the reasons why I resigned from that magazine was that I failed to persuade the editor to change its name. So you see the two attitudes are not contradictory at all; I objected to placing a whole vehicle for the propagation of mine and your culture as well as the culture of the African world in the Diaspora, having it grounded entirely in this European cultural matrix. I don't mean to suggest that we should pretend that the Orpheus lore doesn't exist or that it should not be utilized in a sort of piecemeal way. But to embody everything that comes through that mould which is a creative vehicle of transmission, to refer to it, and condition the mentality of the readership by this reference point, this for me was very subversive.

Agetua: When a man speaks as you do, he is not speaking solely for himself. He's inevitably speaking for others. And he's speaking for something. In other words, he's speaking in the name of, and in favour of, men for whom these values count. Who are these men and what are those values?

Soyinka: The immediate humanity for whom I speak is the humanity that geographically demarcated, is called Nigeria, because it is the entity to which I immediately identify. Beyond that, I think one also speaks for humanity in general. What happens in Ethiopia affects us, what happens in Chile, in Uganda affects us also. So at no time, I believe, does one's writing stay within one's own immediate environment. And you ask what values? It is very difficult to describe. As you very well know, I eschew the very facile ideological programme. A lot of people find it very easy to say what their values are, to encapsulate everything by saying: "The values I stand for are the Marxist values of society." Ask them to go deeper, how exactly are you going to apply this to the situation of famine, of indifference of your government at this particular time and they'd probably reply: "Oh it is not yet the historical moment to confront the reactionary, capitalist elements in society who ultimately are responsible for creating this situation of famine in our country." That's what they will say. They will never commit themselves to a direct activist programme both for the amelioration of this particular disaster or for a confrontation with the indifferent regime which must accept responsibility for it. So you see this is why the question of violence becomes very difficult for me to defend because I do not want to fall into the trap of what I call professional mouthers, the parrots of ideology. I believe implicitly in the values of an egalitarian society and I think that sums it up. An egalitarian society means egalitarianism in justice, in economic welfare in the right of each individual to achieve maximum fulfilment, I believe in the legal robbery of the exploiters and the acquisitive monopolists in society. I believe in retaining the means of production and the material benefits of production by the masses of the people. But I would rather not be bracketed with those pseudo-stalinists-leninists and maoists who are totally unproductive and merely protect themselves behind a whole barrage of terminologies which bear no relation to the immediate needs of society.

Agetua: Are there any political models in Africa which appeal to you especially?

Soyinka: Guinea Bissau, that's an example of a kind of potentially ideal society for a continent like Africa. And those who are still seeking for an ideal model of society should study carefully the organic revolution of that society. Tanzania is another example and there are two other tiny pockets in Africa. For people who suggest that writers don't exactly articulate an ideology, ask just what has been made of the ideologies expounded by Nkrumah, by Nyerere, by the revolutionary leaders of Guinea Bissau?

Agetua: The notion of art for arts sake is alien to your thinking. That of commitment as it has been made fashionable of late is equally so. Taken in its present meaning commitment is making one's art subservient to a policy. It seems to me that there's something which is characteristic of your work that might be called inserting that work into its time. Is this correct? And if so, how do you describe that insertion?

Soyinka: Inevitably, I think, every work belongs to a given moment. But then it transcends this because the ideas, the values, which they project are ultimately universal and external values. There are always ephemeral events which must be taken care of, but I think that even these events are tackled in the context of a larger vision, a larger direction.

I have never really completely understood the expression, "Art for art sake." I know that I love to sit down and put on a record whose music has been created by an artist. I find this very restful, I find that I emerge from this sort of experience a much fuller, richer person, and enabled to cope in a more sensitive way with the direct mundane, day-to-day confrontations of life.

So anything which enlarges the human mind, the human sensitivity is not wrong, is not false. Whether you call it art for art sake whenever it is not associated with a political programme or a reformist programme, I don't know. These definitions sort of wash over my back for the simple reason that I know that what I write is crucial at this particular time. As for commitment, I think one is committed as a human being and that's enough. There is something else; one must not condescend to one's audience, one must not say "I want to write something at the lowest possible common demonimator to make sure that a child in the kindergarten will have to understand it."

I think one should just have integrity. That's the main thing, and the value of his work is residual both in its affectiveness on his audience, his readership as well as in the lasting values as much as by his capacity to lure society to implementing serious progressive changes.

Agetua: At the source of every work there is an experience. It may be a brief and brutal experience—a trauma. For you there was the war and your detention. Have not the last few years been the source of a new experience?

Soyinka: One must never try to rigidify the divisions between one experience and another. All experiences flow one into another. What has happened to me since I consider myself a sentient creative being has never totally finished happening and I think one has enough imagination and projection even to experience right now what he might possibly experience over the next ten years. So I won't like to encapsulate the last few years as denominating any particular territory of experience. No.

Agetua: Could you give us a resume of all that has happened to you since you left Nigeria?

Soyinka: I have been sort of itinerant lecturer at various universities both in the African continent and in Europe as well as in America. Then I did this one year stint as a Fellow in Cambridge and then I came to Accra to edit *Transition*.

Agetua: Now don't you feel decapitated sort of—I remember you once said that you couldn't write if you were cut off from your roots.

Soyinka: I don't find it impossible to write at present. You see, being cut off from one's sources is not completely physical. The physical aspect is there. But in any case one stores enough away, after all, writing is mostly imagination. One stores enough of experience to nourish him for quite sometime. How long it will be before I begin to feel the strophe of those particular roots I don't know. But right now I assure you that I don't feel any dearth of contact.

Agetua: Some observers feel that you succumbed by accepting editorship of *Transition*. They feel that *Transition* is C.I.A. inspired. What's your reaction to this?

Soyinka: There's no doubt at all that one time *Transition* was infiltrated money-wise by fund which could be traceable at the third remove to C.I.A.

There is no question at all about that. You see I am not interested in the magazine's past as such. I am only interested in the uses to which it can be put. Also I know the history of *Transition* and I know about its birth and I know that it was started single-handedly and run on a shoestring by a remarkable individual . . . Rajat Neogy. It was entirely his idea and that magazine ran for a number of years before certain foundations took an interest in it and offered it some grant which as I said was indirectly traceable to a C.I.A. sponsored foundation. My attitude is very simple: I know absolutely that I'm not bought by any interests and that I edit this magazine entirely from the basis of my personal integrity. There is something else. I have noticed that the C.I.A. brush has been used very indiscriminately to smear everything literally that moves and is opposed to the ideas of certain people. Long before I came to *Transition,* believe it or not I was accused of being a C.I.A. agent. Let me tell you an amusing story: there is a boon companion of mine with whom I used to drink who, for reasons best known to him, actually engaged in a conversation with some university lecturers, and swore that he knew for certain that I was a C.I.A. agent. He even assured them that I showed him my C.I.A. identity card. They said he should know because he drinks a lot with me. This conversation was repeated to me by one of the lecturers to whom he was talking. Now, having been subjected to situations like this you can see why I'm so indifferent to these very easy and very cheap smears of unserious people, people who are mostly pseudo-radicals, pseudo-revolutionaires, who for ever find it easy to shout C.I.A. wolf when there is nothing around. My interest is to what use I can put this journal. Also I have satisfied myself absolutely that for at least four years before I took over, there was never any question of any remotely linked C.I.A. money entering this journal. And as I wrote in my first editorial, No. 45, I'm very sorry for the C.I.A. if they thought they ever gained anything out of *Transition* even when their money was percolating into it. The whole of Africa at one time or the other was penetrated by C.I.A. money, all governments accepted aid—now should we say that because C.I.A. money ever entered Africa we should sink Africa and build a new continent?

Agetua: You once wrote, in reference to the genocide perpetrated in Angola and South Africa that given equal opportunity, the black tin-god would degrade and dehumanise his victim as capably as Vorster or Governor Wallace. Recent events in Ethiopia and Uganda seem to bear this out and must be a source of anguish to you. Have you any comments?

Soyinka: In Ethiopia, you may have observed that there has been a universal outcry against the killings. I personally feel once again that the people have been betrayed. You may have observed that in *Transition* 45 we carried a report on the famine in Ethiopia. It is a very outspoken one and really called for what amounted to revolutionary charges. And therefore I was particularly euphoric when the coup took place eventually and this feudal wastrel was finally toppled from his throne. And I watched the progress with keen interest. For me, this recent slaughter is merely a continuation of the brutishness of life which existed during Haile Selassie's regime. But in any case, let's not restrict ourselves to Ethiopia. As I said I was gratified to find that there has been what strikes me as some evidence of the existence of moral conscience among African leaders and commentators. Sometimes, I think it is absolutely dead.

Take Amin, for instance. The only difference is that he has never publicly acknowledged those whom he liquidated. There are still some so-called African intellectuals who deceive themselves that nothing really bad or reactionary is happening in Uganda. They are taken in by Amin's clownery not realising that this man represents the greatest, single curse that has ever befallen this continent. And I think that it's about time the conscience of the leadership in Africa became aroused to a vociferous extent about what's happening in Uganda. In Ethiopia, they acknowledge this execution which has been condemned as barbaric, but I think we shouldn't allow this sudden eruption to override the continuous crime that has been committed against the Africans by this monster, Amin, in Uganda.

Agetua: What impact would the forthcoming All Africa Festival of the Arts have on African Literature?

Soyinka: Little. I think the cultural life of any society should be one continuous festival. Let me qualify that: it's not that I object to festivals. I believe any celebration is good for the psychic health of any people. I like festivals to be intergral. Right now I am not absolutely certain what Nigeria is celebrating. In other words, beyond giving a boost to those who least deserve a boost, and beyond elevating the concept of culture and creativity to what I call superficial dimensions as opposed to making creativity an integral part of life which a really well principled festival can do—and this is the whole point about our traditional festival of arts—and so I take these positions: a festival is not a bad thing in itself. One is not sure that a particular approach both in qualitative, and very likely qualitative approach of this festival is going to be of beneficial effect to creative life in Nigeria or in Africa. In other words, certain values will be promoted by the festival of this nature which are not really healthy to the kind of culture and creative work which is part of our society. I hope I'm proved wrong. Undoubtedly one or two good things will come out. But I doubt whether as an expression of the intergrated cultural life of the black peoples all over the world, I doubt very much if it will be a positive expression of our contribution to that.

Agetua: When is your home-coming?

Soyinka: A lot of people think that the main reason for my staying away is the book (*The Man Died*) and some kind of official reaction to it. That's only a small fraction of the causes why I'm staying away. Most people are not aware first of all, of the pressures which attach to the existence of individuals like myself not merely from the fact that they become famous or notorious but also because of their participation in the political life of their countries. The degree and the levels and the forms they take, these are the aspects of day-to-day living which are very, very important to a majority of people. Even to most writers whose activities are however circumscribed by a full-time commitment to writing. I have, as you know, been actively involved in all sorts of political activities. I participated in a certain way with a number of colleagues in the Morgan Commission strike, at which time we very seriously hoped that the strike would result in some kind of labour revolution in society. It didn't.

Then I was also involved in the insurrection which took place in the West and again I was involved in what I call the Third Movement which was an attempt to find a third ground for the resolution of the civil war. The point of it is that I recognised a long time ago that the problem of Nigeria has moved beyond the remedy of debate and controversy, that the options are very clear. I find it impossible to return at this stage.

You asked me a moment ago what I have been doing and I gave you a brief sketch but I have also been stock-taking and doing a cold-blooded analysis of Nigeria since independence and trying to project it into the future. One thing which I do not see is any further participation on the level of what I may call debate and controversy. I see the disease in the country of such a nature that I cannot honestly with any sense of contributing something useful participate in any particular form of political engagement. At the same time I also recognise that if I'm in Nigeria, it is impossible for me to remain a private citizen. In other words, whereas before, I was content with a kind of catalytic peripheral underground association with activists, and political movements in the country and been quite at home in it because—don't forget that I am not a professional politician—and I don't want to be one—having been involved on that level, it is not possible for me to pretend a lather of creative sweat if I were to revert to what seems to be the only thing possible— the debate—and controversy—political contribution. For me these two options are close; one, of remaining completely an unpoliticised individual and two, the option of pretending to myself that I am achieving anything by the debate-controversy method. I don't because of this condemn, or suggest for a single moment that it is absolutely futile, the debate and controversy method—there is a lot of education which can go on with it, a kind of preparatory work, a kind of retunning of attitudes, . . . I should add by the way that I am not absent from Nigeria; I feel very spiritually there and quite apart from the details of keeping in touch with events there I don't feel absent from Nigeria.

An Interview with Wole Soyinka

Henry Louis Gates, Jr. / 1975

From *Black World* 24.10 [1975], 30–48. Reprinted with permission of Henry Louis Gates, Jr.

Truly a Renaissance man, Wole Soyinka is poet, playwright, novelist, critic, actor, teacher, editor, philosopher. Born in 1934 in West Nigeria, the "Yoruba Pantheon" attended Government College in Ibadan (then the University of Ibadan) and received an honors degree in English from Leeds University, England, in 1957. Beginning in 1958, he spent 18 months as a Play Reader at the Royal Court Theatre in London, where he produced *The Invention,* one of his earliest satirical pieces. In 1960, he returned home to Africa to produce, with The 1960 Masks, his drama troupe, his play *A Dance of the Forests,* which won the competition to commemorate Nigeria's Independence in October of that year.

Four years later, Soyinka formed a new group, Orisun Theatre, which became a vehicle for the more serious political satire, teaming up with the older group for major productions. In 1965, his play, *The Road,* won first prize for published drama at the first Festival of the Negro Arts at Dakar, Senegal. That same year, he was awarded, together with Tom Stoppard, the John Whiting Award for Drama. Shortly after his return from the Commonwealth Arts Festival in Britain at which *The Road* was performed, he was arrested and imprisoned.

Soyinka's first term in prison seems almost humorous. In the Western Region Assembly in 1965, the corrupt ruling party, led by one Chief Akintola, was being challenged for the first time by the opposition Action Group. By "blatant and unrestrained thuggery and ingenious teachery," wrote Ruth First in her *The Barrel of a Gun,* Akintola and his boys snatched away electoral officers before opposition candidates could lodge their nominations. Ballot boxes were stuffed, ditches dug around polling stations so that people couldn't vote.

Just as the local radio station prepared to broadcast the good Chief's prerecorded victory speech, a pirate tape interrupted and announced, "This is the voice of Free Nigeria!" and proceeded to advise, in no uncertain terms, Chief Akintola to leave the country after his startling upset at the polls! On the evidence of a producer, Soyinka was arrested and charged. His first trial was a farce. At the end, he was acquitted, but not before he had gone on a hunger strike in prison to protest the delay in bringing his case to court.

Undaunted, the following year Soyinka took his play *Kongi's Harvest* to the Festival in Dakar. In August 1967, just after his first volume of poems, *Idanre,* was published, again he was arrested. This time, though, there was no humor.

Three weeks into the Nigerian Civil War, Soyinka issued a poignant appeal for a cease-fire. Gen. Odumegwu Ojukwu (leader of the Biafran secessionists), he argued, had at best made a miscalculation; the Federal Government, for its part, was obligated to re-examine its acts of war, since it must accept a sense of responsibility for the massacre in the North of the Ibo people and for the future of the people of Nigeria. The Federal Government, he continued, was faced with a no-win situation: either it had to destroy completely the Ibo people, or it would be faced with the unappealing prospects of attempting to "govern" an implacably embittered people. All this at the moment when it had appeared that "the new generation was about to march together." There had emerged, he wrote in the *Nigerian Daily Sketch,* in August 1967, "the by now familiar brigade of professional congratulators, opportunists, patriots, and other sordid racketeers, the cheer-leaders of a national disaster whose aim was to exploit Ojukwu's blunders to camouflage their own game of power and positions."

In August, returning from a visit to Ojukwu in Biafra, Soyinka was arrested for "spying" for the secessionists. The authorities said he had confessed to helping to buy arms "for the overthrow of the Federal Government." No trial. Two years in solitary confinement, where only the briefest fore-knowledge foiled at least one attempt on his life.

Released in 1969, he assumed a position at the University of Ibadan as Head of the Department of Theatre Arts. He resigned his position and published *The Man Died,* the brilliant and powerful account of his incarceration. Advised that it was unwise to return to Nigeria, he spent a year as a Fellow at Churchill College, Cambridge, England. Recently, he returned to his home in Africa—this time to Accra, where he assumed editorship of the controversial African journal, *Transition.*

He hopes to return to the Chair of Dramatic Literature at the University of Ife in Nigeria sometime in the next two years. He has helped produce one film, *Kongi's Harvest,* which he has vigorously denounced. He has written over a dozen plays, collected by Oxford Press. And his *The Fourth Stage,* an essay on the African tragic arts, is destined to mold the definitive theory of African poetics for the next generation.

Gates: You spent three years in prison for allegedly conspiring with the Ibo during the Nigerian Civil War. After two years of freedom, just before the publication of your description of your prison experience, called *The Man Died,* you left Nigeria, some say rather abruptly. Why?

Soyinka: My decision to leave Nigeria still carries with it some kind of *considered* action. I left Nigeria about two years ago to catch up with some work of mine, to be away by myself, considering a number of things. It just happens that a number of problems have developed from some writings of mine, that have made it necessary to stay out longer than I planned. I don't consider myself as having *left* Nigeria.

Gates: Why exactly were you incarcerated during the War?

Soyinka: Let me say this: there is a lot of confusion over this visit of mine to the secessionist region during the war. In fact, there is a lot of confusion over my role in the war. There have been some categorical statements which have astonished me. I am always rather amused at the certainty with which certain allegations are made. But then, as I think the American press have more recently discovered, I think journalists tend to go more by the statements made by regimes than by individuals or by minorities, or minority opinions within society. I think the expression "clandestine," as my visit to the secessionist region was widely labeled, really belongs to the propaganda machinery of the Federal Nigerian Government, during the war. It's a very false expression, however; I did not make a clandestine visit to the Eastern region. It was a deliberate visit. I consulted a number of people, even those actually connected with the regime. The risk was mine and the decision was mine, and that of a group of people with whom I was actively involved. And again, it has been suggested that I went on a "peace" mission. So far as one of the purposes of my visit was to put an end to the war which had only just begun, you could, I suppose, call it a peace visit. But—and this I suppose was what really bothered the Federal military regime—the real motivation of the visit was to present viable and very concrete alternative solutions to the solution by war. It was a political visit in that sense, I didn't go to the East just to ask the Biafrans to lay down their arms; that would be daft. In any case that's an impractical idea once guns start firing. No, I went there to present a definite political alternative which had been worked out by quite a number of influential people, including my own contributions. It could very well have b en another individual entirely who paid the visit. But, for particular reasons, I was in a position to present these alternatives to the seccessionist regime. And I went.

Gates: What were the root causes of the Nigerian Civil War?

Soyinka: Let me say what the root causes were *not.* The root cause of the Civil War certainly was not secession. Secession was merely a sort of critical event in their long line of national betrayal, desecration of values in the community, an inequitable society, clannishness, petty chauvinism, personal ambition. But, most important of all, the emasculation, the negation, of certain restraining and balancing institutions within the society, by cliques and caucuses within the community. All of which were definitely inimical to the aspirations of the masses of people.

If you want me to be even more elaborate, I would suggest—and I think this is quite tenable—that the root causes of the War can be found in the very lack of egalitarianism within the community. In other words, very deep seated dissatisfactions within the community which were of such a nature that they *could* be manipulated or diverted *into* what I call the "scapegoat syndrome." In other words, if you have succeeded in robbing society blind you can persuade the robbed and the dissatisfied sections of society that the real causes of their dissatisfaction can be traced to a particular sector of the community. And this was what, this was the policy which was very actively pursued by one or the other of the various power-holding sectors of the community. It was not merely tribal—when I talk about this segmentation, it was not merely tribal segmentation; it was, if you like, *class* segmentation. There is nothing *new* about it. The whole history of societies all over the world has always demonstrated this capacity of a very small minority—an elite, or a momentarily privileged and power-holding group within society—to manipulate the masses of people into a belief that injustices which really are due, which have been created by them, have in fact been created by completely innocent groups within society. So the Civil War, the act of secession by the Biafrans, was really a kind of culminating result of very many factors within society. And it really is very distressing to find the very simplistic attitudes taken by so-called intelligentsia within Nigerian society and, of course, outside commentators, almost as if a group of people got up suddenly and decided: "Okay, we want to be part no longer of the Nigerian polity." Of course this is absolute nonsense. In fact, my association and active collaboration with this group, which in certain circles has been dubbed the "Third Force" of the Civil War, was dictated by a conviction that the roots of the Civil War were not to be found in the act of secession of the Ibos or even in the hideous massacre of the Ibo people; but that they reached far deep down into the very fundamental disjunction within the total society.

Gates: Given your incarceration and the unpopularity in official circles of *The Man Died,* did you intend originally to live in Europe when you left Nigeria?

Soyinka: No, I did not come to Europe to live. Since my absence from Nigeria, if you add up the amount of time I've spent in Europe, I think you'll find—with the exception of the year I spent on a fellowship and some teaching at Churchill College, Cambridge—I think you'll find that I spent less time in Europe than in Africa.

Gates: But having lived here at least for the last year, and, one assumes, having associated yourself with some of the more original minds in Europe, how would you evaluate the intellectual climate in Europe?

Soyinka: I think I had better first emphasize that I do not consider Cambridge, or even England for that matter, a place to apply the intellectual barometer for Europe. But I take it your question is really meant in far more general terms. I will say quite candidly that I have always considered the whole of European intellection, I suppose naturally, Euro-centered; because of this, it is a very inaccurate and therefore a very untruthful system of analysis and conceptualization—in fact, of human beginnings and development, thought and ideas. I don't think this is a wholly personal prejudice. You will find there have been quite a number of formidable scholars—Cheikh Anta Diop is a name that comes easily to mind, and also Chancellor Williams— have questioned and backed by research the assumptions regarded as the foundation of "human" civilization, what constitutes "human" development. They have re-evaluated, in fact, the whole theory of social origins which have been postulated by European thinkers and scholars.

I find myself very much preoccupied—if you like, naturally prejudiced—in favor of a wholesale re-examination, re-evaluation of European ideas. In fact, I question very much the intellectual value of a number of the preoccupations of European scholars. And taking as the foundation of my thinking the ideas, the world-view, the philosophical concepts of my society, I find that Europe has for too long brow-beaten the rest of the world, and especially the African world, into an acceptance of the very fundamental system [of evaluation] which is, I suppose, natural to Europe. It is time the paths which have been blazed by a number of very serious African scholars should be followed up very rigorously. And the damage which has already been done—the waste of toil which has been indulged in by universities—seems very ridiculous. Tiny, really minuscule, academic studies, with no relevance at all, to a true understanding of man's situation within the universe—which I think is at the root the most fundamental aspect of all intellectual inquiry. I believe that one of the primary duties of African intellectual institutions is really not merely to question the system of thought of Europe, but to question the *value* of these systems, the *value* of these particular patterns of thought in European thinking.

Now one ready example, of course, is the old question of social development—the idea, the Darwinian idea of human evolution, for instance, which has been applied in a very racist and negative way to a comparative study of societies in the world, always of course to the detriment and the belittlement of Black societies: The deliberate suppression of facts, of historical facts, which are dug up by anthropologists; the biased, the very dishonest selectiveness of material, which then becomes the basis of supposedly rigid structuralism in analyzing social systems; the habit of ignoring or merely treating as curious the systems, the metaphysical systems, the philosophical ideas of African society. In other words, these are made sort of adjuncts to the European artificial systems. I think all of these would make me feel far too prejudiced, really, to make any comment on the European intellectual climate. I find myself completely outside of it. I find a lot of European intellectual structures really of irrelevance to myself as a member of my own society. In fact, the only justification for being preoccupied with these systems seems to me to be a need to recognize what they are, in order to protect ourselves; in order to undo, as far as we can, the immense damage which has been done to our society, and also to retrieve our centers of learning—our schools even, and our universities—from the wrong emphasis, from the time-wasting irrelevancies which have been given a very special badge of erudition, intellectualism and so on. All these things which really have distorted not just the abstract thinking of African scholars, but the *application* of such thinking to social and intellectual development in an African society.

Gates: The motif of self-sacrifice is a common one in your works. Although you apparently reject membership in the European intellectual community, do you think that, perhaps, this motif is a result of the undue influence of a Judeo-Christian tradition?

Soyinka: This, again, I believe is part of the pattern of acceptance of European thought and ideas—this idea of attributing the concept of self-sacrifice to the Christian, to the Euro-Christian or Judeo-Christian world, simply because a single figure emerged from that particular culture to espouse, in very beautiful mythological terms, the cause of the self-sacrificing individual as a kind of, as the surrogate for world suffering, social unhappiness, and general human unhappiness. It is often forgotten that the idea of individual sacrifice—the principle of the surrogate individual—is, in fact, a "pagan" one. Those who attribute this concept to Europe forget that Christianity itself is not a European religion. And that Christ, the central figure of Christianity, is really a glamorization of very "paganistic" ideas: the idea of personalizing the dying old year, the dying season; to insure the sprouting, the fertility, the idea of the emergence, in fact the very resurrection, of Nature. All this is "pagan"—"pagan" as an expression used by the Christian world to describe the fundamentally natural, Nature religions. I see Christianity merely as another expression of nature religion. I cannot accept, I do not regard the principle of sacrifice as belonging to the European world. I completely reject the idea that the notion of the scapegoat is a Christian idea. This scapegoat idea is very much rooted in African religion.

If I may just leave religion aside for a moment, I would like to comment on the peculiar isolation of creativity—the peculiar isolation of the artist as an expression of certain principles, including the principle of individual self-sacrifice. The isolation, if you will, of the artist from the rest of society. If we look at this politically, I think we will find the greatest social manipulators have been individuals who have not scrupled to sacrifice themselves on behalf of the rest of the community. They have also been tremendous organizers. But it is when they failed that the concept of sacrifice begins. To take a modern example: if Fidel Castro had failed in his war of revolutionary struggle in Cuba, he would have been regarded literally as another romantic artist who, inspite of being a member of the *bourgeoisie,* saw himself as Christ did, as a savior of the people, the masses of the people. This transposition always takes place, and the *key* to the particular nature of this transposition—to the concepts and the terminology used—depends very much on whether the practical, organizing aspect (whether in a military sense, or the political sense, or even the propagandizing sense)—whether the sheer political technology of the struggle becomes a successful thing. But if the leader, the visionary—and this really is what is common to all these figures of sacrifice, the visionary—if he fails, then of course he becomes another Christ figure. The moment he seems to struggle—all revolutionary struggles, do not forget, commence by the action of visionaries against supposedly impossible odds. But of course if it succeeds, then you have the transposition of terminologies, which takes place *immediately*. And you now have a revolutionary figure, you now have a man of the masses. So I'm not at all impressed by this distinction.

The writer has—I won't even call it a duty; I would say the field, the scope of the writer involves a true recording of this element, of this *blurred* transition between, if you like, the Christ-like figure of self-sacrifice and the successful revolutionary. I do not think that the writer should be limited if he writes about a particular aspect of this figure, because inherent—and this is the important thing—inherent in all struggle on behalf of society is always the element of self-sacrifice. I don't think Garcia-Lorca set out to be deliberately self-sacrificing anymore than Lenin did, for instance. It is too sharp a division for me to accept. This is a subject I have had to confront more and more. Only recently, for instance, I was giving a lecture at Sheffield University, and one of the members of the audience remarked that he noticed in my recent writing a move from what he called the artist as self-sacrificial, the notion of the artist as a revolutionary member of the community. And this, for me, was a very great simplification of the motivations and the actual futurist goals which nerve the artist as a member of society into action.

Gates: But many of the "Keepers of Blackness" in America insist on the subjugation of self—all, that is, except *their* self—for what they call the "collective good of the community." Do you think it is an African notion that the individual will of the artist must be subjugated to the will of the community, as is claimed by said Keepers of the said Faith?

Soyinka: You know, fascism takes all sorts of shapes and forms of expression. We have to be very, very cautious always when we are confronted by those who say a certain group of people within the community—either as individuals or as species of some strange animal—should always submit themselves, bury themselves within a certain totality. There is always a germ of fascism in the mental preoccupation of individuals, of certain groups of people—their preoccupation with this. I think it is the intensity of this preoccupation which we have to watch.

Of course, the artist, whether he likes it or not, is a member of the community. His concerns, his preoccupations—even his calling, his very profession—depend very much on the security of society. I think he recognizes this. I can count, for instance, on a couple of hands, artists whom I know in African society who consider themselves *separate,* and not a part, of the totality. But while I can say I can count the *artists* on one hand, I can count on both hands and toes and a lot of borrowed digits the number of civil servants, the army hierarchy, plus what I call the colonial aristocracy of African society—in fact, I cannot enumerate them totally, there are so many who do not regard themselves at all as being part of the commonality of African society. So when I hear this concern, this unequal preoccupation with artists, I first of all ask myself what the protestors are hiding above all about *themselves,* what they are hiding about their own personal ambitions; this is very important. In our society we've had artists who've died, who've sacrificed themselves on the altar of war; we've had those, unsung, who have been tortured silently in prisons.

Finally, and this is the most important point: when you listen especially—and I am glad you quoted Black American observers—when you listen to these Black American observers, you find that very often they are those who come to Africa and immediately ally themselves with the power structure. They view the entire society through the spectacles of those who are in power. It's very amusing; but it shouldn't be amusing. It's really tragic and destructive in many ways, because they are the same people who *shout* about the totality of society. They're the ones who complain about writers and artists standing aside. And when they talk about the polity, when they talk about the entire society, they really are talking about a very small hierarchy.

I wish to suggest to you that the first exercise always is to study the background of these complainants, these great champions of the collectivity, these "more revolutionary-than-thou" members of the collectivity. You find they are usually pampered, idle members of the *bourgeoisie,* who have been toasted, wined and eliticized by the ruling powers within society. These commentators, very often who come to aid the revolution in our society, have figures—human figures—in their heads—the top, the leaders in their heads. I don't wish to be cruel, but I would suggest that most of the time these commentators are suffering from a slave mentality. They have not totally eradicated in their mind a slave mentality. They have merely substituted a Black master for the ole white massa.

Not so long ago I had an argument in Kenya over the whole question of our dear friend, General Idi Amin. Now I found out that this [American] brother was not interested in the masses of Ugandans. He was nicely, comfortably situated in Kenya, by the way, and had paid a fleeting official visit to Uganda, had in fact met the "genial" figure of General Amin. And I asked him, "Have you visited some of the refugee camps, have you visited Kisumu," which is on the Lake [Victoria] and is one of the favorite places for escaping Ugandans. . . . No, he hadn't. All that concerned him was that somebody had made a statement publicly criticizing the head, the leader of Uganda. Now this is their sense of collectivity: when a writer, an artist within that society has the courage to expose certain realities, they cannot stand it, because it is a rebuke on themselves. . . .

Now, and the question is: is the leadership of African society today the collectivity? Until those who are so passionately concerned with African collectivity, until they can apply the same rules to *all* sections of society, whether it is the military class, or the civil-service class, or the very top leadership hierarchy—until they learn to study very carefully what is the voice, what really is the aspiration of the masses, and whose articulation is closest to this, I think some people will finally be condemned by the very realities which are constantly taking place within our society. . . . To take the most recent and obvious example: the collective good of the Ethiopian masses, as defined and as recognized by default by the intelligentsia of Africa—this "collective good" has been the benign imperial neglect by the privileged minority.

The magazine I have just begun editing, *Transition,* carried an eyewitness report, a month before the movement against Haile Selassie, of a famine in Ethiopia. In fact, it was more than an eye-witness report. It was a document which also demanded the mobilization of intelligent opinion within Ethiopian society and in the outside world on behalf of the neglected masses against the corrupt arrogance of Haile Selassie. I would like to ask—because I don't really know—how many Black American magazines ever thought fit to publicize and to criticize this criminal neglect of the Ethiopian masses? I want to ask how many intellectual magazines in Africa thought it necessary or saw fit to criticize the banquetry and the junketry and the thoughtless dissipation of the wealth of the Ethiopian people while hundreds of thousands of people were dying of starvation? I want to ask how many African leaders themselves thought it fit while they were wining and dining in the Ethiopian Palace during the O.A.U. conferences, while just a few miles away the people of Ethiopia were dying? How many thought it necessary even to utilize, however indirectly, journals they control to call attention to the plight of the Ethiopian masses? Very, very few.

But the moment a spokesman, a writer, insists that his commitment is to the masses of the people, he is described as a privileged minority who is exploiting a European concept of freedom of speech. I call this a *slave mentality*. I call it a refusal really to be truthfully emancipated as a human being, as a member of society. I use "emancipation" in the Fanonist sense, the revolutionary antidote to Marx's "alienated man." I cannot accept the definition of collective good as articulated by a privileged minority in society, especially when that minority is in power. And when I hear expressions like "collective good," I always want to know whose definition this is? Is collective good to be equated with the self-consolidation, the self-perpetuation of an exploiting minority, just in order to satisfy either our Black brothers from the States, or even to satisfy the constantly proliferating privileged so-called intelligentsia of our own African societies? I insist on reading "collective good" as an expression which refers to the total, to the masses of society, not as expressed, as defined by the propaganda machinery of a privileged minority. . . .

Gates: But how could you concretize this idea of self-sacrifice in your work?

Soyinka: Two things I said regarding your questions earlier: first of all the theme of self-sacrifice, let me try and concretize it a little with examples from my work. In *The Strong Breed* I utilize a ritual which is a very common one which takes many forms among the riverine people on the West Coast of Africa, certainly in Nigeria what we call the "river people" there. There is the idea there of the ritual. The principle of it is that a person takes on himself the entire burdens of society; very often it takes the symbolic form of a canoe-shaped object which is then taken to the river or to the sea and floated away. Other times it takes the form of a mysterious lump which is taken to the river bank or to the sea shore and buried. In certain Yoruba areas the carrier takes the object and dives into the water and disappears for quite a while; he goes down there to bury the object right in the sea bed. Again among the Yoruba people you have a festival called the Eyo festival at which certain human masquerades parade the city.

There is a particular masquerade who is called a Eyo Adimu, who is considered a very dangerous masquerade. He carries the evils of the year in his person: all the diseases, the unhappiness, the evil, all the curses which have hung around society. He takes this away, disappears into a grove or bushes somewhere and all the collective evils of society are taken in his own person and are thrown away. Now the point about all these various forms is that the

individuals who carry, who serve as carriers for the rest of the community,
are not expected to survive very long. The whole demand, the stress, the
spiritual tension, as well as the forces of evil which they trapped into their
own person are such that after a few years they either go insane, or they catch
some mysterious disease, or they simply atrophy as human beings and die.
Their life span is very short, they cease to be useful members of the community quite early. This is recognized, and the Eyo Adimu in particular is exposed to a very lingering illness of the sort that incapacitates him completely
after one or two journeys of this nature, journeys on which he saves society.

Now these individuals whom I have mentioned, they are not artists, or
teachers, or any of these special classifications of society; they are just ordinary human beings like you or me. There hasn't been any concept within
society that these are poor, Christian, deluded individuals. For me it is a great
misconception to suggest that the principle of self-sacrifice, or the principle
of individual sacrifice is something alien to African traditional societies. This
is nonsense. I am not interested in whether the concept of individual sacrifice
is valid or not; obviously these are things which have to be considered on
their own terms, depending on the particular historic or political necessity in
which an individual—whether he is a mason, an athlete, a bricklayer—finds
himself within his community.

I think the obsession with individual salvation—which, if you like, is on
the opposite end of the axis to self-sacrifice—is a very European thing. I am
not aware that it occupied the minds of our people. I think it is a very European literary idea; in fact, the obsession itself is a very Christian principle.
In our society, this kind of event, this process, is inbult into the very mechanism which operates the entire totality of society. The individual who acts as
a carrier and who knows very well what is going to become of him is really
no different, is doing nothing special, from other members of society who
build society and who guarantee survival of society in their own way. I think
there is one principle, one essential morality of Africa society which we must
always bear in mind, and that is the greatest morality in what makes the entire
society survive. The actual detailed mechanism of this process merely differs
from group to group and from section to section, but it is the totality that is
important. I think there is far too much concern about this business of the
Christian ethic of individual self-sacrifice.

On the subject of collectivity, I think maybe after all I should use a very
pertinent example. It sums up entirely what I consider the hypocrisy of these
"more-collectivized-I's-than-thou" revolutionaries who spout these fashion-

able themes so readily. There is a criticism of my book, *The Man Died,* in *Black World* magazine [August 1974 "Books Noted"] which you have just shown me, and this is an illustration of what I consider to be indecisive, the insincerity of many "collective I's" propagandists we have in our midst. On one level this would-be critic [reviewer Carrie Sembene] accuses me of separating myself from the collectivity, from the social collectivity, by certain stands which I take in society and stands which I took in the book and also the very language of the book. In my book I use an expression to describe what I considered an outrage during the suffering of hundreds of thousands of our people and the self-sacrifice which was being made by our people during the War. I referred to the very elaborate, extravagant wedding of the Nigerian leader [President Yakubu Gowon] as "grandiloquent vomit," and she objects to this. There is no recognition in her piece that that wedding event was a kind of a slap in the face for the sacrificing masses of Nigeria. . . . Not only that, but [Gowon] also says that the fall of a town just around the time of his wedding was literally meant to be a wedding present for him, but regretted that it did not happen on the very day of his wedding.

In what I consider a mood of moral outrage (which I know many of my countrymen shared, by the way, even the so-called intelligentsia)—if this critic had read some of the Nigerian newspapers she would have found that one or two actually had the moral courage to criticize in stronger terms this insulting waste of our revenue, especially at a time of national self-sacrifice. It was not just the artist-writer who criticized this. But what strikes me is the fact that the whole of this lady's attitude is governed entirely by the idea that one should dare criticize the first member of the Nigerian society. I don't know if she carried in her head some fantasies of becoming married to some head of state or not,* and resents the idea that some impertinent artist should call such an occasion "grandiloquent vomit." I don't really understand. But it is remarkable that she is applying one set of laws to the power structure, one set of laws to the artist within society. Now it is this contradiction which makes me always question these facile propagandists for so-called collectivism. They don't know what collectivism really is. To believe in a collective society, to believe in genuine communalism means you do not tolerate any act of arrogance or of exploitation from any side of the community: you do not accept the setting aside by itself of a particular class of society. And you

---

Ed. Note: Ms. Sembene is married to Sengalese novelist-filmmaker Ousmane Sembene.

have the courage to criticize and to articulate the voice and the protest of society in this respect. I think people should be a little more honest and regard it as their duty if they are genuine spokesmen for the masses of the people, which is what I understand when they talk about a collectivized society. If they are genuine spokesmen, then they cannot afford this revelation of slave mentality, which says it is all right for the power structure to be elitist but it is criminally elitist for the artist to criticize the elitism of the power structure.

By the way, I think I also ought to take this opportunity to correct a misconception which has been repeated in Sister [Carrie Sembene's review]: that I supported the Biafran cause. Again, this is a result of falling victim to the propaganda of the power structure which, of course, is supposed to be gospel truth. Well I *did not* support the Biafran cause, but I was also very much opposed to the Federal cause. I believe that the Federal regime was responsible for the affairs going as far as they did, for matters reaching the edge of civil war, because of the Federal Government's criminal negligence. In fact, I would prefer to call it tacit approval, by default—let me make it as generous as that—tacit approval by default of the act of genocide committed on the Ibos. But I did not support the act of secession, for the simple reason that I felt that it was not the solution, it was not the way to create a viable society. I believe very strongly that the Biafrans should stay in Nigeria and, therefore, give Nigeria an opportunity to cleanse itself thoroughly of the crime which was committed. In other words, punish those who were responsible and completely re-organize society on principles which would not perpetuate the inequities within society, and the systematic exploitation by a small group of people of the majority.

Gates: How would you appraise the value—spiritual, political or otherwise—of the diasporan Black man's proverbial return to mother Africa?

Soyinka: The move back to Africa by the Brothers from the diaspora is in itself, without any question, a valid desire. By move, of course, I do not really mean the physical move, although this can be a very fruitful and necessary experience or solution for a number of Black Americans. I am more interested in what you might call the cultural move, the spiritual move, even the intellectual move. The rediscovery of the social system, the beliefs, the philosophy of our own society, because this in itself means a long overdue rejection of European habits of thought and life-approach. It is quite true that quite a few who do come, Richard Wright for example, find that they are already far too conditioned to benefit, or even to successfully penetrate the, well, I wouldn't call them secrets—the basic tenets and values of African society. I do not find this strange. I notice that some Brothers tend to criticize others for failing to find "themselves," so to speak, in Africa; I do not consider it strange at all. Those who do, then, it means that there is a gap within—a hiatus within their soul—which needs to be filled from this. I find that to those who are already complete beings in themselves, the rediscovery of Africa would only be an additional bonus if they do rediscover it. Well, they can still survive as revolutionary members of society without actually putting on a dashiki. I am never overly concerned.

I think it's a good thing, this internal movement back to Africa. I think it is one which we in Africa should respond to very seriously. I notice its influence in the cultural product at the moment of Black America in the drama. Again, there are some misbegotten examples of the experimentation, unfortunately. It manifests itself also in the arts, in painting and sculpture; and there is a very, very sadly commercialized aspect of this return, when everything is geared to the business of artifacts and even spiritual commerce and so on. All these distortions are part of a movement of this kind. You will find that even the Roman Catholic pilgrimages to their Holy Lands always carry with them a certain commercial aspect, so let's not worry too much about the negative aspects of this return. It is unfortunate, it is very irritating, it's very often disgusting and it makes Africans—I mean the "home" brothers—very cynical about Americans in general, and I am afraid, occasionally more prejudiced about their Black brothers than about the white Americans. But all in all I think that what we are witnessing is a complete rejuvenation of long accepted cultural forms, concepts, ideas; images, artistic images, even the poetry has benefited a lot from this move.

Gates: How do we gain control of the means of dissemination of information—especially when we are evaluating European concepts?

Soyinka: Now, first of all, I think the most fundamental means is the complete reorganization of our educational system. Some national governments are already aware of this. One recent example is Ghana, whose government has already commissioned a number of educationists, teachers and writers to take time off. Literally, they have been invited to completely re-write, recreate the textbooks which are used in schools; offer new ideas where they cannot actually get to work on them, and try and attune them to the African background, the truthful African reality, and prune away the exocentric ideas of training and mental development which are very often insidiously slipped into these texts. That is one method. And, of course, you move on from the primary level, secondary level to the university level.

When I look at our universities—this, perhaps, apart from the primary-school level—the university level is where the real fight is. I have taught in several universities in Africa, both as a member of staff and as a guest lecturer, and the closer I get, the more experience I have of African universities, the more I become convinced that perhaps nothing short of a *cultural revolution* on the lines of China would do. It's a very drastic method, but I think, not just myself, but a number of my colleagues with whom I speak have a feeling that very little can be done, internally.

Universities are very much the slaves of the system of a bureaucratization. It is impossible really to rid the university of old brigades and old, jaded ideas and Eurocentric evaluation of ideas, even of learning, of discoveries, of research: the emphasis on trivia—on scholastic-sounding trivia—the waste of time, the waste of energy, the waste of intellect on the most irrelevant and generally immaterial details of learning. Sometimes I think nothing short of a real militant movement against the universities—if necessary, the closing down of universities for a number of years while we start over from scratch—I sometimes think that nothing less than this will serve. There may be other methods, but I am afraid I have failed to think of them.

Evolution within our universities is going to take, at the pace it is going, another 1,000 years and will probably just travel the full circle and come back to the colonial system which we have inherited, not only inherited, but *enshrined*—the very pride which a lot of unproductive intelligentsia take in the principle of nonproductivity. By "nonproductivity" I refer to this business of glorification of trivia—independent, autonomous trivia. So, for the process of evaluation and the process of the dissemination of new, valid ideas for our society, I think we must literally gain control ourselves—that is, the real people, the masses of the people, the parallels of the power structure—must somehow gain control of the universities.

A third method of course is again to gain control of journals of thought, of ideas, which probably gives away why I was interested in taking this job of the editorship of *Transition* in Africa.

Gates: Granted that we *can* gain control of the dissemination of ideas, what sort of re-evaluations do you deem necessary?

Soyinka: Just one rudimentary example, regarding the revaluation or re-

orientation of values necessary for the African world, the African intelligentsia. You see, I do not consider it necessary to wait for the Claude Levi-
Strauss' of the world to undo the centuries of Eurocentric blasphemy that
have placed the Black man, the so-called primitive man, under the categoriza-
tion of some kind of semi-human creature possessing some sort of "pre-
logical mentality." It is for me not very important that a Levi-Strauss comes
along and tries to undo the heresy of the Gobineaus, the Humeses—those
who try to glamorize this presumed, this very conceited and racist idea about
the Black man's incapacity for thought. That is a task which belongs quite
naturally to the intelligentsia of the Black world itself. But again, there can
be a level of exaggeration about this. It is as serious, I think, is as *erroneous*
an emphasis of direction to spend time trying to disprove this fallacy as to
try and glorify it as, let us say, some Négritudinists have done—to try and
suggest, to try and agree with the European racist scholars that the Black
man is incapable of analytical thought or ratiocination. To suggest that this
is, however, as laudible a faculty—a faculty of emotion, thought, intuition,
as *opposed* to rationality—to try to laud it and glorify it is to accept, first of
all, the dichotomy between rationality and intuition—subjectivity and objectivity—which is postulated by European scholars.

When I talk about the true intellectual liberation of the Black man, I speak
of a complete rejection, a refusal *even to begin* from the untried axioms of
the white academic—you know, bored with his own society or seeking some
kind of validation for his presumed superiority of his own people before he
attempted to come to terms, in a very self-validating way, with African society. [My position] is to believe very implicitly that the African peoples live a
very complete, rounded, self-sufficient existence, both emotionally and intellectually, and that all the postulations of the European scholar are either
irrelevant, in fact have no bearing whatever—except perhaps in some peripheral cases—or contradict the reality of the African peoples. It amuses me to
find African scholars considering themselves very proud to be Freudians or
Jungians. It betrays a kind of basic inferiority; a lack of self-assurance, which
can only be compensated by resource to European terminologies. I mean,
Freud was a *bourgeois* psychologist whose entire, whose very presumptuous
analysis of the human psyche was based on a peculiar, European, *bourgeois*
society. If we accept the fact that the human psyche can be understood not
only from a study of individuals, but by a study of society, then we must—
coming from a completely different matrix of ideas, of social relationships—
must look warily at the findings of Freud.

The same thing, of course, applies to Marx. For individuals and students and scholars who are concerned with the reform of society in general, a Marxist analysis of European society is of course a very useful base for trying to plumb the various contradictions, the anomalies within our own society which have been picked up and developed as a result of our contact with European society. It is important to try and understand the various, profound, fundamental analyses of European society. But to accept all the tenets of Marx, *carte blanche,* without any intelligent adaptation for the peculiarities of our own society, is really to betray a lingering desire to be accepted on the European intellectual level. There have, of course, been various intellectuals in Black society in the Third World who have been very conscious of this: Fanon is a very obvious example, Amilcar Cabral is another and he, of course, is both a praxist as well as a theorist of African revolution. But all those who inhabit, who *infest,* our intellectual institutions in the majority prove themselves uncritical slaves of European ideas, incapable of critical application to the uniqueness of their own society. They fail to accept this fundamental fact: that theories and ideas *do not exist in vacuo,* but are based on empirical observations of society and tempered by the idealist vision of which every serious and profound thinker is capable.

Gates: What African institutions would you say facilitate the most organic reassociation between the diasporian African and his brothers on the continent?

Soyinka: On the subject of the internal return of our Afro-American Brothers to the Mother Continent, there is yet one more positive advantage which should not be ignored. For a long time, and quite rightly, fortunately the most militant and the most cleansing force for the Black American in the United States has been the force of Islam. The sense of a kind of Islamic nationalism. For us, let me say this quite frankly—for us on the Mother Continent, this has always been a kind of half-way house, a station through which the Brothers had to pass before finding their true, authentic Black soul in Africa. What I am trying to say is this: that we must not underestimate, we must always be grateful for a force which the Islamism of the Black Muslims, the redeeming role it played in recalling the Black American to himself, to a spirituality, a personality, a dignity, which could no longer be tainted or corrupted by the decadent values of American white society. But it must be understood that this is only a half-way house, and that when we in Africa encounter supposedly serious and intelligent Black Americans who have failed to move beyond this point, we get an uncomfortable feeling that there is a genuine fear in such people really to come deep down to where *home is*.

Islam is not an African religion, anymore than Christianity is. For many of us, having repudiated Christianity, we are not about to accept a religion, a way of life, an outlook on life, which is in many ways basically contradictory to the authentic African religions. When we speak of religions, we are not merely talking about an act of worship, we are talking about a whole pattern of cultural mores, a whole metaphysical outlook, a philosophic approach to the world. We are talking about a political attitude as well. There is a very sad lack of understanding, or even curiosity, in many Black Brothers in America about what is the *true* spiritual reality of Africa. And one encouraging fact about this movement back to Africa among our Brothers is that there is now today a lot more genuine commitment to finding out about the true Black African past. I am not apologetic at all about making this distinction; in fact, I think it has become crucial—very crucial—to make this distinction, to emphasize the fact that there does exist a true, an authentic African spirituality, a religiosity if you like, a Black metaphysical outlook. I use the expression "African World," the African World, in preference to others. And this is distinct from both Christianity and from Islam.

To move away slightly from the role, the present commitment of Brothers on the American Continent, to move away from their commitment to what after all was a kind of salvationist ideal for them, to go now to the political emphasis a bit: I sometimes detect to my great discomfort a fear of the true Black heritage discovery. It is something which can be paralleled to the much earlier social distortion in the minds of the slaves, which is that to be quadroon or octaroon is much better than to be *pure* Black. I think that there are still too many Brothers who are very content and who feel very secure in this half-way house. They cannot make the final plunge toward a true, a complete, full-rounded, uncompromising Black authenticity.

Gates: What did you think of the so-called symbolic value of holding the Ali[-George Foreman Heavyweight Championship] Fight in Mobutu's Zaire?

Soyinka: Muhammad Ali, by the way, is one of my favorite heroes, if I may use that expression—which is always a dangerous one. But he's one of my true heroic figures of this century. And I have no doubt in my mind that his Islamic conviction, for instance, is absolute and total. And I don't expect him *ever* to discover the African religions that are a source of his own spiritual strength, his own dignity, because I get the feeling—and this is why I admire the man—that he is grounded in his Islamic calling. But I do wish he would discover some day gods like Shango and Ogun, and find in them sources of strength and the reality of his own being. Very optimistically, I hope a character like this would find that while the Islamic religion was useful to him up to a point, it is merely a transitional, though combative, alternative to the hypocritical, exploitative and racist self-affliction of the Christian Ethic. If Ali had lost his match on African soil, it would have been because he was not viscerally tuned to the Gods who make the energies of the Black Continent. He won because his opponent was even more alienated from those demonic sources of African strength. Ali's psychology was pure African—he stuck pins in Foreman's effigy, then finished the job in the ring. So you see, either way, the African Deities won against the twin usurpers of African spirituality. And that, of course, was the only thing which kept the fight from being a total farce against Africa, against the Mother Continent.

Soyinka in Zimbabwe: A Question and Answer Session

James Gibbs / 1981

From *Literary Half-Yearly*, 28.2 [July 1987], 50–110. Reprinted with permission of James Gibbs.

On Sunday 29th of November 1981 a group of eighty or ninety watched a performance of Ben Sibenke's *Chidembo Kunhuwa* (the smell of the pole-cat), on the lawn of a college in Harare, Zimbabwe. The members of the audience were, in most cases, strangers to one another, yet on the following Friday, barely five days later, those watchers became performers and working together in casts of various sizes mounted seven plays which took up a large part of the morning and most of the afternoon. Some of the plays were performed like Sibenke's on the lawn, others were put on in the lecture theatre and for one the audience moved across the rocks and over the dead leaves into the dappled shade at the bottom of the garden. The plays were about the past and the present, about life in town and life in the villages, and about the moments when the past flows into the present and town rubs shoulders with village. They raised issues of love and death, family obligations and social duties, individual rights and communal responsibilities. They ended in tears and dances, defeats and celebrations, reconciliation and denunciation. They were united in one thing: each play grew out of the experience of Zimbabwe and Zimbabweans.

The plays represented part of the work done during an intensive five-day Play-making Workshop organised by the National Arts Foundation of Zimbabwe in association with the National Theatre Organization and founded by the federal Republic of Germany. It was led by Noel MacDonald, Barney Simon, Mbongeni Ngema, James Gibbs and Nicholas Wright. The Workshop provided a remarkable instance of bringing in and of bringing together.

Zimbabwe has been divided against itself and cut off from much that has been going on in the rest of Africa and the rest of the world during the seventies. The group leaders were able to share their experiences of theatre abroad, particularly theatre in South Africa, Tanzania, Malawi, Ghana and Nigeria. This was part of the "bringing in," but there was also a "bringing together." The Workshop brought together Zimbabweans of various ages, experiences and races: Ranche House College provided neutral territory on which the traditions of theatre in the villages, the educational institutions, the "Reps" and the guerrilla camps could meet.

The workshop provided the participants with opportunities for encounters of various kinds. In their groups they worked at play-making exercises and put together improvized sketches; they explored themselves, their colleagues and their experiences. In the most important of the plenary sessions with the group leaders they were able to see a video-tape recording of *Woza Albert!* and cross-examine two of those responsible for that hilarious and terrifying production, Barney Simon and Mbongeni Ngema. The illustrated answers impressed upon the audience the discipline and dedication required to produce such a polished performance. The whole experience, the tape plus the discussion of it, drove home the lesson that theatre is a matter of minds and bodies rather than of fly-towers and dimmer-boards.

The impact of *Woza Albert!* and of most of the Workshop exercises will be found in the memories of those who took part in the activities at the Ranche House. And, perhaps, in the work the participants have been stimulated to do as a result of it! There is little to be gained from writing here about the week at length. There was, however, one part of the proceedings which benefits from being reduced to print. This was the final encounter of the Workshop: the question and answer session between the participants and Wole Soyinka on Saturday 5 December. Below will be found a transcription of a tape-recording of that session. In preparing the material for the press I took extensive liberties with the questions; in almost every case I rephrased them in order to make them brief and to the point. With Soyinka's answers I was, naturally, respectful. I have, however, removed most of the incomplete thoughts and some of the conversational idiosyncracies. The transcript has also been submitted to Soyinka for alteration and amendment. I made no attempt to rearrange material or to editorialize in a way which would have violated the mood of the occasion. If the movement of the discussion sometimes appears serpentine, this is because of the participants and certain preoccupations to which they rightly and naturally returned again and again.

The document is an important one for students of Soyinka and of African theatre. Soyinka has been interviewed by journalists and critics on many occasions and many of these interviews have been published. He has frequently submitted himself to questions "from the floor," but few of his answers on such occasions have been published. Indeed Karen L. Morell's work is almost unrivalled as an illustration of Soyinka "in operation" as a teacher and as a "cornered" lecturer. In the pages below Soyinka speaks clearly and directly on a wide range of issues on some of which he is generally very reticent!

I suspect that it is the cast of Soyinka's mind and the breadth of his experiences which will impress many of those who make his acquaintance through the transcription below. For instance Soyinka repeatedly draws attention to "parallels." He possesses and wishes to communicate an acute awareness of the ways in which movements find an "approximate duplicate" (the expression is from *A Dance of the Forests*) in other situations and other ages. He is an original and energetic thinker with no time for those who "take the line of least resistance" or are content to reduce ideas to banal simplifications. From his illustrations and allusions we become aware of the variety of his work and of the extent of his involvement in world theatre and international debates. For instance, he refers to productions of his work not only in Nigeria, but also in London and Chicago. He speaks of encounters with English Socialist playwright Arnold Wesker, with Cuban factory workers and with Frelimo leaders. He refers to Ugandan rituals, to *Egungun* masquerades and to *1789,* a "theatrical ritual of revolution." He mentions writers and directors such as Brecht, Synge, Arden, Osborne, Osofisan, Littlewood and Euripides. Yet there is no feeling in all this that he speaks of such people and such things in order to impress that these just happen to be important points on his creative and intellectual globe. Those anxious to explore this world will find that the journey takes them on a fascinating voyage of intellectual discovery.

The questions which Soyinka was asked reflected a wide range of concerns and experiences. It was apparent that some of the questioners were studying *The Lion and the Jewel,* and it was probably for this reason that there were more questions on this play than on any other single topic. Soyinka, who is sometimes reticent about discussing his own work, spoke with candor about the play and put on record some fascinating information about the experience which "triggered off" (to use an expression which he prefers) the writing of the play. But while some sought answers to specific questions on a specific text, others had broader interests and raised more general issues. These included the nature of the relationships between the playwright and the architecture of his theatre, the playwright and the director of his play, the playright and the actors who perform his play, and the playwright and his audience. Soyinka, despite suffering from a throat infection, answered patiently and thoughtfully and, frequently, wittily. I have not indicated the points at which the audience laughed, but a sympathetic reader should be able to appreciate the extent of the humour and through it assess the tone of the whole session.

The mood of creative, relaxed interaction between Soyinka and the participants was most memorably caught at a sun-downer party when, emboldened by days of improvization, a group of young people invaded the verandah of the College and performed *The Arrival of Professor Soyinka.* When they tried to make their exit, however, the real Professor Soyinka jumped onto the "stage" and pursued his impersonator with a barrage of questions! The actor was allowed to escape amidst laughter, but at the question and answer session Soyinka permitted himself no such escape. He was cornered, "nailed down," and faced a cannonade which lasted for nearly four hours. At the end of the encounter, the chairman, Basil Chidyamatamba, thanked the victim-target. I would like to join in those thanks and add a thank-you for the time and trouble Soyinka took to help prepare this material for publication. This final paragraph also provides an opportunity to thank the organizers of the Workshop, especially those at the National Arts Foundation, the National Theatre Organisation and the Federal Republic of Germany whose hard work and generosity enabled us to come together at Ranche House College during 1981.

Soyinka: I have always looked forward to coming to see what sort of a society was developing in Zimbabwe after the Revolution. So this is as much a useful trip for me as it might be for anybody else. I was a little disappointed when communications broke down and the ticket didn't arrive, but I said, "Well, it has probably been postponed." And when I picked up the paper and saw a bit of news about the Prime Minister's brother dying suddenly, I thought maybe that was part of the problem. Fortunately this friend of mine came through from Salisbury and said that the papers were screaming. Then I thought I should try to make it here, so here I am after a series of adventures.

A little bit about myself? There really isn't much to tell. I was born into a typical family. Well is it typical really? It is difficult to say. My family brought together what is generally, simplistically, referred to as the new and the old, the modern and the traditional—which I've never accepted because I believe that society at all times is perpetually fluctuating and I don't think that any society at any given time has ever been without the old and the new. Anyway, my father was a teacher and my mother, who also came from a teaching family, was a petty trader. I grew up among music, performances. I grew up to the sounds of poetry as women hawked their wares. I don't know whether that still exists here—whereby fruit-sellers or market-women don't just sit but actually sing their wares to attract customers. In other words creativity and commerce, creativity and the various processes of living, or of a great deal of social community, went hand in hand. So it was no surprise to me that sooner or later I should find myself putting one or two words together in sequences which you might not call the normal conversational pattern, and that, I suppose, is what writing is all about, especially poetry. I also had the advantage, this is where the question of being born into two societies, two forms, two levels, two patterns of creativity comes in, I had the advantage of actually being raised in a Christian family in the midst of "pagan" manifestations. So it was quite usual for me to be returning from Church and suddenly find an *Egungun* masquerde, that's an ancestral mas-querade cult, parading with very lively music, drums, etcetera, along the street to the discomfiture of the Christian worshippers. Discomfiture, because they felt that their Sundy was being desecrated. I don't know what was so desecrating about it. I thought it was a glorious spectacle, and I suppose for following them around once or twice I received the requisite number of lashes or slaps. But I just thought they were all different forms of worship. I don't remember any time when I felt that *that* particular set of worship or belief was sinful. I am afraid that from a very early age I had a rather pagan outlook on the world, let's put it that way, and I think it has stood me in good stead. In any case, to be frank, their music was more enthralling to my ears than the hymns of the Christian church. It also occured to me that even the missionar-ies, that is the early missionaries, shared this feeling. The reason I say this is that at the end of the hymnal there were some very special songs which were used at Harvest and New Year Festivals, Easter, you know those very seminal seasons of the Christian religion. These were songs, religious songs, Christian songs, composed by the African missionaries using the music of the worship-pers of Ogun, Sango, Oshun, the Egungun chants and so on and so forth. This was a way of gaining the souls of the so-called "pagans" and "hea-thens" through their music. The missionaries grafted onto that music songs in praise of Jesus Christ, God, the angels and so on and so forth and this seemed a very sensible arrangement, you know, very shrewd. I remembered that of all the songs in the hymn book I loved the ones which were sung specially at harvest, Easter, and so on because they had a very, very strong appeal. So I had this advantage of seeing how material belonging to one culture didn't really come to blows with material from another culture. They had a very perfect marriage of convenience with the kind of creativity which you will be very much preoccupied with at this time.

Well, when I went to school I think I continued to some extent. By the time I left school I had begun writing one or two short stories for our then newly born broadcasting station. Then I went onto larger things. I don't really know that some of those very naive stories might not still provide some useful material today.

Incidentally I've just had published a book entitled *Aké: The Years of Childhood*, the autobiography of the first eleven years of my life. That's why I'm able to recall some of these things in such great detail!

Q: Could you sing one of the market-women's songs?

S: O.K. This isn't a market-woman's song. The music of this one belongs to one of the deities, it's either Oshun or Sango. This one goes:

> Jesu Olugbala mo fori fun
> Jesu Olugbala mo f'okan fun
> Ki mmabaa ku gbe ojare
> Ewa, e je K'a sin Jesu

Now that is a song, as I'm sure you realize, that is not a European Hymnal melody at all. It belongs to cultic songs and new words have been put to it. Translated it goes thus:

> Jesus Christ I offer you my head.
> Jesus Christ I offer you my soul.
> So that I may not die in vain
> Come let us worship Christ.

Instead of "Christ" all you have to do is fix in Oshun or Oya and you will realize exactly what those women in the cult used to sing.

Right, so let's move on to what is happening in Nigeria and West Africa theatre-wise. As you must have gathered by now, Nigeria, in fact much of West Africa, the West African coast, has always had a very strong theatrical tradition. In fact, I asked the question in an essay I wrote not so long ago, why the same pattern, the same dramatic liveliness, has not been manifested in much of East and Central Africa. After all we do have here the epic chanting tradition and there are a number of rituals and ceremonies which seem to me to contain in themselves obvious lines of development for theatre. I remember, for instance, the ritual of the launching of a newly carved boat, which takes place among a tribe, in Uganda I think. In it the boat is ritually launched, almost in a replay of the severing of a child's umbilical cord. The boat is decorated, there is singing and dancing, the boat is ritually washed and so on and so forth. Curiously many of these rituals have remained within almost a kind of purist structure. They have not been stretched in a theatrical direction. Then there are what one might call "Flyting Matches," the hurling of poetic abuses, which are undertaken, among other tribes, between two teams. In the matches teams compete to see which can "knock the other one down" with a barrage of abusive verbiage and also which team asserts itself with its own self-glorification. Patterns of enactment like these have remained very much within the original formal structures in East Africa, while in West Africa the situation has been somewhat different.

The early *Egungun* ritual, to name one example from among the Yoruba. . . . The *Egungun* ritual began as a ploy—I'm quoting historic sources now some of which contradict one another—but the background is that this *Egungun* masquerade began as a ploy for bringing the dead body of a king into a city. The king had died outside his own domain and kings were not supposed to travel in those days! They were to stay permanently in their palace. This king had sneaked off, probably on some little private affair, and he had died outside. Somehow he had to be got back into the city, and so mummery was invented and under the cover of mummery the body of the king was brought back in. Those who invented this show were later given chieftaincies by the king's heirs and were given the monopoly of annually performing this rite, this masquerade, in town. Well that is one of the sources for the origin of the masquerade. One of the interesting things about the emergence of the cult is that it started as a serious, solid, ritualistic masquerade, but shortly after, it developed secular aspects, so that the masks instead of being the masks of ancestors with all its solemn moments became masks for satires, for commenting on the local situation. The masquerade developed into masks for various animals, the crocodile, the snake, and many of them began to typify certain human characteristics. Over the years the masquerade actually developed an entire secular repertory of its own with stock characters like, in modern times, the policeman, the white man also came into it as the District Officer, the Portugese trader, the slave-trader, the courtesan in society, the *nouveau riche* and so on. So that when the masks came out, the solemn ancestral masquerade went round visiting the families of those who had been bereaved, speaking in a gutteral voice—rather like the one I have got right now with my cold—which was supposed to be the voice for people from the other side of the world. At the same time in other parts of the town, the village square, in front of the palace there were these *Opidan,* the magicians, the conjurers and there was, of course, the enactment of short scenes in which recent events in the society would be satirized, would be re-enacted. Maybe some hostile tribes would be brought in and ridiculed. In modern times, you have modern theatre borrowing from these stock characters and a kind of *commedia dell'arte* developing from what was originally a mysterious cult.

Well in the nineteenth century—this is the earliest record we have of the kind of theatre which today we call "Folk Opera." The Folk Opera borrowed from the masquerade tradition, but, as we know it, it started out from the church. I would like you to see the parallel development of this to the development of the mediaeval mystery and miracle plays. During the Easter and the Christmas seasons certain religious but dramatically inclined elements within the church began to stage special performances of what we call "cantatas": Easter Cantatas, Christmas Cantatas. This meant taking the basic songs, the seasonal hymns, the Christmas carols, putting new words to some of the tunes and then enacting the Crucifixion, the Resurrection, the Nativity, whatever, for the religious instruction and also for the entertainment of the local populace. Not satisfied with this, however, what happens when you have a body of hymns and then improvize actions between one Easter hymn, one carol, or whatever and the other? Gradually other Biblical stories followed: The Trial of Neebuchadnezzar, The Wages of Sin. . . . Well, inevitably history came into it, the history of the people, kings, wars and so on. Again the same format was observed, songs would be written and learnt by everyone. These were the constants. Then the action would be improvised from one point to the next with songs between the scenes. At the beginning these plays derived most of their instrumentation, even their dramatic structure, from Westernized sources, but beginning with characters like Hubert Ogunde, who is one of the most famous of these folk-opera composers, they went backwards and began to draw on dramatic motifs, symbols, metaphors, from the kind of secular masquerade drama which I have just described. So that by the time you got towards the 1930s you had a very mixed bag of theatrical fare in which in the midst of, let us say, the Crucifixion of Christ or Temptation of Christ the devel might take the form of an ancestral masquerade! So that you have the meeting of the two streams of various fronts. Now, the Western world encroached more and more on the theatre—a very flexible theatre. For instance, when the films of Charlie Chaplin first appeared, the scenes of comedy slap-stick were immediately adapted by the Ghanaian dramatists like Master Yalley. Some of the characterizations were pure Charlie Chaplin! And then there was the influx of the returnees; American slaves in Liberia established a kind of vaudeville theatre in Liberia and in Sierra Leone. This imported tradition of vaudeville moved eastwards along the coast to mix itself with the kind of Concert Party which Master Yalley had begun in Ghana and with the kind of Folk Opera which Hubert Ogunde was producing in Nigeria, to produce performances which have mixtures of bawdy sailors' music from Liberia, Master Yalley's adaptation of Anansi the stock-trickster in Ghana, and in Nigeria, of course, many episodes from Nebuchadnezzar mixed with the appearances of *Egungun* masquerades!

Well, you can imagine what an exciting, absolutely unpredictable, un-uniform theatre this was and this is the tradition on which we, the so-called modern dramatists, in various forms, have attempted to build—not non-consciously, but this material was there, and we tried as much as possible to make use of it. One of the earliest things that we did after Independence was to run a repertory theatre to bring together the work of Ogunde and Duro Lapido with the poetic, so-called modern, Westernized drama of Wole Soyinka, J. P. Clark, etc.

Q: In what direction is Nigerian drama going now?

S: Oh, multiple directions. The folk opera troupes are still as lively, as catholic in their repertoire, as ungovernable, as ever, as outrageously innovative. We have new troupes like Baba Sala's. In fact I was talking to someone just now about a shoe-string film which has just been completed called *Efansetan Aniwura,* based on Akin Isola's play. In the credits to this film are listed thirty-five acting companies! Now, not all those companies are very well established, some of them are one-man companies, but in order to get a good foot in they went round very quickly to the bar and hired some bar-girls and went to the garages and hired some hands at the garages and said: "OK, we are now performers. Come along." And so the leaders of those groups were able to negotiate on an equal basis with larger troupes. That will give you an idea how pertinent to the Nigerian scene these groups are that when the film project came, they had to go and gather all the various troupes together and put them in a huge cast. As I said, in the credits are listed *thirty-five* different groups, some of them are very well known, some of them are one-man companies.

Now that's on one side, on the other side is the so-called modern theatre, the more literary theatre of young, comparatively less well known writers like Femi Osofisan, Kole Omotoso, Bode Sowanda, and a number of new names in the north. This theatre is taking a very strong ideological direction now, the theatre is being used directly to make statements about the future of society, the way society will be transformed.

And, of course, there is institutional theatre. One of the things which Independence did for Nigeria, with the splitting of the oil money and the splitting of the country into various states, is that it produced a very healthy rivalry between the various states. Every state wanted to be culturally prominent. Arts centres—or rudimentary cultural centres—were built in nearly all the states. Companies were raised or at least supported by the state purses. Festivals of the arts encouraged the competitive spirit. On the school level, and in colleges and private companies there's a great ferment of theatrical writing or the traditional Concert theatre.

Q: How much of the drama is in English and how much is in African languages?

S: I'd say that about 75% of it is in African languages, about 25% in English. And there are many companies which switch easily between an African language and English. For instance, in my university, the University of Ife, our acting company, which is a laboratory for the Drama Department and which travels any time it has a bus, performs both in English and Yoruba.

Q: Ngugi has turned to writing in Gikuyu. What do you think about writing in African languages?

S: This is a very vexed question. I think it is possible to give it undue emphasis, because, first of all, there are political considerations. Let me remind you, for instance, of a discussion I had some years ago with some FRELIMO combatants before the independence of Mozambique. I was promoting one of my very ambitious schemes: the idea of making Swahili a language accessible to all of Black Africa. In other words making it a compulsory language in schools so that there would be at least one common language between all Black Africans and that language would not be a language of the colonial period. And the combatant's reply was: "We are in the midst of a struggle and we already have problems of ethnic rivalries, clashes, and sometimes these are very expensive and dangerous in a revolutionary situation. The Portuguese language we have moulded to our use, we have decolonized it. We are using it as a weapon against the Portuguese oppressor and for us to embark now on the idea of a national language would not only be divertionary, but it would also create suspicions! It would create problems which we don't need to cope with!" Now, others disagreed with that and when you think of the political advantages and the cultural advantages you really cannot come to any hard and fast conclusion. In the case of theatre I would also like us to remember that theatre is not always literary—a lot of theatre in fact started out with no spoken language at all. In some of the improvized things which we do in Nigeria, especially for making immediate statements on social situations, the spoken word is sometimes of very little importance compared to the various messages the performance wants to convey. So, while I agree absolutely with the idea of encouraging creativity in *all* existing languages, there is no question about that; in fact the mother tongue should be the first level of communication and therefore of creativity. But, at the same time, in, let us say a country like Nigeria which has "God knows" how many languages at the last count, it would be ridiculous to limit oneself to producing in only one of those languages because that way you are not reaching the rest of the community. Where the problem starts is where people substitute what is a mechanism, a mechanism of communication, for the substance of communication. It can become a ploy, it can become a sort of messianic design or theme which diverts a lot of creative energy away from its natural outlet.

Q: Some people write plays in order to make money. Have you aims or conscious interests in writing your plays or do you write to make money?

S: That depends very much which play it is. There are moments when you must speak directly, very directly, on an issue in society. There is no question at all in your mind. I can give you an example: recently we had what we called a "Rice Scandal"—I don't know that I should use the word "scandal," but in the ideologically backward society in which I live every event is a "scandal" so the word loses meaning after a while. Successive governments were responsible for creating a situation of food scarcity whose remedy, the recent government decided, was just to continue the pattern of importing millions and millions and millions of Naira-worth of rice, palm-oil, all sorts of things. The members of the government distributed the contracts for the imports among themselves. This meant that prices were outrageously inflated and that millionaires were created overnight merely by sitting down, collecting the contract and selling it to the next person. They didn't have to lift themselves from the chair—they became millionaires just like that! It was really outrageous and everybody was up in arms about it. One of the things we did with the "Guerrilla Theatre," which we tried to get going for quite a while (it has been on and off, on, and off) was a "Rice Scene." We rehearsed the scene very quickly and took it to Lagos. We performed at what is known as "The Kitchen," the Museum Kitchen Theatre, which is just next to the House of Assembly. We played this scene several times over and then all the actors got into a bus and carried placards saying: "From him who has not plenty shall be taken; and to him who has much even more shall be given." We also carried sacks stuffed with "rice" and piled them, stacked them, in front of the House of Assembly. Then we fled before the police could take action. The protest was a spectacular event which clogged up the traffic around the area—which was our intention since everyone had to slow down to see the performance going on repeatedly in the Museum grounds. But the interesting thing was that only *one* paper, I think, *one* paper reported it. The others, even the opposition papers, did not speak of it. For the simple reason that the opposition legislators too have a share in this rice bonanza. One single paper, *The Daily Sketch* I think, carried a report. It was on the back page and from the way it was reported you wouldn't think that a very indignant protest was being lodged about the exploition of the masses of the people by their chosen representatives. Now that is one form of writing and performance which is totally unambiguous. It is provoked by a situation, as I've just said, and addresses itself directly to that situation. It is what I call a "Shotgun Writing," a "Shot-gun Performance," you discharge and disappear. There are many forms of theatre like that in which there is no question at all about the social impact.

There are others, however, in which society is studied in a far more leisurely, relaxed and even complex manner. This partly happens because if one is a writer, one's imagination is engaged by the very complexity within society, the interaction of the characters that make up that society. Whether one is merely working out a personal problem in relation to one's own place within that society that also motivates a number of writers I think.

Then, I think, there is also the fascination of a theme just coming into your head which you want to work out dramatically—which again is one of the functions of literature. Although it is very fashionable these days for certain schools of criticism to refuse to consider the possibility, or even the legitimacy, of a man with any kind of imagination wanting to work out a motif, a motif of human interaction which has occured to him as having artistic poten-

tial. I think that one or two of my plays belong to that category very definitely.

I don't think, apart from my adaptation of *The Bacchae of Euripides* which
was a straight-forward commission, that I've ever written a play specifically
to make money. But *The Bacchae* was a commission from the National Theatre of Great Britain which I had no problem taking up because *The Bacchae*
has always been one of my favourite plays. I jumped at it immediately. This
again was an opportunity to work at a play from my own point of view, a
play which had always fascinated me. I don't know if that answers your
question.

Q: It raises a further one: a lot of Western drama is preoccupied with the
problem of the individual in isolation. You specify that you study a community as it were. Have you any comments on that difference.

S: Yes. But I also mentioned in passing that one is also engaged in the
working out of one's own relations as an individual with the society. That
may be at the level of social commitment and the problems *that* raises for the
individual who, after all, is a human entity. Every individual is, in a sense,
unique—and that combination of psychology, sociology, or history, or environmental affects, of human strengths and weaknesses—these are also legitimate and inevitable areas of fascination for any writer. It is true that in a lot
of Western writing a great deal of emphasis is placed on that individual who
stands as the pivotal element in the drama. One modern example is Osborne's
Look Back in Anger. While it deals with an intolerable, and in effect stifling,
bourgeois, English society and with the struggle of an articulate indecisive
rebel, the society is only a background to the main action. The main emphasis
is on the mini-titanic rage of this single individual. And I don't find it surprising at all that the writer should be fascinated by the working out of the
individual psyche in society.

Q: Could you say some more about the Egungun masquerade?

S: The Egungun masquerade is an ancestral masquerade. It is one of the
devices for reconciling society and individuals to the trauma of death. The
Egungun continues the line between the living and the dead. The masquerade
comes out each year in symbolic habiliments of the dead man. A compound,
for instance, can even hire someone from the Egungun cult to come and perform within that compound. The masquerade speaks in the gutteral voice, with
certain tricks of speech which they remember as belonging to the dead per-

son. The Egungun arbitrates in quarrels which have emerged over the year and he blesses the family. That way and through the performance a link is preserved and the trauma of death is reduced a little. The world of the dead is brought closer to that of the living and that is the social and psychological purpose of the Egungun. It is also a festival: everybody comes out in their best clothes; there is feasting everywhere. The Egungun, being from the other world, is not supposed to eat or drink, but the food that is left for the ancestors rapidly disappears when he moves from house to house!

Now another festival—to choose a famous one—is the Oshun Festival, which is the annual festival of the river goddess called Oshun and which takes place at Oshogbo. Once again this festival has the effect of bringing together a community. The festival is a purgative: it wipes away all the evils of the old year. It is also a communion service in effect. There is a ritual performance during the course of which the chief is symbolically captured and then redeemed. He manifests all the qualities of patience, of tolerance, of forgiveness, and this, of course, serves as a kind of moral lesson, an example, to the rest of the community. By his self-sacrificing demeanor he takes away all the various offences of the old year and prepares for the new year.

There is a ritual of the New Yam which is rather similar. During it the new yam is symbolically eaten every year. There is a lot of ritual attached to the festival and before it no one may eat the new yam. This again has economic significances as well as bringing everybody together in mutual, communal participation.

Q: Has it been proved that drama, because it has a popular base, is a more powerful force for making social analysis and criticism than other art forms?

S: I think the very property of the theatre, which is one of enactment, lends itself to many interpretive channels and this makes it a more powerful force for social comment than other forms, the novel if you like. The question in a play is constantly being re-examined, re-examined in the light of new information, of new developments in society and of the increasing awareness of the participants in any play. Since theatre, even at the most audience-remote in the West, is still a participant medium—I mean the company cannot go on the stage and act to itself, it has to interact with the audience, so there is always a level of participation. And this interrogates constantly the situation within the place, this permanent question and answer being given in any performance. Of course in societies where the level of participation, of interaction, is even greater the theatre becomes very obviously a tool for social analysis.

Q: How far has the theatre in Nigeria proved a threat to the established powers in the country?

S: Well, to give you one immediate example, the gentleman I mentioned just now, Hubert Ogunde, was banned by the colonial powers and then, after Independence, a play of his was banned by one of the regional governments, that of the Western Region. When the man gets it from both sides like that he must be saying something really dangerous, or something worth listening to.

In Ibadan when we were doing our own sketches—before I went to Ife we did a series of direct sketches like those I have described—the situation was so dangerous that I taught our acting company how to look after themselves in times of assault. How to use the fire extinguishers to great effect. We were constantly under threat, and that is a regular pattern in Nigerian theatre.

Q: Could you tell us more about the background to the writing of some of your own plays? Why did you write certain plays?

S: I wrote the first draft of *The Lion and the Jewel* towards the end of my student days in England. It was actually inspired by an item which said: "Charlie Chaplin"—see how much this fellow keeps coming into West African theatre!—"a man of nearly sixty has taken to wife Oona O'Neill" who was then about 17 something like that. Now no one reading *The Lion and the Jewel* would ever have imagined that is the authentic genesis of the play. From Charlie Chaplin, and again thinking of the old men I knew in my society who at 70 plus, 80, would still take some new young wives—and always seemed perfectly capable of coping with the onerous tasks which such activity demanded of them! I just sat down and that's how Baroka came into existence. I knew that some of these old men had actually won these new wives against the stiff competition of some younger men, some of them school teachers who came to the villages. Lakunle was based on those who thought: "This girl has got to be impressed by my canvas shoes." Mind you the younger men didn't speak the language that those girls understood and they were beaten by the old men. That's how *The Lion and the Jewel* came to be written.

By contrast a play like *The Swamp Dwellers* was triggered by the first report I read that oil had been found in the delta regions at the time. I began thinking about the effect—I had no idea what the reality would be though—about the effect that kind of sudden access to wealth would have on interpersonal relationships in a rural, largely peasant, society, which literally always lived on the edge of poverty. I'd seen examples like that before, where sudden access to cocoa wealth had created a crisis for society.

A *Dance of the Forests* was, of course, triggered by Independence, by my knowledge of the leaders who were about to take over the reins of the country. I realized that after Independence some of those new rulers were going to act exactly like their forebears did, just exploit the people. I was interested in taking another look at that history and saying: "The euphoria should be tempered by the reality of the internal history of oppression." In our society this included the slave trade, in which the middle men, who were Africans, collaborated actively! In other words, I thought that Independence should be a sobering look at history, not just euphoria, and so on.

Break for tea

Q: Do you consider that the classics, such as *The Bacchae* and Shakespeare are relevant? Is the theme of *The Bacchae* of particular interest?

S: First of all a kind of general statement: I seem always to take the view that a great deal of caution has to be exercised before consigning the literature of any society to any category of irrelevance to another culture, another society, especially African society. It is true that there has been a deliberate excision of another part of the world by our colonial eduation. I speak, for instance, of Asian culture. It wasn't until I went to study in, of all places, England that I was even aware of the immense wealth of Japanese theatre, Chinese poetry and drama, Indian poetry and drama. I remember my enormous resentment that any system of education should have been devised by a colonial power which deprived the people it ruled over of material which was accessible to that particular colonizing society. I remember going to Leads Public Library, browsing through Noh drama, going through Chinese plays, encountering *Sakuntala* for the first time and wondering: "What is wrong with this kind of literature?" Wasn't this closer in many instances to the culture, the literature, the creativity of my own society? I wonder what sort of diabolical thinking should have consigned us to a fare of Bernard Shaw and Shakespeare to the exclusion of these vast areas. I think this kind of resentment can actually lead to one coming to a decision, a feeling, that the literature of Europe has no relevance whatever. There could be a kind of vengeful consideration whose background one is not even completely aware of. Before we go on a little to *The Bacchae of Euripides* for instance, look at the plays of John Synge, or indeed the characters whom you will find in Sean

O'Casey's plays. I agree entirely with Joan Littlewood, the British director, who was very fond of referring to Brendan Behan, another Irish playwright, as a "white Yoruba." And conversely she would jokingly refer to me as a "black Irishman." But what she really meant was something quite well observed, in that in Irish literature, in its songs, poetry and in the plays of these two writers among others, the characters and the scenes in a number of these plays could very easily have been a close study of a number of African societies which belong to the same class and have the same richness of dialect. So it is very easy to throw the baby out with the bath-water, and the reasons for doing so are very valid and quite understandable. But I think that when one examines the actual material with complete objectivity we find there are many models, not for slavish imitation but at least *inspirational* models, to be found in a lot of European literature, drama, as well as very often in their style of production. What Sean O'Casey, for instance, tried to do in his plays is not too dissimilar from some of the theatre I have been describing, the theatre of Hubert Ogunde, Kola Ogunmola, Duro Lapido, for instance, in West Africa.

Now to *The Bacchae*. What is the story of *The Bacchae?* I've spoken about rituals, communion rituals, rituals which deal with the regeneration of earth and I've spoken about societies which are at a particular productive level which we cannot compare with, let us say, modern industrial Germany. In other words we are speaking about a people who were still very close to earth, whose whole economic structure is bound up in the actual products of the earth. Industries did exist in the Greece of that period—yes—but very much on the level of the mining industry which you have in some villages in Africa today. And so this rutual is an integral part of the very economic processes and level of that society and in that period, where the regeneration of earth, the guarantee of the continuing productivity of the earth, was crucial to the people not only at a religious level, but also on a mere survival level. And this ritual which was used by Euripides in *The Bacchae* has to be seen as one which covered the entire spectrum of soci-economic consiousness as well as the religious experience of the people, a condition which applies in a lot of Africa today. That is the relevance that I really want to emphasise.

Secondly, there is the religio-political aspect: the attempt to destroy the hegemony of a priest class, a priest class which held the monopoly of belief in their hands at a very secretive, cultic and revealed level, instead of making religion part and parcel of the total social participation. The Dionysiac impulse was a counter, in effect it was a revolutionary religion, a movement right across Phrygia and Asia Minor into Greece, which tended to destroy the monopolistic hold of the priests on the Elusinian mysteries. It was a direct challenge to the city state, which, at that time, was contiguous with the priesthood autocracy of that society. In other words, in this play you had all the makings of a revolutionary movement. You had a statement, if you like, on the integration of the working community into the productive mechanisms of that society and you had the liberation—to go back to the individual—you had an attempt to liberate individual impulses, the total energy of the individual within the workings of society. Therefore the Dionysiac religion was not welcome, it was not welcome to the city, the state, to the state power, it was not welcome to the religious hierarchy. But it was welcome to the oppressed masses, the slaves, the women, the harlots. They welcomed Dionysus. He was the Messiah of Liberation, religious liberation, individual-psychological liberation and agricultural-economic liberation. He was a Messiah and he was welcomed. *The Bacchae* is a magical play, a play which deals with magic, of course, as a play must do which deals with the entire energies of the cosmos, of the earth, the very magic of fructification, of renewal of earth itself. So it is a magical play in that sense, which, of course, is not strange to us in Africa because of our rituals here. Now it is these various aspects which I've described which have always fascinated me in this play of Euripides. *The Bacchae,* incidentally, was a rather unusual play for Euripides the cynic to write in his old age. He was one of the more secular of the classical tragedians and suddenly he turned to this magical evocation of nature in this final play.

I was not content merely to re-work *The Bacchae* in terms of either European or Asiatic mysteries. I saw the parallels, as I said, with the many nature mysteries of my own society. I saw Dionysus, for example, as a figure of Ogun, as a twin brother to Ogun, who is a Yoruba god of creativity, of war, of the lyric. He is the creative-destructive paradox, the two sides of the coin which exist within our nature. So I put into this play some of the liturgy of Ogun. I was a little bit dissatisfied with the mysterious denoument of the play as written by Euripides. In other words, there is this all powerful God: he can hypnotize, he can mesmerize, he can conjure illusions, and he uses his powers indiscriminately. At the end he dishes out sentences to everybody who is opposed to him in a very high-handed manner. I felt the play would be far more rounded, far more consistent, if it went along the mystery of communion, if the resolution was within the msytery of communion. And you must realize I'm not talking about Christian communion. (Christianity itself is a pagan religion, as we can see from the origin of Christianity.) I'm talking about the universal communion which I could bring out with the symbolism of wine. In the original ending Agave is made to tear her own son, King Pentheus, to pieces when she is possessed by Dionysus and carries the head onto the stage thinking it is a lion's head; finally the mist of illusion is wiped away and she realizes she has killed her son. Dionysus is triumphant of course; he sentences this woman, banishes another character and so on. He removes, at any rate for me, the collective force which has been manifested in the presence of Dionysus. Dionysus I saw as the communal will, the collective will, the effective principle of the mass of the people merged together with the forces of the earth. So what I tried to do was to restore that element of the collective power, and try to resolve the conflict which had existed through the symbolism of the communion wine. When you read it or see it you will decide whether I succeeded or not.

This was the main change I made: I tried to remove the image, the presentation, of Dionysus as an individual tyrant—because I don't like Gods anyway! Gods for me have meaning only as expressions of human will, human strength, a superhuman aspect of human energy, of collective being. So I tried to remove Dionysus from that arbitrary, autocratic, mysterious power and present him as a symbolic representation of a movement of the masses, a movement of the earth, a movement of the totality of the community.

So that's a Greek myth which I found relevant, one in which I was able to find very close parallels with the myths of society. I tried to make something of it which removed it from its Europeanized orbit.

Q: Do you agree that the characters in *The Lion and the Jewel,* Sidi, Baroka and Lakunle, are "flat"? Did you make them "flat" intentionally?

S: Well, first of all, let me say that I don't see how anybody can say that Baroka is a "flat" character or a "caricature" character. I think this is one of the richest and most mischievous characters I've ever created. I love the old man. I think he is a wily, reactionary bastard, but he is so thoroughly grounded in his roots that he wins. I mean, never mind whether he is on the side of tradition or reaction, the important thing is that he has no doubt whatever about where he comes from and where he belongs. He even knows how to manipulate, how to keep under check, in control, the putative forces of a new order which threaten his being, his contentment, his entrenchment in his little backwater of African society. It is a vignette, but one which is very, very real. I've met old men like that who are not ignorant of the march of progress, they are not ignorant at all. They know how to manipulate and

how to handle those who are confused by the ideas which are just coming in.
They will pretend ignorance, but in actual fact they are forestalling the event.
It is important to know this, to know how to deal with innovations. But for
anyone to suggest that Baroka is a "flat" character. No! I don't see how they
can. I'd like to see a case made for that!

Now, it is very different thing for Lakunle and Sidi. I think that the reason
why people think that they appear "flat" is that they represent a particular
phase of development. They are in fact not fully developd beings in their
milieu. They are creatures who responded, especially Sidi, she responded
instinctually, to new experiences of a culture—a foreign one—in a glossy
magazine, for instance. It is just the kind of reaction any village girl would
have. You know immediately her self-estimation rises considerably. She
judges the magazine by certain yard-sticks of a society of which she is totally
ignorant. The impact on her of this magazine is, of course, on a very superficial level and that is correct. That is absolutely accurate. She has no other
means of judging what her photographs there represent. She has no idea. She
has never heard of "cheesecake." She has never heard of "glossies." She
judges instinctually and, in so far as that is concerned, she is only to be
sympathized with if we think that she particularly needs our sympathy. But
to say that she is "flat" . . . I think that has to do with her being caught in a
little vignette, the play covers only a day, of village life. She is caught also
in a phase of development and to try to suggest that she is more complex
than she actually is just to be dishonest. She is not more complex than that
and you must have encountered girls like her! She is not being criticised,
she's not being put there for very rigorous social analysis. No. It's a little
clipping and there are plays which are perfectly valid just like that—as little
clippings. . . . In fact there is no attempt to take in a whole march of history
and sort of interrogate that march of history in terms like *A Dance of the
Forests* or *Kongi's Harvest.*

Now Lakunle—for me he is a caricature. We have caricatures like that in
our society; there are walking caricatures all over the place. The "been-tos"
are caricatures! I suspect sometimes that those who say Lakunle is "flat" feel
uncomfortable, they feel they are being got at. Even though they are a little
more sophisticated than Lakunle, because they have "been-to," but in actual
fact they are caricatures like Lakunle. I know some of my friends who belong
to this class of "been-to," professionals and so on. They are ready to sack
their servant, to raise hell, to really embarrass you at dinner-table because
their house-servant, if they can afford one, has placed the fork on the wrong

side of the plate. They feel disgraced and they apologise to you: "This boy! I have taught him. These boys—They never learn!" You say: "What's that you are talking about? What's the matter with you? Put the fork back where you think it ought to be. I can pick it up anyway." But for them—their whole world has fallen down because the fork has been placed on the wrong side. It is their notion of "culture." These are caricatures. How else can you treat them except as caricatures? You can, if you like, give the colonial background and say "This man is like this because he has been oppressed for so long and then he travels overseas and he came across the socio-economic contradictions of his society." Yes-if you have the time and patience for that, and if you have a six-hour play instead of a dance drama which is supposed to celebrate life in some sort of way. But Lakunle is a poor, struggling schoolteacher, hundreds of whom I know, who think they can match a character like Baroka with imperfect weapons, with half understood weapons, with notions of what a modern city should be. Of course Lakunle is a caricature. Since when have caricatures been banned in plays? So long as one does not suggest that they represent the norm. . . .

So, maybe, that is what bothers people. They are expecting a different kind of play. Many people come to the theatre with their own notions of what a playwright ought to be doing and doing all the time. For me that is a very strange position. But, as I said before, the genesis of this play should teach one a lot of things about writing, about what inspires literature and therefore about what fascinates a writer in the process of construction. There was a famous film star who took a new wife, a very young wife, and it reminded me of parallels in my own village.

Incidentally, I think that Charlie Chaplin is a genius in what he does, a genius! But you only have to read his autobiography to realize that his I.Q. must be about half that of Baroka, I'm sure Baroka would lick Charlie in any straight-forward contest. He would defeat Charlie Chaplin anytime! I found the autobiography very fascinating, but Charlie Chaplin had one of the least analytical minds I have ever encountered. I couldn't believe that a man who created such delight for so many millions of people all over the world, who was such a genius on the screen, was so shallow as a mind. I couldn't believe this. But, anyway, he was the one who triggered my recollection of all these dirty old men back home and I celebrated their virility. What's wrong with that?

Q: What is the ideal number of characters for a play?

S: Well, if you are in the United States of America and you want to write for Broadway, you have a choice of extremes. In other words there are producers who will not look at your play unless it has a cast of thousands. You know, the Hal Prince kind of producer who loves huge spectaculars on stage. On the other hand there are probably even more producers with whom you will score if you can write a play with only two or three characters. In the European and American theatre about half the plays which are enjoying any kind of a successful run have just two or three characters. It's purely an economic thing. It costs them so much to put on a play that only those who have access to bankers and consortiums could actually consider a play with a cast of half a dozen; the others will look asquint unless there are only two or three parts. A form of criticism has even developed—very fascinating to me—in which they looked to see if someone had ever written a play with a cast of more than six—if he had, then he was a renegade and a reactionary. But that's by the way.

Since you and I, however, are not, I think, basically concerned with Broadway or the European theatre, it is very likely that we will continue to write plays which are numerically determined by the theme of the play, the situation. I think what will happen is that you will tend to leave that headache to the director who decides that the play is fascinating enough and, however many or however few characters are in it, will decide to do something about it—because I always insist that between the playwright and the audience stands the director. Plays which have been written for casts of a hundred have been performed successfully sometimes with a cast of ten or fifteen. Something is lost in the process, but other things miraculously are gained. Suddenly there are new perceptions, new precisions, which would have been diffused by the multiplicity of minor roles in the play. Shakespeare's plays today are being performed by casts half the size he ever intended for them. So I would say, "Don't worry about the size of the cast when you are writing a play."

But if you are writing for a company—that again is something I have done—in which I have a particular group in mind, a group with which I am working all the time. There's a theme I have in mind and we literally create the play or the sketch together. But that is an instance where you are governed by the company, because you are acting there both as a playwright and as director.

Q: Do you know exactly what will happen in a play when you sit down to write it or do you just have a basic idea?

S: A very good question and one which is answered "yes" and "no." "Yes" there have been plays in which the idea was so compact from beginning to end, everything was set and it followed the pattern in my mind, straight, all the way through. An example is *Death and the King's Horseman*—there was no doubt at all. The same thing with *The Lion and the Jewel.* On the other hand you have plays, like *Madmen and Specialists,* which did not follow the original conception. So . . . it happens both ways.

Q: Should a young playwright try to incorporate music and dance into his play?

S: It is important to make the play organic, do not incorporate music and dance in a contrived way. There is no question at all that any play which succeeds in integrating music, dance, masks and so on is at least one dimension richer than the purely literary form of theatre. And there is no shortage of themes at all in African society which provide the opportunity to indulge in musical drama if that is your forte. The South African theatre is an example of that: a lot of South African plays grew from street music and other areas provide similar examples.

Q: What have your experiences been with National Theatres?

S: Again, that's one of those very, very delicate questions. You see, "National Theatre" very often means prestigious theatre. All the resources of creativity, at least the lion's share, go into this prestigious institution, whether it is a national dance ensemble, or a national theatre, or a national musical ensemble, whatever it is "National, National, National!" Especially for the newly independent countries, there's an instinct towards a symbol, it's an understandable instinct. It's an expression of the spirit, the future, the hopes and aspirations of the nation. Yes. We know that. But then what is National Theatre in Britain? National Theatre in Britain is the same kind of expression, the prestige, "Culture" with capital letters. Big names, a big, large budget. The lion's share of the National Arts Council funds to the detriment of the smaller, regional groups, lots and lots of which contain much more talent, more originality of talent let me put it that way, in their little sphere than the entire common stock of the National Theatre of Great Britain. It is an opportunity for attracting the national theatre of other countries in a mutual national self-glorification, of speaking culturally on a level over and above the actual creative productivity of the masses.

Those are the dangers of a national theatre. Bureaucracy steps in, the civil service mechanism takes over. There is also the business of intrigues, political intrigues, the death the smothering of talent under the amount of energy required to stay on top of the level of intrigue all the time. These waste a lot of the creative energy of those involved in national projects of this nature. They become administrators first and foremost and stop producing the very material which got them into that position in the first place. But I agree that there has to be some form of national expression and I think my favourite model is the Cuban model—at least what it was when I went to Cuba in 1962. In which the arts, and theatre most especially, were decentralized. Any group could get itself together—this was at the height of the revolution in 1962/3, any group could form a company and then invite the Council, which was manned by some very intelligent, and democratically elected people, to come and take a look at their efforts. If it was not yet worth investing in they were given advice, they were given expertise, to help them, to raise them up to a certain level. And then the moment they proved themselves to be serious both in terms of discipline and in terms of the quality of the production they received subsidies from the government. In fact, they became paid workers of the state. They were encouraged to tour, to mix, to interchange with other groups within the country. The resources which were available for the arts were evenly shared in that way. I think, for instance, there was an international occasion when the Government's Council went round and selected something from anywhere to represent the nation on that particular occasion. For me, that is a form of national theatre programme which is valid. Out of the material available you select progressively, two, three, four—and this is my own elaboration which I suggested to my own society—you select a constantly increasing national theatre repertoire of plays. I wanted Duro Lapido's *Oba Ko So*, for instance, to be literally the first of that kind of national repertory which would be maintained. In other words the company would be paid a certain amount to keep that play permanently in its repertoire so that it becomes a National Treasure. The company can be called upon to perform it at any time, at short notice, the government will aid the company to keep the selected piece in its repertoire, it is available at any time, it is part of the National Theatre. There are many elaborations which can be made but that is my basic idea of a national theatre.

Q: Isn't there a danger that a National Theatre will become too much of a Big Brother watching over people and using its power to manipulate groups and individuals?

S: There is a danger, but the danger is considerably less than if you have the kind of monolithic structure which National Theatre tends to take to start with. In other words if you build up a National Theatre from the grass roots, you wait for the people, for the creative artists themselves, to offer something, you let them do something that is germane to their own particular environment, their own experience and which is within the capacity of their talent, and then you go and see it. There is a danger that the body might become a body of political appointees, but the danger is less if you decentralize, go round and see what is being produced and then encourage the ones which are of real artistic and thematic interest to the rest of the community. In this way you will build up from down, not start from up and say "You do this, you do that." I think the danger of manipulation is considerably reduced by a programme of this sort.

Q: Does *The Lion and the Jewel* show the clash of Western culture and traditional culture?

S: No. There is no clash, because there is no Western culture there. What you have is a misconceived, very narrow, and very superficial concept of Western culture as stated by Lakunle. You also have the old man defending his turf against any encroachment from outside. So it would be wrong to say that Western culture was represented in any way. Lakunle is *not* a representative of Western culture, he is a representative, of a sort, of Biblical gleanings, the occasional magazine, low-brow/middle-brow magazine, poorly digested! There is no Western culture in that play.

Q: Some teachers claim that the theme of the play is "culture clash" and that the playwright was concerned with "culture clash."

S: Not just the teachers, the Western critics too. They always follow the line of least resistance and see the clash of cultures. There is no clash of cultures in that play. How can you say that Lakunle represents a culture?

Q: The teachers refer to Lakunle's concern with "breakable plates" and with knives and forks, and to the way Baroka rebukes Lakunle when he meets Lakunle with "Guru morin, Guru morin. What is that?" They say Baroka stands for the preservation of his culture.

S: Baroka's attitude to the "Guru morin" is on such a jocular level that it can't be given much weight. To have a clash of cultures you have to have a much more complex play. *The Lion and the Jewel* does not pretend to be a complex play. And you've got to have a more equal representation for each side.

Baroka himself does not represent any culture as such. He is somebody exploiting certain aspects of his culture for the benefit of Number One, Baroka. I wouldn't say that Baroka represents tradition as such, he represents a last ditch defence against external intervention in his little pocket. Lakunle is certainly in limbo. There is no culture in limbo! The analysis of the play in terms of "culture clash" is just the line of least resistance, adopted first of all by the Western critics, analysts, those looking for evidence of clash of cultures. Remember this play came out at a time when African writers themselves were agonizing about their being torn between two cultures. I read some really execrable poems which came from around that period. Really phoney. I mean *angst* isn't in it: "Where shall I go? Backwards or forwards?" Well, stand still! A lot of it was very, very artificial. It was just easy material and the play came out during the period when everyone was writing it.

I always criticised that kind of poetry by the way. It is so ironic to find a play I had written for the enjoyment of Baroka (as a character) being taken to represent that theme. I thought I had very studiously ensured in that play that nobody could mistake Lakunle for a representative of Western culture. The funny thing is that people still make that mistake. I would never suggest that someone I might meet in the street like Lakunle represents Western culture. Would you?

Q: How can the theatre compete with soccer and music for the attention of Zimbabweans? How can we encourage the public to go to the theatre?

S: Well, I have to consider that I have a problem here—a very serious problem. This problem has to do with the fact that I come from an advantaged area, one in which people go to see plays. I mean all that one of the folk opera troupes has to do is arrive in the morning, drum through the city, go through the town in a hired lorry with posters on it saying: "We are appearing at so-and-so place tonight" and believe me two hours before the play is due to begin the place is already full. So I have a problem in answering your question.

To move away from that and to keep looking at parallels outside to assure ourselves that some of the problems we are discussing here are not unique, I remember a quarrel I had with Arnold Wesker. Wesker belonged to the bossy Social Reality school which began in the late '50s, towards the '60s, the departure from the old drawing-room drama of Agatha Christie's *The Mousetrap* and so on. I saw Wesker's *The Kitchen,* which is one of the most beautiful plays I have ever seen, it is a strong bit of working-class slice-of-life and shows the pressures which in humdrum employment can build up to an explosion in an unrelieved, desocialized environment. But I began to wonder about this when Wesker began complaining about the working class being apathetic towards his theatre. (He felt, I suppose, he should have been supported because he was dealing with working-class conditions. He was writing the history of the working class movement in England, in plays such as *Chicken Soup with Barley, I'm Talking about Jerusalem* and so on). He sort of felt that the working-class should be flocking to see his plays and I said: "Why the hell should they? This reality is so much part and parcel of their lives that maybe they don't want to see it on the stage." And in one particular play I felt he was very condescending and I was really angry on behalf of the people he was supposed to be representing. This was *Roots*, where there is a family which doesn't appreciate modern painting, the heroine says the family doesn't "talk," they don't discuss among themselves, they just sit down and drink their beer. And I asked myself: "What right have we really to demand that the working-class, the masses, come to our plays? Who the hell are we? What really is the total sociology of the theatre? What does it do to and for people? And how are we so sure that the people, the masses, need theatre? Whatever psychological well-being is derived from theatre, I challenge anybody to prove to me that the same kind of psychological well-being cannot be obtained from sitting in a pub playing darts and drinking beer among your own people and feeling part and parcel of the community. For me it is a real problem and one of the reasons why I've never taken it to heart is because also the question of earning a living comes into it, because maybe the reason I want them to come is that I am desperate to earn a living from them, if they don't patronize my play here I am going to starve! Why should they be concerned about whether I starve or not?

If you say: "We want to win audiences," allright I'm with you, I agree with you. You want to win audiences. You want to create audiences for new commodities, which could be a new play. Well just find out tastes of your "audience" first of all. You must take it in that serious, workmanlike way: "What are their tastes? What are the themes which are closest to them?" But at the same time: "What are the themes which are not so close, the themes that they don't live with all the time?" Because there are some themes which they live with and don't want to see decontextualized and placed as a piece of special event—which theatre is. The moment you remove something from reality, even in conditions of mutual interaction, you are already saying to your audience: "This is a special event." Maybe the audiences resent this, maybe they resent the misery derived from their labour, their sweat, their agony, being presented as a special event. I don't know. I remember we faced the same problem in a drama workshop in Cuba at which, in a huge seminar including many workers, factory workers and so on and so forth, one of the group got up and said: "Look, when I've finished working eight hours a day I don't want to come here and watch the problems of the working-class *there*. I want something else." And a lot more spoke in that vein. And perhaps this also leads to shifting ideological programs for the arts in many revolutionary societies, societies in which the program moves from the dictat of a former social realism to anything which says "Wait a minute, don't be gloomy." Remember that Mao Tse Tung admonished the artists of the Republic of China and said: "Why are you getting so gloomy? Come on, put some music, some romance, into your work! Why do you think people are going to come here and look at all these grimy and gloomy faces? Inject some romance into it." That's one of the most ridiculous things I ever heard, but I think there must be a reasoning, there must be a questioning, which went on before this rather simplistic directive went out to the artists. So I refuse to be categorical about these things. As I said, one must make sure that one talks relevantly to his prospective audience and that means relevant in terms, in terms of structure, form, symbols, metaphors. You must be able to engage them in a mutually creative way. They themselves must feel that they are part and parcel of the creative process. But at the same time there is a danger in getting too close, in which case they will say: "Oh, I've lived through *that!*" "I don't want to see *this* as a special event."

Q: Isn't this the question of national theatre—without capital letters? Isn't a national theatre one which is not imposed surfaces? It is particularly important in a revolutionary or changing situation that the theatre and the relationship between the "artist"—that's a word I don't like because it sets up a separate category of people—but the relationship between the writer and the people must change.

S: Yes. I would very much agree with that. In fact you've put your finger on one of the ways of ending the separation of the so-called "artist" class, of de-glamorizing the entire creative business. Now, of course, we are reaching into the realm of the political structure of society. For society to transform itself so that the artists are seen and treated just like any other working cadre in society, it, of course, requires a transformation of attitude, a transformation of self, the abandonment of any kind of elitist feeling which still attaches in *most* societies, curiously enough in *nearly all* societies, to the artistic worker.

Why this should be so I do not know, but it is a kind of heritage which has developed with the change in productive relations in society and no kind of society seems to be immune from it. But definitely an effort can be made. I believe, for instance, that all artists, all kinds of artists, who form the structure of a national theatre such as I have spoken about, should be salaried by the state like any other worker. That way the idea, the glamour, which attaches to the suffering artist, you know, starving himself to death in the garret, will be lost. And we'll stop having—even in my own society—the complaints: "Artists are not encouraged!" "Isn't it a shame that art is not encouraged in society!" Each time I hear that I want to stuff up my ears. Not because it isn't true. I know it is true. But that statement also contains the claim of a special category for artists. When I hear it, I always say: "Well, look at the rest of your society. Have you ever seen the farmers, the agricultural workers, encouraged to set up cooperatives and the government ready to really subsidize much needed crops within society so that at least the farmer does not feel he has to be a poor relation of society? Why should it be different for the artist?" In other words, the entire structure has to be changed. The very firm grounding in the ideological purpose of society is essential before we can even seriously consider the transformation of the artist as a category of workers side by side with other categories of workers in the community.

Q: What has been your experience of building plays through improvization and how do plays constructed by this means differ from those created by more conventional methods?

S: Well, the plays which have come out of improvization—I always use the term "sketches" because that's really what they are usually, short "sketches"—I find them very rewarding because they are usually directed at a social anomaly, they are meant to challenge the corrupt or repressive authority and that, of course, brings out a level of commitment which is proportionate to the artistic energy which writers bring to their work. So improvization has always been for me a period of intense participation and activity, total involvement, because one not only actually sees the work itself taking shape, but one is reexamining all the time the problems which produce the sketch in the first place. One is, in effect, debating the socio-politics of the situation all the time and, of course, this goes on during informal discussions, and one gets far more educated as a result of this activity. And when we present it before the public there is instant communication, an instant learning-teaching session and, of course, one of the effects of this is that it is highly embarrassing to authority. But it is a different level of creative involvement from sitting down at a typewriter and bashing things out that way.

Q: How should a young playwright start or begin his career?

S: Well, my recommendation, from my own experience, is that a young writer should not try to write the big play to begin with. Trying to write the big play is what discourages many people, just try to write a short, brief play, perhaps for radio. Write for radio, study the techniques of writing for radio. It may not be a bad idea to have a workshop sometime on radio plays. That is a wide field and a marvellous field because it reaches mass audiences. During fifteen or thirty minutes you are able to experiment with sound-effects and it's really a very flexible medium. Write short plays like that.

Write on themes which are meaningful to you, on actual situations. Don't do like many of our West African playwrights did at one time—go all out for ritual. Every play had to do with some mysterious, cultic thing, taking place somewhere. Oh, man, they were lost in sacrifices and drums and that kind of thing, and couldn't get out of the labyrinth of the grove. Write on things which are immediate to your experience and after you have found that you have acquired the technique and facility for deploying characters on an increasingly wide canvas, then you can expand.

Q: Do you learn much from your critics?

S: Very, very rarely. I don't think I have ever learnt anything. In fact I stopped reading any criticism of my work for a number of years and only started again when a new pattern of criticism developed from within my own immediate environment. This prompted me to take a look at even what others had been writing for some time. All it did was make me take up my pen and start criticising the critics for ignorance, for basic ignorance as to what theatre of literature is about. In fact there is an on-going battle, a battle royal, right now in African universities on that score.

Lunch Break

S: Some of the interrogators (at the party last night) raised questions and maybe I should deal finally, definitively, with one of them: this strange problem *vis à vis The Lion and the Jewel.* I realized that, when one young fellow spoke to me, that maybe the problem is slightly more complex than I thought originally. It would be a very great mistake if some problems which obviously have been raised in the teaching of *The Lion and the Jewel* are lost, because I find them to be of value. My assessment of the problems which were encountered by the students was that maybe the teachers of this play, because of their background interests, tended to emphasise them, in such a way as to overbalance the main theme of the play. For example, he raised the question of fertility and the contrasting play of sterility with fertility in the drama. Of course, that is there. But the whole joy of creativity, of creating anything around a certain theme, is that one is constantly being, not so much provoked, one is being stimulated. It is almost like a rose bush—you carry a rose bush and, of course, the thorns snatch at various little twigs, creepers, on the way. Meanwhile your eyes are focused on the flower. I think, it is the same thing when you play variations, because that's what it really is. If you play variations on a theme, it is not going to be a straight-forward one-dimensional drama, play variations on it, but only in different proportions. So the fact is that Baroka represents—whatever else he is—he represents a certain virile and therefore reproductive force in society, while Lakunle's approach is a pretty sterile and unproductive one. Yes, that also is there. I don't think your teacher who mentioned that is wrong. No. What the problem would be, I suspect, is that for many such teachers who've grown up in the English school, teachers who have been weaned on Robert Grave's *The White Goddess,* on Frazer's *The Golden Bough,* and who encounter plays like this in a kind of environment which is still very close to the material of these mythological worlds, it is quite natural that they will focus on what is triggered off in their minds by this counterplay of different forces within society, especially a close-to-earth society. So it won't surprise me at all if some undue emphasis is given to the fact that, yes, Baroka represents a vital force in that society, whether you want to interpret that in terms of creativity or procreativity. And that Lakunle is taken as being a dead-end, a purely transitional character, who in *that* sense anyway can be considered the obverse of Baroka—or at least who cannot be seen in the same light as Baroka's procreative energy. So that is there. And the whole thing about plays, especially poetic plays, is that there are constant dimensions which are created not even so much in the action as by the metaphor, the metaphorical language. Inevitably they trigger off these associations. These references are there, they are part of the joy of using words and one can never cut sharply a kind of line of association in any work of drama, especially in a poetic play. So it is a question of proportion; to reiterate: this is a question of proportion.

But one must not, because of that, because of these deeper associations, lose the enjoyment of this play—*The Lion and the Jewel.* I've directed it myself so I speak as a director. For any group which has tried to produce this play there is a kind of joy, a theatrical joy, a kind of pleasure, about the play and I think theatre is also about *that,* creativity is also about *that.* Creativity is not so much about the academic analysis, the post-facto analysis. This is not what creativity is essentially about. You must never permit yourself to be so ensnared by all these very fascinating ideas which are provoked by the play as to lose the sheer theatrical joy which most dramatists that I know, including Bertolt Brecht, are interested in. Brecht was one of the most consciously didactic playwrights, but when you read his texts or produce his plays, you see the creative animal, the demi-urge, is really at work, is really redolent in the manipulation of the characters you see on the stage, the song, dance, jokes and so on.

Q: Does "The Dance of the Lost Traveller" show us creative energy in Lakunle?

S: Absolutely yes! Lakunle is a performer, he enjoys his role. And that is why at the end of the play I made sure that he is not a tragic character. In the final dance he is already creating for himself a new madonna. He responds to the provocative dancing of a beautiful girl and we can see another madonna in the making, for Lakunle is never down for long.

These are some aspects of the theatre which, I think, teaching occasionally obscures.

Then, over lunch, we were talking about an old mutual friend and I would use her as a reference for some of the things we were concerned with. That's the great British director Joan Littlewood with whom I've worked on a number of projects. The history of Joan Littlewood is very, very fascinating; it is the history, in fact, of the African travelling theatre. I use the expression "Mother Courage," for her because even though I didn't know her at the time, this was shortly after the war, the image that I always have of her is that of Mother Courage with her cart, you know, trundling through the morally and ideologically devastated streets of Europe, both West and East. There she was with her company of actors with all their belongings in a travelling vehicle, which very often they had to pull, which carried their set, costumes and so on. They just travelled and performed, sleeping in church-yards, schools, and factories, and performing anywhere at all where they could have an audience. And really *living the theatre* because they believed passionately in it. Very often they had to hawk some of their costumes to be able to provide something of a square meal, and sometimes, when everything was lost, they would pile into a train, and share one ticket among them passing it along the window when the conductor came along. Finally she found a home for her theatre in Stratford Fast. She revolutionized British theatre in terms of production techniques, the interaction between the stage and the auditorium. She really turned this workshop—it was called Theatre Workshops and justifiably so, it was a workshop—turned it into a Mecca for the sated and bored West End theatre patrons. They used to make the journey all the way to the East End, which is the seedy side of London, to see this marvellous experiment in creativity. She had numbers of successes, she discovered numbers of playwrights, in the sense that she took their raw scripts, raw material and turned the scripts into something really formidable: Shelagh Delany, Brendan Behan, Lionel Bart. And many of the actors whom you see today on British television, Morecombe and Wise and a number of other comedians, started out with her, they were Joan Littlewood's products. But again, and this is what happens to jots of theatre, success occurred, success overtook Theatre Workshop. One production after the other went over to the West End, to the Sodom and Gomorrah of British theatre, the bright lights, and so on. The actors became highly successful. Now I believe very much in tightly knit repertory companies. That's really what I enjoy working with, a small group, maybe a large one, but who develop a style of their own and can interact so that when one person says: "I was about to do this," the next has sensed it already and has responded. That kind of theatre is for me far more vital and more creative than the kind of commercial theatre where you assemble famous names and faces and do a prestigious production, which is the kind of thing which happens in National Theatres. But anyway, she became very successful and one after the other her productions went to the West End, the bright lights, and stayed there for long runs. So she would set off again with a new production, bringing in new young actors, sometimes not even actors with any names. Some of these people who become actors and actresses started out as bar attendants in the place and she just said: "I need some extra person to walk on in that scene! You! Leave your bottle. Come. Walk in there." And suddenly she said: "The way you walk is not bad. Let's try that again." And suddenly a real talent had been discovered. Well all these people went to the West End and at one time she had three full-scale productions running there. That would strain even the most elaborate, the largest, repertory company. And so Theatre Workshop went from professionalism to an improvizationary character of a different kind, of an amateurish kind, the critics—you could see they were being kind to the new productions, they were being patient. She just could not attract back those actors, the whole sense of company, of belonging, was lost. That was the fate of Theatre Workshop, and it contains very useful lessons for us here. It reinforces the point I was making earlier that when these regional localized theatres are set up the state policy should not be to start creaming off the talents. That creaming off destroys the grass roots, the kind of community theatre, for the glorification of the white elephant in the capital city. They should be subsidized so that they can continue to grow in their own right, with their own specific characteristics. This multiplicity of talent and variety, this healthy competition is a very solid basis for a national culture.

Q: To what extent do you regard directing a play or the production of a play as an essential part of creating of that play? Is the production a separate part of the process or merely a continuation of the initial impetus?

S: A sensible question and the answer is very simple—for me a play on the page is really cold and dead and my real instinct has always been to see the play fleshed out. I don't feel that the play is completed until I've actually seen it live on the stage. I think I am as much a director as I am a playwright, and when I begin to direct a play I have no respect at all for my text. This has shocked a number of the actors I've worked with. You know actors love their lines. They come and say: "Wole, How can you do this? These are the best lines in the play?" I had this experience most tellingly when I directed *Death and the King's Horseman* at the Goodman Theatre in Chicago. The actors would love these lines and so on, but the lines were just not working for that particular production and so they had to go. They just couldn't believe it. "You can't do this to yourself!" "Oh yes I can!" The two functions, of writer and director, are not really separate. I think I've found that I just look at the text very coldly when I'm directing. It doesn't mean that the lines are useless, but if they are not working for any reason either because of the actor, or the time factor, or something else, say the actual environment. . . . This example was very interesting actually. We were doing *Death and the King's Horseman* in a theatre which was used for Saroyan and Arthur Miller and Eugene O'Neill, the occasional Greek play, one or two modern American playwrights with their very peculiar language—which they call English. I don't know it is! I was working also with black actors who came into the theatre thinking that because they were black therefore they understood the play. So I had to break that down and make them understand that they were just as much strangers to the play as any whites, because this play was from a totally different society. In fact at one time I swore that if I ever met the man or woman who invented the saying that "Black people have a natural sense of rhythm," I was going to decapitate that person immediately, because if there was anything more humbling to those black actors, it was that they could *not* move to the rhythm of the African dances, drums and so on because they had become so accustomed to the disco culture. For everything which had the slightest bit of subtlety beyond the disco beat, they were lost. Many of them were tone deaf, which they could not believe. They were used to singing all the "yeah, yeah, yeah!" and they had ear-phones clamped to their ears! When I played them the tapes which I had brought from home of some of the songs and said: "You have to learn this now," they weren't into what they thought. But by the time they finished they admitted that they had learned from the experience. They formed themselves into a repertory company and they said they didn't want to go back to whatever they were doing before. Again that was part of the training programme. I just would not settle for their approximations. I felt they really had to break down their bones, get them to learn new auditory habits, hear new sounds, sounds they never knew existed. That meant that even though they spoke "English" they had to learn to read it in a rhythm that was not British R.P. That is a rhythm I needed for what the language of English is saying in my own language. They had to find a totally new way of saying those lines and, in fact, one famous actress who was playing the lead role had to drop out after two weeks of rehearsal because she could not do it. She had done the classics but she couldn't cope with this! It is an interesting experience working on one's own script if one can divorce oneself from the role of playwright.

Playwrights are a nuisance anyway in the theatre when you are rehearsing. I always lock them out until a week or so to the performance, then their suggestions are welcome. Their advice may not be taken but at least I can afford to listen.

Q: Do you allow those who are directing your plays to take the same unsentimental attitude to your text?

S: Yes. I stay out. That is what caused the problem with *The Bacchae of Euripides.* I stayed out of rehearsals till it was too late. I stayed out till about two weeks before the opening and then only looked in because the actors were sending me S.O.S.es where I was to come to rehearsals.

Q: Do you mind if directors change your text?

S: I no longer have any control over the text and I believe that new insights come to a production during rehearsal and also when a play is looked at by somebody else. But, at the same time, I don't believe in undue liberties. I feel free to criticise in the harshest language whatever anybody does wiht my play—if I agree to see it at all! In the same way as I expect the playwright to chase me around with a club when I've finished with his play, I have to accept full responsibility for what I've done to his play and I don't want him to interfere. If I need clarification, which of course one does from time to time, we'll go out together for a drink and just talk around the subject till I draw out from him—without his knowing—what I really want to know and that's enough. That's all the help I want.

Q: How do you audition actors for a production?

S: Auditioning is very difficult, it is very easy to goof. Whenever possible—I'll let you into the secret: when I have a production on, I find an excuse for somebody to, not necessarily "throw a party," but to have a "function," an occasion at which the potential actors will be at their most relaxed. Let's say, you organize a meeting: "There's going to be a meeting for the play and all whose who are interested . . . " (You can do this sort of thing in a university atmosphere). And before the meeting starts—maybe by "accident"—you reveal that someone is celebrating a birthday, there are going to be drinks around, you invite them to come a little earlier, you watch them when they are unselfconscious, watch them very closely and make notes about their temperaments, the rhythms of their bodies, of how they react in dialogue with other people, that sort of thing. That tells you a lot, I find, about an actor's potential for a role. After that, you build on it; you do a reading, in which sometimes I make people just read the dialogue. And after that you begin the process of really winnowing down the possibilities, you have a few more individual auditions. By the time you have reached that stage you are pretty sure who is getting to do what. I find that I derive most of my information from throwing the actors and actresses into an unselfconscious situation where you can observe without being observed.

Q: What is the best relationship between the actors and the audience?

S: Well, again, that depends very much on the kind of theatre it is. Take Grotowski for instance, this Polish playwright/director, essentially a director, who approaches theatre from an almost monastic point of view. He takes the view that actors should be disciplined like monks and the space relations of the theatre should be such that the audience become almost like mystical voyeurs, peeking on some masonic ritual. He wants the actors to be like organisms under the microscope. He has all sorts of theories about this, essentially that the theatre is a monastic profession, the outsiders are really involved in watching a very private mystery. (Now I don't hold with this view). That is absolutely valid so long as you don't try to apply it to all kinds of theatre and that is why I say that not too much should be made of audience participation, audience involvement. It depends what kind of play it is. What kind of space is available. The proscenium theatre, for instance, I think is a monstrosity. I find I've never been able to work in the proscenium theatre. The kind of theatre which I enjoy working in, the kind of theatre I enjoy *producing* in, is not one which is determined by the proscenium arch. I have seen productions which very clearly belong behind proscenium arches, to the whole idea of looking at the stage as if you were looking through a frame at a picture. The proscenium theatre is appropriate for certain kinds of play.

Then you have celebratory theatres, like Joan Littlewood's theatre, one constant celebration. Well for that you do not attempt to restrain the stage or the audiences in any way. You really want maximum space.

The development of a certain kind of theatre, with which I have never felt the slightest sympathy, which to me was just an expression of American gross self-indulgence and faddism—I think it is called "Liquid Theatre" and it went in different directions like "Theatre of Smell" in which nothing was left any longer to the imagination. If you burn incense on the stage, you've got to make sure that incense is burning in the audience. Things reached the point where the audience was excoriated, was supposed to have become insensitive, to have lost the human touch and therefore the only way to restore that is to have actors clambering over members of the audience. Usually naked! I have always treasured a remark of Kenneth Tynan's during one of these sessions we had. He said: "If I'm sitting down and someone comes climbing over me with her tits bulging I just hope I have a lighted cigarette in my hand to really apply it where it will hurt most!" This kind of excess begins to appeal to the senses instead of to the mind. The theory is that there is no contact between the actor and the audience unless there is *physical* contact—how much more reductionist can you get? This form of theatre went way out on a limb and I am absolutely appalled by that kind of theatre because it oversimplifies the whole business of contact between the audience and the actors.

Then there is the travelling theatre, "folk opera" theatre, which is actually stopped and the audience is appealed to: "Does it seem right to you? What do you think?" If the tradition is worked into the text then there's no problem with it. It is when you take a play from a totally different and incongruous set of cultural circumstances and try to impose this kind of audience participation that you just look like a fool. There are times when I want to sit in the theatre and I don't want anybody to talk to me: "For God's sake just get on with your business. I will extract from it what I need, I will feel satisfied!" I feel that I am being patronized, being talked down to, by the fact that the actors are constantly winking at me, let's put it that way: "Hey, what do you think of that then?" One resents it with certain kinds of plays. On the other hand, in a different kind of play, you don't even wait for the wink, you get up and say: "Hey that's not the way that should go!"

Let me tell you an amusing episode we had. Recently we did a production of *Inquest on Biko* by Blair and Fenton. I directed it as the Congregation production at Ife and later took it to the U.S. (In the U.S. people had to do a double-take when they saw that the company was all black and yet it was doing a play on apartheid and the murder of a black nationalist. Well that's by the way.) In Ife we had this veteran, this labour unionist, Michael Imodu, who was being given a long-overdue honorary degree by the University. He was present at the performance and in the middle of the play—those of you who know the play will know that the medical evidence is, of course, a disgrace—when one of the medical doctors was giving evidence, Michael Imodu got up and said: "But that's a lie! I demand to say something! No, no, she can't get away with that." (It was a female playing the role). "She should not be allowed to get away with that!" Imodu is an old man, about seventy, and he has been an agitator, a politician, all his life. He is used to making speeches at the drop of a hat and suddenly he lost the difference between reality and the theatre. He wanted to get up and challenge the falsification of medical evidence on the stage. He said: "Oh no! It's impossible." He was pacified by his "aide-de camp," one of my colleagues, who was with him. But from time to time he still persisted "No! No!! This is impossible! This is impossible! We cannot allow this to go on!" At the end when the judgment was passed and the South African police were found to be totally innocent of the murder of Steve Biko, he literally erupted: "I said it! You didn't allow me to talk at the time. That's what you get. See! See!! The murder of justice!" And so on. Well that's an extreme example, but if you've watched audiences in Africa responding to play in a travelling theatre or sometimes even in the cinema responding to films, you can notice the same degree of involvement. Commentaries like: "Oh, that's a lie"; "Oh go and sit down"; "Who do you think you are going to fool with that?" Either on that level or else on the level, in the thrillers, of "Look out!" He's behind you!" And so very often you will find that the conscious effort to involve audiences on an elementary level is a waste of time. The audiences are not mutton, they are not logs of wood. They have their own systems and language of reaction, sometime this language is a language of silence and of later contemplation, of digestion of the various factors in the play. There are many, many languages of audience response and I think very often there is an excessive worry about how we are to involve the audience or how we are to involve the audience *more*. I've never heard the audience say, interestingly enough: "Why don't you people involve us more?" For the simple reason that they have had their own quota of involvement. Most of the time anyway.

Q: Which very modern playwrights do you regard as most significant and why?

S: That is a difficult question because in fact I went through a couple of years during which whenever I travelled to Europe or America I didn't go to the theatre. One reason was that I found that I had lost the capacity to enjoy theatre for its own sake. I found that I was constantly analysing the production. It was a real hang up and I would be so fed up with myself because I was not submitting myself to the theatrical experience any longer that for a couple of years or so I'd rather go to a musical concert or visit the opera or whatever. Any time I was in the theatre it had become a totally cerebral process. And within the constraints of that it is very difficult for me to say today what kind of playwrights represent for me truly modern theatre. I can, however, talk about a few plays, a few theatrical experiences.

One of my favourite playwrights by the way still is Arden, but that's quite some time ago. I've not seen anything he's done recently.

I loved Ariane Mnouchkine's *1789,* which I saw in Paris a few years ago and which was a festival of revolution, a ritual of revolution, which did not stint on sheer theatricality. Its use of commedia dell'arte, improvizational theatre, audience direct contact and space was really fantastic.

I was fascinated by *Le Regard du Sourd,* by an American Bob Wilson, who has experimented with a kind of theatre which is almost like an animation of paintings. He used to go on for hours and it was largely mythological. His work has been interpreted in terms of Jung. It is difficult to describe and you really have to see it: a slow-motion animation of paintings. His first work in this direction was *Le Regard de Surrealist du Sourd,* translated as *Deaf-man's Glance,* and it's like getting into the mind of this deaf-mute girl. This playwright was working with a school for the deaf and that is where the idea came from. It was really like an animation of the collective symbols of society seen through the mind, the vision, of this deaf-mute girl. But after that first one I found that he became very self-indulgent and when I went to see his next production I walked out noisily because I thought he was carrying it too far.

The work of Derek Walcott, the Caribbean playwright, fascinates me a lot. He is a poetic playwright who also deals with contemporary sociology. Again talking about the individual in society, he is very much concerned with plotting dramatically his own sensibilities, his own development, in a multi-racial and class conflict ridden society.

Among the British playwrights I have seen Shaffer. I am fascinated by Tom Stoppard's wit, his urbane, intellectual wit and word play, but I derive no real, gutsy, theatrical satisfaction from his work.

I don't think any modern playwright really captivates me, not on the same level as some of the classical playwrights.

Q: What about other African playwrights?

S: There is a lot of work going on by African playwrights, especially by the young ones who are very ideologically motivated. I've mentioned a few. Ngugi wa Thiong'o is, of course, another. In fact I think a lot of the African dramatic genius is being poured into film right now, Ousmane Sembene, for instance, and there are one or two of Ola Balogun's films which are worth mentioning. The young Francophone cineastes seem to be very exciting today and a lot of dramatic talent seems to be siphoned off to the cinema.

Q: Do you find that you are inspired to write by the books you read or by your environment?

S: I think it's a mixture. I've told you, for instance, of the initial genius of some of my plays, so what "inspired" me is a tricky question and I prefer the expression what "triggers off" the idea of a play in one's mind. And that can be an accident, a study, a situation, an immersion in a continuing situation which can only placate itself by turning to the written word.

As far as environment is concerned, I find I can lock myself in a hotel room and write.

Q: Have you ever been anxious to write a play about the clash of cultures?

S: No. I don't know that I ever have been consciously anxious to do that— except perhaps in *Death and the King's Horseman,* which is, they will tell you, of an actual piece of history in which European colonial officer's ethos came into conflict with the practices of the society of which you are a part. Apart from that I have never been really interested in the clash between two cultures, culture conflict, and seemed to agree with one when he said: "OK, you've got conflict. The whole point of society is to resolve the conflict. So if you have got a conflict don't make so much noise about it, resolve it!" And I take that attitude in my writing because I believe that culture is not static anyway. It never has been.

Q: Would you comment on the use of rites in drama.

S: The use of rites? Well, rites, rituals, ceremonials, festivals are such a rich source of material for drama. They are instrinsically dramatic in themselves, because they are formalized. Apart from being visually clarifying, their representation is so precise that even when the meaning is obscure you are left with a form which is so clear that it reifies itself into a very concrete meaning for the viewer. So, for me, rites, rituals are inevitable metaphors for the drama of life, for many, many human situations.

In *The Strong Breed,* for instance, I talk about the ritual of purification at the end of the year. Which again is tied up with the whole business of sacrifice, of self-sacrifice, the acceptance of the role of the carrier in society on whatever level. Whether one speaks of this communally or whether one speaks of it individually, the fact is that there are beings in society who accept the role of sacrifice. As in this text by the Zimbabwean freedom-fighters I was reading, who very readily accepted the possibility of death and self-sacrifice in a particular case. It seems one of the pivots of social regeneration all through history. And of course I come from a society where these rites proliferate and where even Christian rituals are part and parcel of the same formalism of rites.

Q: Can you tell us about your involvement with the Mbari school of writers?

S: There was no attempt to start a school of writing, of creativity. No. Mbari was just a place. It was obvious that we were never going to get government patronage for the arts except in one or two selected areas and we had lots of young people who were anxious to write, to debate, to sculpt, potential architects. For instance, once we invited printer Berhman, who was a South African exile, to come and so some workshops in design for potential architects from the point of view of trying to assert some relevant aesthetic awareness in the building of society. This really was our aim. It is not enough to sit down and complain that our cities are sprouting up all over the place without any design, that imitations of sky-scrapers are being brought to a society which obviously has options, has alternatives, that even traditional architecture has lessons for society, and there is no point, in an underdeveloped place, in raising the kind of buildings which in turn require air-conditioners for human beings to be able to live and function in them when you could build houses in a cheaper way which don't need air-conditioning. And you could utilize local materials in developing the architectural styles which have served society for so long. This is, for me, where tradition becomes critical and important. Not just in the question of song and dance.

Of course the painters also benefit from motifs for styles and expression. Instead of being enslaved to schools of expressionism, impressionism, pointilism, etc., etc., and any other-ism which artists get fascinated by! At least they must recognize certain valid, applicable and adaptable patterns in our culture. They must be made *aware* of them to start with, then at least they might be able to make an original contribution to the whole process of art.

So that's why we came together and found a place, encouraged by the well-known writers of all types, from the so-called primitives like Amos Tutuola, who was one of the founding officers, to the modernist novelists like Chinua Achebe, J. P. Clark, Wole Soyinka, and popular writers like Cyprian Ekwensi. Just a home where you could come, could experiment, could discuss any problems. We put on programmes, but there was no attempt to create any sort of school of writing or sculpting. No.

Q: Do playwrights benefit from working with other artists and in other art forms?

S: An artist in any medium shouldn't feel a sense of isolation, he should understand very early and very succinctly that all these various art forms flow into one another. An atmosphere in which we can actually see that, actually see images in the lyric of a song, or the lyric of a play, where he can actually see those images reflected or associated with images in a painting, a sculpture and even hear equivalents in musical compositions which his words might trigger off, is very often useful and *vice versa*. And also he can see that sculpture can inspire a dance, see all these things at work and see how even environmental design speaks to the decorative arts, the plastic arts, one also speaks to the other. I think this is very, very useful so that he doesn't get locked up in a kind of block. Someone was asking me about "writer's block," I told him I experienced it quite often myself, this sort of block very often can be dissolved simply by moving outside of one's own medium to a different matrix of art. That in itself is very often a help. So any kind of atmosphere in which these various art forms can intermingle . . . no force . . . just let them be there, that's all.

Q: How do you get sponsorship for your group to travel around?

S: To begin with we didn't have anybody to sponsor us. In fact this was the reason why the acting group which I formed in 1960 was made up of people who were working. They all had their jobs. We met in different places to rehearse and put on productions. Later on, when we became better known and were attracting large audiences, we made some money, and I started a second group which was going to be a company of young professional performers. We did some programmes for television, but just, barely, made ends meet. But the fact that a large proportion of the original group was willing to perform free of charge in order to bring up this kernel of professional theatre artistes helped a lot. Later on, when I teamed up with the University of Ibadan, when the Theatre Arts Department was being formed for the first time. I transferred this group of young professionals to the University as its acting company, the laboratory for the Department. So for the first time the University was actually maintaining an acting company in Nigeria. It went in various steps like that.

Q: I find a similarity between Segi in *Kongi's Harvest* and Simi in *The Interpreters*. What point were you trying to make by creating two such similar characters?

S: Well, it's not so much a point that I intended to make as that both Simi and Segi were modelled on a certain kind of woman who is very prevalent in Nigeria. A very strong kind of woman with very strong influences on men and events—I'm sure you have them here too. That kind of woman held a certain kind of fascination for me. They are a very independent type of woman and at the same time very feminine. It wasn't that I was making a point but one draws one's pictures from models very often and these characters are no exception.

Q: Is it true that Segi represents Life and that's why the Oba is frightened of her?

S: Not so much that she represents Life, but that the Oba would be afraid of women like Segi, definitely—because she doesn't conform to the kind of woman he would keep in his harem. So it is not surprising that he would be frightened of her, but not because she is made to represent Life. She just is not the kind of woman he is accustomed to.

Q: If, as you say, culture is dynamic, do you think that a writer like Ngugi wa Thiong'o is right to turn back to his roots? Doesn't he recognize the dynamic nature of culture?

S: Well, you see, Kenyan politics is very complex—as you know very well. And the strategies for combating the reactionary politics of society can be puzzling to those of us are on the outside. It is possible, for instance, to commence revolution within society by recourse to a very strong cultural base. That is possible. I do not know if that is Ngugi's strategy. I know he is a believer in social revolution. He even says he is a Marxist, although I wonder about that claim in view of some of his strategies for his society. But there are many reasons, which I cannot pretend to know, why he has moved deeper in this direction. I've tried to understand it. I've tried to understand even the sudden passion he has for advocating a language-culture as the basis for national self-liberation. I don't really know. I find quite frankly that he contradicts himself in many ways, since you've raised the question. But then I always say to myself: "I'm looking at it from the outside and the dynamics of politics in countries in East Africa are very different from those in West Africa." So it is a question you will have to ask him when you get him nailed down like you've got me nailed down.

Q: What is your advice to anyone contemplating managing a company?

S: First of all, you get yourself a club and a whip—metaphorically speaking. That's the only way you'll ever run a company. Actors, I don't know why, are the laziest beings in the world! Actors do no like discipline and you cannot have an acting company without discipline. I'm not talking about Nigerian actors only, this has been my experience in Europe and America. I think it has to do with a certain confidence in themselves that when the day comes they will be ready. But I am afraid that their work is not superior to the work of the director, the scene designer, the costume maker, the make-up artist and the property makers, and the director must know just what everyone is capable of at every stage. So you have to do a lot of frowning, so to speak, to put a group together and keep them on their toes. I don't give a damn whatever anybody says about democracy in acting companies. It has not worked for me. Actors must know who the director is—it's the only way. Then, of course, you must be totally honest with your group and flog yourself as much as you are ready to flog them.

Q: What happens if you have a theme which is exhausted after 80 or 90 minutes and yet to be acceptable on the local stage it has to last 120 minutes, three acts of 40 minutes each, or two acts of 60 minutes? Have you any suggestions to how a dramatist can go about teasing out the theme?

S: The answer to that is for me to digress with your premise. I don't think that any play has to be 90 minutes or 120 minutes or whatever. When a theme exhausts itself the play should come to an end there and then. Then it is the business of the entrepreneur or director who wants to present the play to decide whether to have an evening of a 60 minute play or have a double-bill. And that is why little theatres, lunch-time theaters, street theatres, are so important in any society. There are so many different kinds of spaces, of environment, even times. People tend to want a heavy meal of cultural diet in the evenings, but in the afternoon, lunch-time theatre, you can go and watch a different kind of play between having a bite and the time you go back to work. I think that's the forum for the kind of play you are talking about. It would be a mistake to tease out a play, teasing out will show.

Americans went through this, as many of the American playwrights admit. In fact it still goes on today with the producer sending the script back and saying "Flesh it out. It lacks just another 15 minutes—or 20 minutes." And so the poor sod goes back and stretches his dialogue here and adds a scene there. When the play from beginning to end is compact, and already a finished, acted piece. Now he loosens it up. I've seen plays like that which at their first outing, let us say at the Theatre Upstairs of the Royal Court Theatre, London took 40 minutes. When you see it next on the full stage it lasts one and a half hours and it is no longer the same thing. So I disagree with your premise.

Q: What are the differences between writing for radio and writing for the stage?

S: Well, briefly, I'll give you one obvious example. You just have to remember that the actors, the action, cannot be seen and therefore your dialogue must be written in such a way so that you do not frustrate your audience, your listeners. By using dialogue the listeners must know that the actors are seeing things which the listeners cannot see. If you don't it is very frustrating for the listener. In other words dialogue must be written in such a way that either it creates the physical objects which are involved in the action or the physical action itself is translated into words. The sound effects can be used also, of course, but they should be at the bottom of the list. What you must do is transfer the physical reality into dialogue. Far more than on the stage, that is essential. You can get away with action on stage. You can involve the audience in the action on stage. But all that has to be transferred to the language of people in between, into dialogue. You can use narration if you like but that is copping out. We should use narration as sparingly as possible, everything has to go into the action between characters.

The session continued with an exercise in improvizing radio drama. The Chairman chose some of the participants, called them to the front of the hall, lined them up and asked them to improvize a radio drama. The scene which emerged drew on a recent confrontation in the local sporting world: a team went on strike and refused to turn out for a match. After the lively improviza-tion, Soyinka drew attention to the instances of the "language of action" and to "the graphic expressions." Then he drew out of the participants examples of some of the ways in which characters can be identified or can identify them-selves for a radio audience without sounding excessively artificial. One of the problems of radio, he said, was to make listeners familiar with the identities of the characters involved.

Q: Do you think narration should be used more in radio plays than in stage plays?

S: Radio plays definitely require narration far more than stage plays. But again I wish always to qualify whatever I say: there are certain forms of theatre, certain specific types of theatre, especially where there is constant rapport with the audience, and in these instances it is part and parcel of the expectation of the audience that the characters will come out and address them directly. In fact a lot of yardage of laughter, of wit, is accumulated by the very means of narrative. It is almost like "narrative counter narrative." What is obvious is introduced in a language which connotes the action and in fact puts the audience in a very receptive frame of mind. So it isn't that narrative is being condemned as such. I am just warning about the fact that it must not be used to replace the skill of the writer, the director, and the actor.

In radio the same thing happens. There will, from time to time, be situa-tions whereby you must use narrative. But even the narrative should be writ-ten in a way to enhance the rest of the production, to promote the action, rather than make it very, very static.

"We are now before the castle of Elsinore, and Hamlet is about to walk the ramparts. It is moonlight—"

And so on and so on. No! Everything I have just said just now can be put into the first two sentences of dialogue in the most natural way. That's what I want to say.

Q: What do you think about the proscenium or picture-frame stage and its suitability for African drama?

S: First of all, if it is there you can use it, utilize it. And remember you can break out of the picture-frame stage any time you like. I remember a production in the Arts Theatre at Ibadan where I ripped out a number of seats in the front rows and extended the stage there and I used a ramp which went from the stage down the sides of the auditorium. This totally destroyed the picture-frame effect, and I used three levels on the stage for *Madmen and Specialists.* So, if it is possible to make structural changes to the theatre, you can totally destroy the picture-frame effect. You can break out of it, meanwhile you are conscious that the frame is still there, and thereby turn the tables on the picture-frame itself.

Now for the strict picture-frame. Yes, there are plays for which it can be used. I remember we did a production of *You in Your Small Corner* by Barry Reckford. All we had was a picture-frame stage and it seemed to me that the play suited it anyway. The same thing with Sarif Easmon's *Dear Parent and Ogre,* which is a drawing-room kind of play set in Sierra Leone. It raises certain social issues which I thought were of interest, in fact I found them fascinating. I decided that instead of fighting the picture-frame, I would produce this play exactly like a picture, so that it was as if you were looking at a slice of reality in a very clinical, a very, very clinical way. The audience was manipulated—I hope anyway—into viewing the play as if they were looking clinically at some characters on the stage as objects of curiosity. So in those productions, in that way, I collaborated with the picture-frame, but only because the two plays were of a certain kind. They were plays in which one could say: "Let's look at this piece of humanity, this particular situation in the most clinical way possible." I think that in that setting nobody, none of the audience, felt: "Oh what a shame, we didn't have a different kind of stage." No. It never even occurred to them, I think, that they were watching a play on the picture-frame stage. That's why I don't want to condemn the picture-frame stage outright.

I can't write for it and I prefer not to use it—ever. But I have seen productions in which the material fitted perfectly into the picture-frame.

Q: What kinds of theatre forms are there?

S: Theatre forms are constantly being replenished all over the world. There have been, as I said earlier, in the last decade at least twelve theatre forms to the best of my knowledge: from Environmental to Liquid to Living. And each one has very distinct features, both in terms of the material written for it and the method of production, the spatial use and the manipulation of scenes and audiences. For instance, one form employs the concept, that instead of manipulating scenes, you manipulate the audience. You put the scene there and light it. Then you shift the audience. That is to say at the beginning of each scene the audience is told: "Go, over there!" Next one: "Go over there," and so on.

There is no limitation to theatrical forms and I am sure that you will develop a new theatre from here in Zimbabwe.

Realms of Value in Literature Art: Interview with Wole Soyinka

Biodun Jeyifo / 1985

From *Contemporary Nigerian Literature: A Retrospective and Prospective Exploration.* Biodun Jeyifo, ed. Lagos: Nigeria Magazine, 1985, 23–37.

Jeyifo: You have been writing for more than two decades now. During this same period you have been very active in cultural movements and institutions both in Nigeria and the continent at large. Moreover, your international contacts as Secretary-General of the Union of Writers of African Peoples, the production of your plays around the world, all these have placed you in a rather privileged position to see literature and art in terms of broad social and historical forces.

Has the situation of the African writer changed in the period of more than two decades that you have been writing? Can one in fact generalise about the situation of the African or Third World writer?

Soyinka: I do not believe that one can generalise. . . . Obviously there are important, even critical differences in the situation of the Nigerian writer, and that of Mobutu's Zaire even though the politics of these two countries do not differ ideologically. I cannot imagine, for example, the Zairean writer being passionately concerned with thoughts on how to stop the recent South African raids into Angola . . . he's far too desparately involved with the "throwback" whose continued existence in power in his own country threatens his very existence, should he step out of line. (That, incidentally, quite apart from the "amnesty" announced by Mobutu which is being quite sensibly ignored by his opponents who remember what happened to those who were foolish enough to believe such offers of "amnesty" a few years ago . . . a decade or so ago . . . remember he just hanged them publicly . . . in the market).

By contrast, the Nigerian writer can actually afford to be positive in his concerns with the movement of world-wide forces. . . . such as are gathering around Southern Africa or even Latin America. . . . and the Middle East of course, even as he attempts to utilise his craft in the immediate context of desired changes within his society. We are of course speaking in general terms. Twenty-five years ago, to use me as an example, I was almost exclusively concerned with the problem of black liberation from the settler-colonial and apartheid obscenities. As a student just beginning to write seriously, I saw the political background in Africa as being situated in Southern Africa, nowhere else. You see, in West Africa, for instance, we were thrown right in the midst of the nationalism of people like Enahoro, Oged Macauley, Azikiwe, right from the very beginning, from childhood. So colonialism, for me, was already dead. For me. . . . I was already thinking of it in the past tense, as something already dealt with. . . . just a matter of time. . . . obviously could not last. Perhaps that's why my political attention centred so squarely on Southern Africa at the time . . .

My first two "serious" plays were on Southern Africa. One of them was a melodramatic piece which after going through about six versions of it, I realised that it was just "wrong" and I destroyed it in a sober moment.

The other was *The Invention* which marked my debut on the stage in London. Neither of course was very satisfactory to me later on. . . . and I understood why. The passion was there, it was "correct" and genuine and honest. . . . but I was experiencing the situation vicariously. I also threw myself frenetically into the collective production of *Eleven Men Dead at Holla* also at the Royal Court Theatre which was a sort of haven for a number of aspiring writers at the time. This was a dramatisation of the scandalous beating and stomping to death of eleven suspected "Mau–Mau" detainees in Kenya and I remember contributing quite extensively to the writing and even to the music. I acted in it also.

Well, there were other things I did in preparation towards the "day of liberation." Now the change when it came, it was an abrupt change, a total change. I took one look at our first set of legislators . . . you know partial self-government at the time . . . when they visited the U.K. and talked to students. I listened to them, watched them, and I knew . . . that instant, I think I received what the Japanese might term "political satori," you know, I just had illumination. I realised that the first enemy was within. If there was any shadow of doubt left hanging, it was soon removed by the pattern of thought which developed among my erstwhile "comrades" for whom all thought of liberation in Southern Africa, etc. suddenly disappeared. They could not wait to return home and get a slice of "independence cake," because that is all independence meant to them . . . step fast in the shoes of the departing whites before other people got there. It was then that I began to write *A Dance of the Forest,* writing first the lyrics, the verses there. And I suppose since then

I've been doing nothing but the "danse macabre" in this political jungle of ours.

Jeyifo: Some critics have commented on a supposed "generational divide" which translates into an ideological point of departure between Nigerian writers of your generation and the new wave of writers who came to the scene about a decade and half later. What do you say of this observation?

Soyinka: Now this "generational divide," a lot of it of course, in ideological terms, a lot if it, you will admit is, a lot of blather. One disappointment which I've had in the, what you might call the new wave of writers, the ideologically inspired writers, is for me, a self-cocooning amongst themselves, a kind of conspiracy of comradeship. I distinguish very sharply, as you might remember from some of my remarks and writings in the past, I distinguish between the very genuinely ideologically committed and those for whom it is just a convenient point of departure in literary style. In other words those in whom I do not see this ideological commitment percolate thoroughly, not only in their writing, but also their positions constantly *vis-à-vis* what happens within the country.

And when I talk of "self-cocooning" I discover habits of protecting even the obviously dishonest amongst themselves. In other words, I would like to see a greater clarity of commitment, of recognition, so that it does not seem when one is attacking that particular group that one is attacking all of them. But as long as even within its fold the so-called "second wave" ideological left insists on gathering all strange birds under its umbrella and keeps a conspiracy of silence about the obvious shallowness, hollowness and opportunism, that is really, the word, there will always be this seeming divide. But it's a very artificial divide. For me anyway this is the reality, it's mostly artificial.

Jeyifo: In between your many involvements as a writer, teacher, theatre director and publicist, do you manage to keep abreast of new writings from Nigeria and the Third World in general? Specifically, are you familiar with the works of writers like Omotoso, Osofisan, Emecheta, Iroh, Okri, Ofeimun, Sowande and others?

Soyinka: Yes, . . . well, it's yes and no. It's true that I never lengthen, I never increase shortlists of the books that I want to read. In fact they are usually by my bedside and in a fit of sudden desperation I usually attack six of them at a time, so I'm very, very familiar with the works of Omotoso, Osofisan, Iroh, Emecheta, Okri, Ofeimun, Sowande.

But in the Third World in general I have to confess, beyond the occasional, obvious names like García Márquez, one which is familiar to all of us, I have not been able to keep pace with the output, although a lot of the Third World poets, a number of them, I read from time to time in poetry magazines, I read their works. But I've not been familiar with their works during the last. . . . eight to ten years, as I used to be in my younger days.

Jeyifo: Has your conception of your audience changed from what you once described as minds out there in the world with whom you can communicate? At any rate, what views can you offer now as your thinking on this issue of who the audience of the writer is or ought to be?

Soyinka: No, my conception has not changed about this belief in the fact that I cannot write for myself, that it is impossible for me to write something that is entirely and solely for myself. But I think there is a lot of mystique over this business of who one reaches in one's writing and who one ought to reach. It's a mystique because whenever one has to speak to a specific issue, and to a specific situation and people, anytime, anybody who is as socially and politically committed as I think I am . . . one will always find the means for it. It won't always be a *tome* and I consider literature, all writing, all creative work, a joint social operation. There are various media of expression and one can employ any of these media at any time to address a public. In the early sixties, for instance, and in Ife in recent times when I've been able to gather groups together, we've been experimenting . . . indulging in what we call the guerilla theatre . . . the political and social sketches are very different in content, the tone and style from, for instance, a novel like *The Interpreters* and the purposes are different. *The Interpreters* was an attempt to capture a particular moment in the life of a generation which was trying to find its feet after independence.

By contrast, all those sketches, Orisun Theatre Sketches, the recent "Ethical Revolution" sketches and so on, are an attempt to reach a much larger audience and make certain statements which are pertinent and even critical to the ongoing economic and political situation within the country. It's a kind of sensitizing the political and social conscience and consciousness of the people. And at the same time the idea of even putting the songs on record also came into being to me because of the approaching elections, which I consider very critical to the remote possibility of a future for this country. Well, a desperate consciousness of the critical moment in which we are, gave me the idea, for the first time, of actually making a record out of some of the songs in our sketches of political satire, and even writing a totally new one for the other side of the record. So you see, this business of who one is addressing at any given time, I believe there is a lot of angst about it because, as I said, writing, creativity in general, is a social phenomenon, and therefore, somewhere, at any given time, what needs to be said has a way of coming to be said in whatever form . . . it's a combination of various pressures of learning to think slightly out of your normal routine and finding a new form of expression which says very desperately and urgently what needs to be said in that particular form.

Jeyifo: This conception of literature and art as social phenomena relates to your strong activist bent, your fame as a polemicist, a publicist or doesn't it? But art also has a personal dimension and literary art in particular has a privacy at certain levels of creating.

Can one separate the private and public domains in the life of an artist? Is there a satisfactory complementarity between these two domains, in your own experience, or is the relationship one of tension and conflict?

Soyinka: Well, separation of public and private domains . . . it's a very difficult question. I know that I guard very jealously certain areas of my privacy and these areas include, for instance, moments of certain forms of creativity. There's no way in which I can collaborate with any soul, any human being at all, when I'm undertaking certain forms of creativity. At the same time, my private life, I try to guard it as much as possible. It sounds incredible I know, and many people will not believe it, but I would rather I was not a public person. I find that being a public person, (having to be a publicist for certain causes), I find it very demanding. Somehow, inspite of the fact that I am politically and socially very active. . . . it's paradoxical, and I've been privately amused at this "contradiction" within me, I really would not be a public person, a publicist for a cause. And that is why when certain causes have been taken up, and taken up effectively, I do not feel the slightest need to open my mouth or take any action towards it, unless of course, it becomes apparent that additional effort, additional pressure is required and there is a kind of abdication in not participating in that form or event. I'll give you an example. I forget the particular event. It happened here about two years ago, in fact it was more than one event (I forget the particular details). These journalists came to me and said, look, every body is talking about this, you've been quiet lately, we haven't heard from you. Is the wild, radical, controversial Soyinka that we know, is he getting tamed, and so on.

So I asked them to name me the various events in which the wild Soyinka should have participated in. And they named one and I said "do you remember there was a movement from Ahmadu Bello University, there were articles in the papers, so just what more do you want? What is there left to be said?" They mentioned another event, and I said, "you think one should just put one's face in something for the sake of being there? Is there anything which needed to be said or done about these events which are not being said and done?" There was no answer to that of course, and for me, it happened to be a period when there was a lot of participation, very direct and immediate response on certain ongoing wrongs in society and I didn't feel the slightest need to join in. And of course another consideration is that sometimes one knows really what needs to be done, one knows that the most effective means are not available at that particular time. At such moments, I prefer just to be silent and either work quietly with others, and even hope that such means will arrive. But I will not pretend to be vocal if I do not feel that it is going to achieve any purpose. I'm just punishing myself because I lose my privacy during that period and achieve nothing.

Jeyifo: All this of course has to do with the issue of far-reaching changes in our society. What do you think of revolutionary theory and practice in Nigeria? Are we in a period of stabilised reaction? Is there a credible left alternative in the country today?

Soyinka: Revolutionary theory and practice in Nigeria and in the continent? Are we in a period of stabilized reaction in Nigeria? I don't think so. I think we are witnessing in Nigeria one of these marvellous moments when the various forces of history, our history in particular, and the contradictions in society are reaching such a level of both qualitative . . . what you might call the attainment of critical mass by matter. I think we are reaching that level in this society, and who knows (well, let me not be Godspower Oyewole predicting). . . . if there's any society in the African continent today which is reaching that state of critical mass when all our revolutionary theories will be tested and there will be no more ambiguity, I think Nigeria is that society. And for that reason, inspite of all the seeming hopelessness, the constant betrayal by so-called progressive forces, the self-exposure of opportunist leftists, I think that Nigeria may actually be one place where our various theories and our commitments too, will be tested. There is a credible left alternative emerging in Nigeria. I can see it, but I just wonder how effective they will be at the critical moment of crisis.

Jeyifo: It is generally thought that you are rather ambivalent about the left in the country, especially in relation to the leftist critique of your work. What really is the essence of your reaction to the leftist criticism of your writings?

Soyinka: Well, much of it, I find, is the result of a very vulgar concept of Marxist theory and I have written extensively about this. Some of it is due to a mis-understanding of the intent, the purposes of literature, i.e. total purposes of literature. You see, literature is supposed to serve, it's a product of intellectual labour, and any such product is directed towards more than one end. Literature does not have to serve, all the time, a particular ideological theory. It's a point I insist on and if that view seems to be reactionary, well the opposite view is also unnecessarily dogmatic and even authoritarian. I think a lot of it has to do with what I usually call the *surrogate power complex.* One wants to possess, to take control over the labour of the other person, without even considering for one moment what triggers off, what are the mechanisms within the writer which trigger off any work of literature. You see, the only reason it bothers me is that I think it destroys potential literary productivity in our society. It terrorises new, unfledged, insecure writers. People like me, I think, we are beyond that kind of terrorism, and the reason why I bother to reply it is that certain general rules are being made up, in other words these critiques move beyond being merely critiques of Wole Soyinka's works, rather, they become general rules and these rules are confusing a lot of writers and even inhibiting their productivity.

This is my only resentment. I also hate to see opportunist critics—I'll mention one name, for instance, like Gerald Moore, who is one of the most reactionary critics. His critical works are basically reactionary in tone, but of late he too seems to be trying to get on the bandwagon of leftist criticism and of course, his insincerity is apparent in the way, first of all, he interprets Marxist theory, the very almost simplistic terminologies which he uses. Just read the section on Senghor (in his book *Twelve African Writers*); he makes this pronouncement, but by the time he comes to analyse Senghor's works, it's a kind of reverential approach. So you see, that kind of opportunist criticism, I think, should just be ignored. However, the sum total of it—and this is where these critics must beware, watch their language more carefully—the sum total is that they are inhibiting potential works of literature and I think this is a great pity.

Jeyifo: You once expressed—in a private conversation—your admiration of Shakespeare, Beethoven and Picasso above all others in Western culture and art, for their **protean** range and mastery of diverse styles, forms and subjects. But Proteus, as a metaphor of the creative principle, comes from Western culture while you have also adopted Ogun as an essence of the creative artist.

Similarly, in your important essay, "The Fourth Stage," you conjoin classical Greek and traditional Yoruba deities and idealities as expressive paradigms of the psychic aspects of art in general and tragedy in particular. Such procedures have drawn a label of "Europhile" intellectualism from certain African critics. What is your reaction to this?

Soyinka: Well this "Europhile" criticism used to be the favourite terminology of people like Chinweizu, and there's so much nonsense in this accusation that I don't think it's even worth replying to. For a start, many of these people are not even critics, they're merely "throwback" activists, the kind of criticisms which they make about literature they will also make about the bearing of foreign names, as if this is what the radicalisation of society in thinking is all about. That pattern is not my conception of what the African heritage is. If I want to name my son after Fidel Castro nobody is going to stop me, if I want to name him after Lenin, after Garibaldi, for reasons of sentiment or optimism, whatever, nobody is going to stop me. . . . because I don't think that constitutes a betrayal of my African resources. So these throwbacks—I call them "Neo-Tarzanists"—who lack the intellectual capacity to even first of all appreciate the kind of exploration which I am making into points of departure as well as meeting points between African and European literary and artistic traditions and quite unabashedly exploiting these various complementarities, or singularities, or contradictions, in my own work. For me, they are missing out on a lot that can be enjoyed intellectually in the entire creativity of man. There's no way at all that I will ever preach the cutting off of any source of knowledge: Oriental, European, African, Polynesian, or whatever. There's no way anyone can ever legislate that once knowledge comes to one, that knowledge should be now buried as if it never existed. Oh, incidentally, curiously enough, I'm not a very great admirer of Picasso. I think of all his works that I've ever seen, I've only genuinely admired may be one out of four. I think most great artists—he's a very great artist, I recognise that—but somehow I find a lot of what I think . . . all great artists have their moments of "jokes," and self-indulgence. I've referred to one of his paintings in the UNESCO foyer as . . . I think that's one of his "jokes."

Jeyifo: Still on this issue of points of departure and convergence between Western and African traditions, there's the case of Christianity and its historic contact with African art and culture. Do you think Christianity can inspire significant artistic or literary expression? You have spoken very strongly on Christianity as an inimical force on the creative roots of our culture.

Soyinka: This relates to the former question. Of course Christianity can inspire, and has inspired significant artistic expression. You see, a work of art very often leaves its moorings its sources of inspiration and becomes an object in itself. Shall we put it that way? So whether it started out in Bhudism, or Islam, like the work of Boghossian, or Ibrahim el Salahi, whose works started out as an attempt to stay within the Islamic culture which sort of frowns on direct human representation, and so he began working with the caligraphic motifs, the caligraphic idiom and created the most incredible you know, beautiful works of art, Skuder Boghossian moved in a different direction and started exploring the symbols of productivity in general. So these were people who were conditioned, at least at the beginning, by a religious point of view and then either deviated or exploited the very constrictions within those religions.

And the same thing goes of course for Indian Tantrik art, medieval architecture, medieval "naive" painting, which are admired today. I derive great aesthetic pleasure out of my encounters with such works so I can never rule out any religion . . . To do that is to deny that in my own society our religions have not produced, have not inspired great works of art and we do know that they have . . . the artefacts, the objects themselves are all around us, magnificent carvings which have also inspired European artists like Picasso himself, Mondrian, the entire Cubist and Expressionist movements all owe much to the encounter of these artists with works which were inspired by our traditional religions.

So how can we have a kind of "valve system" of artistic contact? Of course it must open both ways. Yes, it is true that I have stated that the Christian faith has been inimical to, and even destructive of the creative roots of our cultures and sensibilities. But this is a historic fact. I've documented it in some of my essays. We know how the early missionaries—but you see they were philistines, they were barbarians—how they used to go out and literally create bonfires out of our works of art, how they banned traditional music and instruments in the churches, in their religions. How in fact we lost quite a sizeable heritage of dances because they were not only satisfied in converting our forefathers and so on . . . they actually warned them that their cultural activities, their habits of thought and so on, were works of the devil. The same thing with Islam; these two religions have, for me, been very, very destructive of a number of aspects of our traditional cultures. These are historical facts.

Jeyifo: To take the whole texture or "oeuvre" of your literary works, one is struck by certain all but irreconciliable antinomies: a constant evocation of a communal ethos, a communal spirit, side by side with an implacable affirmation of individualism; a strong celebration of *joi de vivre* almost amounting to literary hedonism, side by side with a deeply and profoundly tragic and pessimistic outlook. How do you react to the observation that these antinomic tensions are barely contained or integrated or resolved in your works?

Soyinka: Yes, the "antinomies" in my writings. But are these not a reflection of the human condition? Nobody can say that he's never been through moments of intense pain or pessimism, whether on a very private level, or even of viewing what I've termed a "recurrent cycle of stupidities," an expression which distresses those who want human existence to be so obviously and patently, without any qualification, optimistic. But what Nigerian today, what Nigerian this very moment that I'm talking about, looks at this country and does not experience absolute moments of gloom? Well, is one to pretend that such gloom does not exist? When Fidel Castro's comrades were destroyed during the very first attempt to invade Cuba, I try to get into the heart of a man like that, at the moment when he was the sole survivor of a band of revolutionaries who tried to over-throw Batista and the rest perished in the swamps or were shot down by Batista's goons, what did he experience? This is the moment of tragedy. But the human spirit constantly overrides the negative side of it, not always, but those who interest us are those who succeeded in overcoming the moment of despair, those who arose from the total fragmentation of the psyche, the annihilation of even their ego, and yet succeeded to piece them together, piece the rubble together to emerge and enrich us by that example.

But how can we ever be enriched by that example if we do not recognise the tragic prelude to the moment of triumph?

It's there, tragedy exists in human life and I do not believe that the function of the writer is to ignore the tragic aspect of the human experience, that tragic experience of truth. This is just to write propaganda, to write one-dimensional works, and to even ask ourselves what was all the victory about if it was so obvious anyway. And it's true that one can get seduced by the poetry of tragedy but why not? If tragedy enforces its own music, its own poetry, if this tragic grandeur can be expressed only in beautiful tone or masses of music, of sounds and the placement of words in a particular way which we call poetic, what is wrong with that? That is part of the property of the tragic experience, and that is part of the richness of literature.

When the moments of celebration come in, and you are quite right, I do experience my *joi de vivre,* but it is beyond mere sensual existence, no, the kind of *joi de vivre* which I'm referring to is the kind which is experienced at the moment of the acceptance of a challenge. That's why, for instance, I was able to write *Ogun Abibiman,* that's what I call a "revolutionary *joi de vivre.*" For me that moment when Samora Machel accepted the challenge of Southern Africa, and remember what I said at the beginning, that this sore, this festering toe of the continent of Africa, has always been my pet obsession, even though since my early days I've re-defined my immediate constituency—even so I never fail to experience the acceptance of a challenge in those areas which still constitute my larger political constituency. For me the acceptance of that challenge is not a tragic moment at all, even though I know it predicates loss. But suddenly there's a statement to the people of a continent, to myself personally, that somebody thousands of miles away has finally rejected further dialogue or compromise with an uncompromisable situation, so for me it's the same kind of *joi de vivre* that I experience in that moment as I experience when I drink a good, heady glass of wine, there's no difference.

So this antinomic tension is not something to be contained; in fact it's at the very heart of my creative existence, the acceptance of the tragic face of life, the tragic face of even the acceptance of responsibility, because the acceptance of responsibility of commitment is, unless one is an out-and-out unreflective optimist, even the acceptance of commitment cannot escape the historic experience in other areas by other people, and therefore the simultaneous awareness of the history of others gives it a tragic tinge.

The history of betrayals is constantly at the back of one's mind, the knowledge of the possibility of betrayals in the whole history of political movements in the world, yet the knowledge that one must go on, which you might describe as fatalism, but which I consider the very essence of life, of existence, of change, of progress within society. So is there a tension in my work? Yes, but the tension has sort of become the reality, the very material on which I work.

Jeyifo: On the psycho-affective level, how do you write? What sparks off or ignites the creative urge? Is this even an appropriate metaphor to use for the subjective aspects of the creative process?

Soyinka: How do I write? What sparks off or ignites the urge to write? I do not know. I refer to myself often as being basically lazy in the sense that I would rather not write. I suppose recollection sometimes, a sort of intense recollection of a former experience can trigger off the need to write. And of course there's the other kind of writing when writing is merely a medium for expressing what needs to be expressed, like an urgent political situation for instance. You address yourself to that instant and that one is plain enough, that's why journalists write, columnists write, that's why our troubadours sing. But in general, what ignites the creative spark, I honestly do not know.

Jeyifo: You have called for the adoption of one single language for the entirety of black Africa and have translated from Yoruba to English. Yet you continue to use English and are uncontestably entirely self-assured in that language. Are we now beyond the *Prospero-Caliban* syndrome of the complexes which attend the adoption of a language of colonial imposition?

Soyinka: Yes, I have called for the adoption of one single language for the whole Africa—*Kiswahili*—and I believe very much in it. I do not believe that I will ever write in *Kiswahili,* although I will write a few poems in it, a few careful verses, you know, I certainly will experiment in it. But I will set up the machinery, assist and participate in setting up a machinery for translating works, my works, into *Kiswahili* and that comes to the same thing. A lot of works come to us in translation, what's wrong in that? They lose something, but they also gain in other respects.

I have said I consider, and very seriously too, literature as a very social activity, even though very often it takes place in the privacy of one's creative space. But it is a social activity and so the continuity of it, the criticism is part of the continuity of a work of literature. So translation occupies its own place within the overall social activity.

English of course continues to be my medium of expression as it is the medium of expression for millions of people in Nigeria, Ghana Sierra Leone, Gambia, Kenya, who I want to talk to, if possible. And I want to talk also to our black brothers in the United States, in the West Indies. I want to talk also even to Europeans, if they are interested in listening. But they are at the very periphery of my concerns. I do know that I enjoy works of literature from the European world, I'd be a liar if I said I didn't. And I also enjoy literary

works from the Asian world, Chinese literature, Japanese literature. I teach
Japanese drama. I've taught Chinese poetry, when I was in the Literature
department. I always interjected the translations of poetry from the Asiatic
world because I wanted to open up that vast area. I enjoy the works of Tolstoy,
Turgenev, Gogol, etc. So I find no contradiction, no sense of guilt in the fact
that I write and communicate in English.

And I'll tell you something, when I receive letters from totally unknown
people, totally unknown, from the Soviet Union, from the United States, from
Cuba, from Asia, Japan, from the Arab world, who were only able to read
my works because it's in English well, totally different strangers—I've received a hundred letters from all corners of the world since *Aké* came out, for
instance, from people, from some school-children . . . to say that this does
not give me joy, some kind of very special pleasure, is to lie. I'm glad that
I'm reaching all these people. But that should not prevent us adopting some
means of reaching, first, our own people on this continent. I would like everybody on this continent to be able to read the works of Kole Omotoso, Odia
Ofeimun, Iroh, Sowande, Iyayi, as well as the works of our comrades in
Ghana, Kenya, and so on.

The *Prospero-Caliban* syndrome, I think, is dead. In fact those who are
suffering from the *Prospero-Caliban* syndrome are middle class, bourgeois
upstarts, the noveau-riche, and the medium of that syndrome for them is not
of course words, but jet planes, the most sophisticated stereo equipment, the
very latest in whatever happens to be the most expensive cars going on in the
world . . . the superficies of material indulgence without even the slightest
understanding of the mechanisms, the operations, the technology, of these
things which they consume. I think they are the ones within that syndrome at
the moment, not the artists.

An Evening with Wole Soyinka

Anthony Appiah / 1987

From *Black American Literature Forum,* vol. 22, no. 4 [Winter 1988], 777–85. Reprinted with permission of Anthony Appiah.

Appiah: Now that you've had three months or so to think about it, can you tell us what you think the significance is of the award of the Nobel Prize, first of all to you and then to you as an African?

Soyinka: To me, it's been hell. (Laughter.) On one level, yes, I understand what Bernard Shaw meant when he was given the Prize and he said he could forgive the man who invented dynamite, but it took the mind of a devil to invent the Nobel Prize for literature. I share some of this feeling, but only to a certain extent. The other side of the coin, of course, is that it increases one's literary family, increases one's awareness of the need of many activities, many paths, many concerns of the common Earth we inhabit. It increases an awareness of the need of people to fasten onto a voice, a representative, and that refers to your question about Africa in particular. So, it's of great importance, I think, not so much to me as to the literary craftsmen of my continent, to those who share my political concerns for the continent, to those who share the longing for a brotherhood/sisterhood which transcends the African continent and reaches out into the diaspora. The way in which the Prize has been received by people all over the world, particularly the African diaspora—in the West Indies, in the United States, and across the various language boundaries—has reinforced my insistent conviction that the African world is not limited by the African continent.

Appiah: I noticed that when you gave your Nobel lecture, you chose to discuss apartheid and southern Africa. Did you feel that that was a particularly important thing to do at that moment?

Soyinka: A lot of my writing has been concerned with injustice, with inhumanity, with racism, inside and outside of my immediate environment, which is Nigeria. This is a world platform, and I could not think of any more appropriate moment for voicing this particular level of my literary concerns. I thought it was most appropriate, yes.

Questioner: So, in that way, the Prize gives you the right to speak to the world and also to the West.

Soyinka: That's right.

Appiah: How does it enhance or change your position when you're speaking within Nigeria?

Soyinka: I've always insisted that I do not accept any kind of double standards. I do not accept a distinction, excuses on behalf of either our own black oppressors or the white oppressors of our race. In other words, the more one emphasizes the oppression which we receive from outside, the more we obtain the moral strength and the moral authority to criticize our own black oppressors. So this is equally important. Many African heads of state sent messages, personal telegrams, telexes, etc., and for me this means they have already accepted the imperative of the moralities which guide my work. So now it becomes a little bit more difficult for many of them to say, "Oh, you are criticizing us to the outside world!" when they understand that a kind of moral authority attaches to events of this kind and they have identified themselves with it. Otherwise, I'll tell them, "Take back your congratulatory telegrams." (Laughter.)

Appiah: I wonder if this wouldn't be a good moment to go back a bit in time and ask you to comment on *Aké,* your book about your early childhood. Could you say something about the process of writing about your early life?

Soyinka: You know, one recaptures certain aspects of some elements of smells and sounds, either by actually smelling and hearing them or by suddenly missing them, because something triggers off the memory. You suddenly realize that a certain slice of your life is disappearing, and you get a feeling that you want to set it down in one form or another. This period of my childhood belongs to that sudden realization of a lost period, a lost ambience, a lost environment. I don't like autobiographies, because they're mostly lies, but there's a period of innocence in which one can write down things quite frankly. Even *Aké* is not totally truthful. (Laughs.) You have to expunge some things. You are embarrassed by some things, so you leave them out. But this is obviously more truthful because of the lack of inhibition than many other things I write about my life. It's not lying—you don't tell untruths, you just do not tell all the truth. It's part and parcel of the protection of human dignity. I've always been repelled by the general Euro-American habit of telling all, revealing all the dirty secrets of human relationships, even without asking permission of those who share this personal relationship with you. (Laughter, applause.)

So the childhood is one period in which there is really nothing much to hide, and I'd always wanted to set it down. I spoke to my publisher, he gave me a small advance, and I spent it. It took three years after that before I could enter the frame of mind to recapture this particular life in the way I wanted to set it down.

Appiah: *Aké* was very successful in this country—it's a widely read book—, and that success makes plain how intelligible you have made the world of your childhood to those of us who in different ways didn't share it, because we lived either in other parts of Africa or in other parts of the world. There presumably are, however, problems in presenting your work, especially as a dramatist, because of the different traditions of interpretation of theater and performance in Nigeria, in West Africa, in Africa, and in the rest of the world. Could you reflect a little while on some of the ways in which these problems affect the production that you're now engaged in, *Death and the King's Horseman*?

Soyinka: It's interesting that you ask that question apropos of *Aké,* because in one of the sessions with the company, some of the cast expressed their difficulty in finding a sort of corresponding experience in their own lives with the content, theme, and characters in *Death and the King's Horseman*. I have to confess that I was very impatient about this kind of difficulty. But, remarkably, one of the actresses—and a white one at that—said to the others, "Well, why don't you read *Aké*?" At least one portion is, in fact, very significant in terms of the position of the women in *Death and the King's Horseman*.

But, as I said and admit freely, I have a very impatient attitude towards this. I grew up, as many of us did, on the fare of the European literature. Even in school we didn't have too much problem understanding the worlds of William Shakespeare, Bernard Shaw, Galsworthy, Moliere, and Ibsen, and, frankly, I'm irritated when people from outside my world say they find it difficult to enter my world. It's laziness, it's intellectual laziness . . . especially today when communication is a matter of course. There are economic relations between all the nations of the world. I see in Nigeria millionaires, multinational corporations, a constant exchange of films, video tapes, radio, music; Fela comes here with his music. I find no difficulty at all in entering into Chinese literature, Japanese literature, Russian literature, and this has always been so. I think the barrier is self-induced. "This is a world of the exotic, we can not enter it.'' The barrier is self-created. By now it has to be a two-way traffic. There can be no concessions at all; the effort simply has to be made.

But at the same time the work of a director principally involves responsibility towards the audience. He must always find idioms, whether in the field of music, poetry, or scenography, to interpret what might be abstruse elements. The director must bring out images in concrete terms which are merely in verbal terms within the book. When he moves a play from one area to another, the director seeks certain symbols, certain representational images in order to facilitate—because you're encapsulating a history of a people within a couple of hours. If you take *Coriolanus* to Africa, it's the responsibility of the director to try to transmit the metaphors within that particular language, the visual images, in terms which cannot be too remote. But then again I believe that the audience must not be overindulged, and once (as a director) I feel I have satisfied myself, that I've eased the transition, the rest is up to the audience. They can take it or leave it. (Applause.)

Appiah: I take it that part of the passion of your remarks is in response to some of the ways in which your work has been received in the United States and in Europe, perhaps more in the United States.

Soyinka: I have to say Europeans are a little bit—if one can make comparisons—more receptive. Americans are very insular. I suppose that's because you have so many cultures in America, and Americans don't feel they have to go outside what is already here. But there's a great deal of insularity in America, and that applies not merely to culture, but to politics. Americans don't even make an attempt to understand the politics of outside nations. They think they do, but they do not. And I mean this on all levels. I speak not merely of the taxi driver who asked me, "Yea, what's happening, man. You're from Neegeria. Is that in *Eeran*?" (Laughter.) I find the same attitude even among university lecturers. Not so long ago there was a professional, very intelligent, highly trained, and I happened to remark that one of my ways of relaxing is just to go into the bush and do some hunting. And he said, "Oh, what do you use for hunting?" What he was asking was, "Is it clubs? Or bows and arrows?" I mean we've been fighting wars with cannons and guns in Africa for I don't know how long. I said, "No, it's catapult." (Laughter.) So, it's the same thing with culture. Americans are far more insular.

Appiah: I'd like to talk a little more about *Death and the King's Horseman*. Is this a political play, or would you rather read it as relatively apolitical, by contrast, for example, to *A Play of Giants*?

Soyinka: Of course there's politics in *Death and the King's Horseman*.

There's the politics of colonization, but for me it's very peripheral. The action, the tragedy of *Death and the King's Horseman* could have been triggered off by circumstances which have nothing to do with the colonial factor—that's very important to emphasize. So it's political in a very peripheral sense. The colonial factor, as I insist, is merely a catalytic event. But the tragedy of a man who fails to fulfill an undertaking is a universal tragedy. I regard it as being far, far, far less political than *A Play of Giants,* yes.

Appiah: You've said that *Horseman* is fundamentally a metaphysical play. That might invite the speculation that it is a difficult play, since *metaphysical* is a word—I know this as a philosopher—which invites difficulties. Is there something you want to say, in advance of people's seeing it, about the metaphysical issues, the issues of death and transition, which the play addresses?

Soyinka: All his life, the principal character, the Elesin Oba—the Horseman of the King—, has enjoyed certain unique privileges for a certain function. At the critical moment he fails to fulfill that function, so he's doomed. That's straightforward. But then, one asks, how is it that, in the first place, such a function was the norm for a community of people? We can ask that from this distance. And that's not so long ago. In fact, societies like this still exist.

I've given my company current examples from India, for instance, of human sacrifice and so on to the goddess Kali, which were in the newspapers quite recently. So one must begin by understanding what is the spiritual context of a people for whom this is not an aberration, not an abnormality, and one finds it in the world view, the metaphysical beliefs of the Yoruba people.

We believe that there are various areas of existence, all of which interact, interlock in a pattern of continuity: the world of the ancestor, the world of the living, and the world of the unborn. The process of transition among these various worlds is a continuing one and one which is totally ameliorated. For instance, the function of ritual, of sacrifice—whether it's a ram or a chicken—, the function of seasonal ceremonies, is in fact allied to the ease of transition among these various worlds.

So, in effect, death does not mean for such a society what it means for other societies. And it's only if one establishes this kind of context, through whatever symbolic means, that one can begin—distanced as you and I are from this particular kind of society, even if we are part of the world. It's only by exposing this world as a hermetic, self-regulating universe of its own that a tragedy of a character like Elesin can have absolutely validity. So within that context, this is what enables him. For him it's not death.

At the same time, even journeying from New York to Boston is an activity of loss. You leave something behind. It involves a pain. How much you want to live in this world which you know very well, which is concrete, which one can only relate to in symbolic terms. And so for Elesin the difficulty does exist as a human being within this world. But he's been brought up to believe, and his whole community believes, in the existence of these various worlds which are secure and even concrete in their own terms. And his failure to make that transfer from one to the other, *that* really is the tragedy of Elesin.

Appiah: You spoke just now of *Horseman* as a tragedy, which of course it is. I think the concept of tragedy tends to get used in our culture very much and in a debased form and with very little sense of classical tragedy. You chose, very deliberately I think, to frame *Horseman* as a classical tragedy. Is that not a difficulty, turning once again to the problems of production? Is it not difficult to produce a tragedy for a contemporary American audience? Not because it's alien or exotic or African, but because the concept of tragedy required to enter this world is a distant one to many people?

Soyinka: Yes. But that's only if one begins by accepting the European definition of tragedy. I remember my shock as a student of literature and drama when I read that drama originated in Greece. What is this? I couldn't quite deal with it. What are they talking about? I never heard my grandfather talk about Greeks invading Yorubaland. I couldn't understand. I've lived from childhood with drama. I read at the time that tragedy evolved as a result of the rites of Dionysus. Now we all went through this damn thing, so I think the presence of eradication had better begin. I doesn't matter what form it takes. (Applause.)

Appiah: Nevertheless, whatever their origins, tragedy does have a specific, formal . . .

Soyinka: But I've never made a claim that I'm presenting tragedy in European terms. *Tragedy*—quite apart from the misuse of the word which we know about—whether we translate it in Yoruba or Twi or Ewe, I think we'll find a correlative somewhere in which we're all talking about the same thing. Just as the equivalent of the word *tragedy* in Yoruba can be debased in Africa, so it can be debased in Europe. But ultimately there is a certain passage of the human being, a certain development or undevelopment of the human character, a certain result in the processes of certain events which affects the human being which has that common definition of tragedy in no matter what culture. And it is to that kind of linguistic bag, that symbolic bag, which audiences in theater must attune themselves, whether it is Japanese tragedy or Chinese tragedy.

There may be difficulties, but I think they're very superficial. As I explained to some of my company, "You say you have difficulty looking for some parallel experience in America. But what do you call what happened to Richard Nixon? If ever there was a tragic character, that is it. Being from here." (Laughter.) Just begin from there. We all have these experiences; it's universal. It's only in the details we differ. What happens to a man psychologically in terms of his valuation within the community in which he resides, the fall from—to use a cliché—grace to grass, that's the element of tragedy.

Appiah: I think we'll turn over discussion to the audience.

First questioner asks about the Ali Mazuri program.

Soyinka: Americans cannot tolerate anyone's saying one good thing about anyone they've already condemned as satan. That's their problem. (Applause.) It's very very different. But I think we Africans must do a very objective critique of Ali Mazuri's *The Africans.* The two programs which I saw were a travesty of the African reality. And I'll be dealing with that when I've had time to sit down and look at all the programs.

I object very strongly to any notion which suggests that Africa is either traditionally Christian or Islamic. (Applause.) Africa was conquered by civilizations which claimed as their authority both Christianity and Islam, and our authentic being, authentic culture was submerged and really subverted by these two religions. I object to any program which claims to speak for Africa, which suggests in any form at all that Africa is basically, naturally Islamic. This is a lie. (Applause.) A historic lie. And this is what I have to deal with with Ali Mazuri's program. Uncle Sam's problem, that's their own. (Laughter.)

But I agree about the necessity for Africans to begin to speak in their own right in their own name. We have had centuries of anthropologists who have claimed to know Africa more than we do, the experts. Of course, some of them have been really marvelous scholars and have been very humble. You see, when you go into any culture, I don't care what culture it is, you have to go with some humility. You have to understand the language, and by that I do not mean what we speak; you've got to understand the *language,* the interior language of the people. You've got to be able to study their philosophy, to enter their philosophy, their world view. You've got to speak both the spoken language and the metalanguage of the people.

Many of these people who go to Africa do not even have this—I've repeated this in many essays, so I don't want to keep repeating myself, but you're absolutely right. It's not out of a necessity of wanting to express oneself to other people—who cares about that?—it's just that lies must be constantly corrected and pools of ignorance must be filled if there's going to be any communication between cultures.

Questioner: Whose responsibility is that?

Soyinka: These external cultures like to go only halfway. Ali Mazuri has himself declared that he is not really a black African but is part Arab. He's said it quite often.

Questioner: But that doesn't matter . . .

Soyinka: No, no, it matters. (Questioner tries to interrupt.) Sorry, sorry, sorry, excuse me. When I speak, I speak for that part of Africa which is black. Black Africa. (Applause.) I do not accept anybody who says they are half-European or half-Arab to speak for me. You see, there's alienation. There's internal alienation, there's external alienation. One can call himself an African and yet be alienated from the true resources of his own society.

There are people who are comfortable with a halfway house towards Africa, and I happen to believe that intellectuals, scholars like Ali Mazuri, represent this halfway house. That's all.

Remember, I want to insist I have not seen all the programs, but the two which I saw made me mad. I've ordered the remainder because I want to sit down and view them and give my response. I just want to be clear. I do not want to leave you in any doubt about my feeling of the direction of what I saw.

I agree with you that the efforts must be made. They must be made by African governments; they must be made by writers, by cineasts. A lot of work, a lot of African writers really dig into the resources of our society, of our world and are doing a lot in that respect, even if they're iconoclastic. Even if they're criticizing what is contemporary and only obliquely pointing to the authentic and really valuable positive forces in our society. There are very many ways of going about it. I just do not believe that what I saw in that series is really what we should be heading towards.

Appiah: I'll take a question over here.

Questioner: Is Elesin a traitor? Does he have any redeeming qualities?

Soyinka: I do not believe that Elesin is a traitor. He's a weak man. All cultures, all societies have their weak people. They are people who undertake more than they're really capable of delivering, who divide themselves along the way to a goal and find themselves thereby weakening towards the fulfillment of an undertaking. Not only do I think that Elesin is a product of that environment, but I also happen to think he's a universal figure. We can point out examples in the literatures of the world in which we find various Elesins. I don't consider him a traitor as such; he's a failed man. He's a man who failed. That's all.

Appiah: It's always fun talking to you, Wole. And I'm glad to have done it here. (Laughter.) It's the least relaxing conversation we've ever had, for me, but I hope that some of you have enjoyed it, and I hope that you'll all come to see *Death of the King's Horseman.*

Wole Soyinka in Stockholm

Nii K. Bentsi-Enchill / 1987

From *Literary Half-Yearly*, 28.2 (July 1987), 1–6. Reprinted with permission.

Bentsi-Enchill: How best do you think African/black peoples may build on the fact of your winning the Nobel Prize?

Soyinka: I will simply refer to my experience on returning to Nigeria, my time in Nigeria, the announcement of the prize, and my coming here. [With regard to] the reaction of the whole population, especially the literary section, you can see that by the way they have reacted, both as colleagues in the same profession, younger mostly, and as citizens, as black peoples, they felt it as a stimulating event, an inspiring event.

Seeing what they organised: for instance, evenings of poetry readings, performances, formations of special committees to celebrate the event, artistically of course, readings taking place of their own, creating special sketches in honour of the occasion; well, if you begin just from that concrete manifestation, you can see how it has been accepted by people of our literary profession.

So there is no question at all in my minds that this is a boost, a jolt in the arm of not just literature generally, but specifically dramatic literature and poetry, because these are the fields in which I really consider myself most at home. The response of the literary community in Nigeria and outside Nigeria is difficult; you know you can't just say you will go by the number of telegrams or letters; that's nonsense. We're talking about the way literary people have responded. Very clearly, for them it has generated a momentum.

And not just that. Let's think about the suppressed writers in Southern Africa. I have no apology to make for constantly returning to it over and over again, because that is one of my "frustrating constituencies," frustrating in the sense that we all know what has to be done, but that there is little we really can do, immediately, about it. Having received invitations from people like the Medupe Writers' Association, having had theatre companies named after me in Southern Africa, having received invitations to visit them, lecture, hold workshops and so on, which I wasn't able to do because the South African government wouldn't give me a visa to visit these communities, and from meeting actors from *Woza Albert, Sizwe Bansi Is Dead* and so on, this is *specifically* for the downtrodden writers, the dehumanised writers in Southern Africa.

So when I weigh the admittedly negative considerations attaching to prizes like this with the positive, I come down very heavily on the side of the positive.

B-E: Has anything happened while you have been here to make you feel some of the negative aspects? Have you felt overly on exhibition as a unique specimen of the black man?

S: No. One thing that has been wonderful about it—and I would have reacted immediately if I had seen this particular one—is that for most of the people I have encountered, their source of pride is in that they discovered African literature and Wole Soyinka long before the Nobel committee did. Don't forget that quite a number of my works have been translated in Sweden. There is the case of a student who spent four years on her thesis, and the first three years were spent entirely on her own, and her professor said: "Who is this Wole Soyinka? Never heard of him . . . don't be ridiculous; go and find something else." After three years when she began the work, he began to read this thesis, became curious, and became really interested. When her citation for the thesis was announced, this supervisor said: "It's all her own work. I only came in the last few months. And she taught me the value of this literature." I mean, this was a fairly public statement. So, obviously, with that kind of situation you cannot talk about tokenism, a unique, accidental freak. He has now gone heavily into African literature, and he is receiving quite a lot of illumination about human society, and about African society from the works of other people apart from Wole Soyinka. This experience is repeated in many, many areas of the world. There are letters, including one from the United States from someone who taught his professor about African literature and Wole Soyinka.

I have not encountered this [negative aspect]. In fact, I have had what I call expressions based on intellectual, and intelligent curiosity by a number of Swedes.

B-E: Do some "federal character" politics govern the selection of Nobel prizewinners?

S: I don't believe this for a moment. But I do know that all juries are human beings, and when all things are equal, factors can come into it. But the expression is: *when all things are equal.* So it wouldn't bother me in the

slightest if we discovered that in reality, the Nobel Prize, the Academy of
Letters here which is responsible, decides that . . . "wait a minute, it's about
time; why is it that we have never . . ." It wouldn't surprise me in the slightest
if all things being equal they said: "Let's weigh our judgement on behalf of
this neglected area."

But I'm a member of the Royal Academy of Arts and Letters, Great Brit-
ain; I'm a member of the Academy of Letters of the German Democratic
Republic; I'm a member of the American Academy of Letters; I have received
prizes, citations, reviews, I have been invited to adapt plays for the National
Theatre of Great Britain, and so on and so forth, so . . . I don't have any false
modesty about me. No. None whatever. I mean, I've won the AGIP Enrico
Mattei Prize for humanities, the first ever, awarded this year long before
Nobel, and the AGIP people are beating their chests that they discovered
Wole Soyinka long before Nobel.

So that aspect of it, that *maybe* an additional thing came into it, I'm not
interested in the slightest. One would be stupid, I think, to think that as human
beings we are not sometimes affected by factors slightly outside. But an
Academy of Letters has its reputation to protect. They must be able to defend
their decision in strictly literary and artistic terms. Otherwise they would not
be worth their salt. They have their self-interest to protect. So I don't have
any false modesty if I've been selected to win the Nobel Prize. I have never
aspired to any prizes. When people offer me prizes, I do not turn them down.
I believe it is good for the profession. It is a recognition that is a demarginali-
sation of the arts among the entire productive corpus of society. So, it's
possible. I'm not going to hold brief for the Academy. But I insist that anybody who thinks that people just go and dig in the dustbin and take out
something from a certain region because they have never considered that
region before, I think such people must be mad.

B-E: But there is a theme in your lecture though, which one might use . . .

S: Aaah, good. And I've noticed that a few people have tried to use it. But
what I said, I still insist on. I accept this prize, I can reconcile myself to this
prize *only* because I have taken the attitude that it is recognition of a neglected area of the world, that it is we from that part of the world who most
deserve the prize. In fact it seemed the very opposite to me. But I accept on
behalf of all those who should have even received it before me or who even
deserve it even at this moment.

B-E: What names come to mind?

S: I don't want to start a fight, but let me tell you those, for instance, whose works I admire tremendously, such that if I were on a jury I would definitely put on the list of prizes on this level: one, obviously, is Derek Walcott, the poet and dramatist of the West Indies. The others who, qualitatively, I would also mention, but who quantitatively would face a problem . . . definitely people like Senghor. In fact, I have supported the candidature of Aimé Césaire for instance, of Senghor, for this prize, among certain other writers. So, when I say I accept it on behalf of all those others, this is what I'm really talking about.

B-E: V. S. Naipaul has said of black (American) literature that once it has made its profitable protest, it has nothing left to say. Your observations?

S: As for Naipaul, who I know the British literary establishment would prefer to win prizes of this nature because they consider him an Englishman, and he also considers himself an Englishman—I have no hesitation at all in saying that because he has said a number of things really discreditable in terms of the black race, and black self-regard and self-esteem, so I've no apologies to make for singling out V. S. Naipaul. He is an unfortunate creation of the British literary establishment. When he talks about protest literature . . . I have ceased to take seriously anything V. S. Naipaul has to say whether about black culture, about African culture, African society, the serious problems which assail the retrieval of society, whether it's in terms of liberation, in terms of "protest literature," in terms of even the integration of an authentic African culture in a universal concept of human society, all subjects along that line. I think it is more serious to ignore V. S. Naipaul and not spend energy on him. I try to leave V. S. Naipaul to his Caribbean colleagues to deal with.

B-E: What is your view of the debate over the language in which African literature is written?

S: I advocated and still advocate the use of Kiswahili as a common language for Black Africa. Because for me Black Africa is a nation, is a tribe, is a community. In spite of all the various cultures that exist there, Black Africa is an often neglected entity which exists in its own right, and constitutes a nation.

I don't believe in going back and elevating a local language. The function that a language serves at the moment, whether in Ghana, in Nigeria, our indigenous languages, those functions are perfectly legitimate. The promotion of literature in those languages is absolutely important. There is no question, no dispute at all about that. But in addition, I believe the *solution* to this language question is to have a common language, like Kiswahili for Africa.

When someone like Ngugi wa Thiong'o says he's going back to writing in his own local language (Gikuyu), I believe he is really depriving me of something. That's his right. But I don't see anything revolutionary about it. What I consider revolutionary is that idea which African teachers, artists, writers, have come to from time to time, whether merely as a concept, or even in terms of promotional activities, that "we must have a language of communication to translate the literature written in colonial languages, the literature written in indigenous languages, into that language which serves the entirety of the black continent." To go back and say you will write only in your local language is, for me, very defeatist. I consider that as a dramatic gesture.

B-E: I thought it was meant to be allied with the promotion of translation into other African languages?

S: Well . . . if it is allied, beautiful. But then look at it this way: where is that language? It now has to be translated into a hundred other languages; among those, its literature in that language has to be translated into a hundred other languages. I believe it is better to have all those languages centering on one common language; it's more economic, it's more political; it gives that sense of duty which we so desperately want; it reminds us of a belonging, that applies to the Caribbean . . . I mean, what language do you want our black brothers in the Caribbean and America to study? How many languages? If they had one single one, they would form even a literary/economic unit, which simplifies and certainly aids the dissemination of our thoughts, of our culture, our projection into the future, of our ideologies, our economic programme, scientific, technology programmes; all this is not utopian, this is a realistic approach to this unfortunate problem of language transplantation which is inherited as a result of European colonisation.

I will not go back to writing in Yoruba. No way. Because within the boundaries of Nigeria, we have at least 200 different languages. Why should I speak only to the Yoruba alone? I will not accept that. I will be willing and ready to use a language that not only reaches all those people within the continent, but actually expands outside the continent. For me, [Ngugi's] is a gesture which is grand, which is magnificent, but which for me does not relate to realities of the African continent.

Wole Soyinka

Jane Wilkinson / 1990

From *Talking with African Writers.* Jane Wilkinson, ed. London: James Curry, 1992. 91–110. Reprinted with permission.

The first of the three interviews included in this volume took place in L'Aquila (Italy), 7 June 1985, during a conference on African theatre; the second in London, 16 July 1986; and the third in Rome, 24 May 1990, after two "Meetings with Wole Soyinka" at the Italo-African Institute, where the author talked on "The World of Wole Soyinka" and "Beyond the Berlin Wall." Extracts from the first and second interviews were published in Italian in *L'Unità*, LXIII, 259 (2 November 1986), p. 13, and *Rinascita,* XLIII, 41 (25 October 1986), p. 24, and from the third in *Rinascita (nuova serie),* I, 19 (17 May 1990), pp. 72–74.

L'Aquila, 7 June 1985

What would you say are the major problems facing the Nigerian writer today?

I don't know that there are any major problems facing the established writers—I don't think so; I don't imagine that writers like Chinua Achebe, Wole Soyinka, the younger writers like Femi Osofisan, Iyayi, Osundare have any major problems. The only problem which we all face is one which besets not only writers but citizens in Nigeria: the problems of our unbelievable and unacceptable socio-political situation, which gets more and more reactionary and inhuman with every succeeding regime. So that's a general problem. For the younger writers I think the main problem is what I call an ideological confusion. During the last decade, I think there has been far more criticism than creative work and this I have attributed to the stridency of what I call the ideologues *vis-à-vis* the kind of literature Nigerians should be producing. I take the attitude that it is better to have lots and lots of literature and creative material for people to work on according to the various ideological and critical schools than to have none at all. I have in fact accused these critics of inhibiting younger writers by confusing them about certain priorities that are not even very clearly defined. There's a very crude, vulgar school of Marxist

143

criticism, or so-called Marxist criticism. Placed side by side with criticism, Marxist criticism, even from the Eastern European countries like Hungary for instance, Poland, even contemporary criticism from the Soviet Union, this kind of so-called Marxist criticism—not just Nigerian—also of socialist thinking countries, its level of crudity is a form of authoritarianism, back-to-Zhdanov-Stalinist school. The damage it is doing to very talented writers is incalculable: they're inhibited, they're threatened, they're bullied—some of these critics are their teachers who have a captive audience among these students, some of whom are very talented. And the problem is that some of these new writers cannot give free range to their creative bent without constantly having hovering over their head accusations of being reactionary, subjective—all the usual terminology which in the end means absolutely nothing. This for me represents the greatest problem that the Nigerian writer has, though naturally people like me are totally impervious to this crudeness and in fact we respond only because we are also teachers and we feel that certain wrong things are being taught. Otherwise I don't see any particular problems.

You didn't think the crisis in publishing in Nigeria is creating difficulties for the young writers?

Yes and no. I don't really consider that a major problem. It is true that Western publishers have shown less interest in African literature since that first flush of curiosity for what was coming out of the newly independent countries. Now they've become far more circumspect, more critical, more choosy. Frankly, a lot of literature got published that should never have seen the light of day and most of those writers have fallen by the wayside, because there was never really much talent there. As we say in Nigeria, "water has been finding its own level." The other point I wanted to make is that there has been a growth in indigenous publishing: Ethiope Publishers, which is constantly looking for scripts; Fourth Dimension, which has a *number* of writers, especially from the Eastern Region post-war school: literature, criticism, poetry, essays; Onibonoje Publishers; Fagbamigbe Publishers; so there has been a lot of very healthy growth which is very good for Nigerian literature. In fact I began reserving all Nigerian rights for my works from about ten years ago: Ethiope is publishing a couple of my plays, for instance. So there has been compensation for that loss of foreign outlet. In fact the situation seems very promising.

How do you see the present political situation in Nigeria?

Very sad. Very distracting. In a statement I made last year I referred to my generation as the wasted generation and I was thinking in terms of all fields, not just the literary: the technological talents that we have which are not being used; but I also had in mind our writers of course, the fact that a lot of our energy has really been devoted to coping with the oppressive political situation in which we find ourselves. A lot of our energies go into fighting unacceptable situations as they arise while at the same time trying to pursue a long-term approach to politics such as, for instance, joining progressive-looking political parties, but of course each step is always one step forwards and about ten backwards. I find the political situation very, very frustrating, personally frustrating. I mean, forget even the amount of let us say personal work one could have done, writing and so on, and just think in terms of the amount of time one could have spent on training, in theatre for instance, would-be actors, or devoting more time to would-be writers, many of whom are constantly inundating one with cries for help; the qualitatively different kind of creative community atmosphere, structures that one would really love to give more time to—look at what we started in the early '60s, the Mbari club with its movement, its discovery of new writers, workshops. I know, very definitely, that I feel a great sense of deprivation in terms of what I could have contributed to the general productive atmosphere of the country in literary terms and I'm sure a lot of other writers feel the same. That is one of the penalties of the political situation we've been undergoing since independence and which has got *progressively* worse, progressively more lethal. The penalties for the wrong kind of political action in this situation have become far more depressing.

You were talking yesterday evening about problems of censorship. Would you like to go back to that question?

Censorship is a very real thing. First of all, the decrees that have been passed amount to a total penal control over all activities. There is first of all Decree No. 4 which was aimed primarily at journalists, at the media. Two of the journalists, Tunde Thompson and Nduka Irabor, were jailed in very disgusting circumstances: the imprisonment, the judgement, everything about it was criminal. They were jailed in effect for publishing the truth. The decree says it is not a question of whether what you print is factual or not, if it can be proven that it's brought the Government into ridicule or created disaffection—not just the Government but any official, any servant, any employee of the Government—that decree gets you. Now this has affected a number of things one can say to people, because the media have to practise self-censorship. But, as if that were not enough, the Chief of Staff, a few weeks ago, bothered perhaps by the fact that universities and university writers and intellectuals carry on business as usual at least within their own walls, made new threats. Universities are saturated, literally *saturated,* with the NSO, the National Security Organization, so maybe they had reports on seminars, lectures and symposia on the state of the nation, on current affairs. Not so long ago there was a production, a convocation production, which was an adaptation by Biodun Jeyifo of Brecht's *Puntila and His Man Matti*, and the opportunity was seized to call attention to a number of those who had been detained without any trial, for a year without any trial whatsoever. You should have seen the kerfuffle! There were letters from the Chief of Police, the University Vice Chancellor had to call a meeting and I went to represent the department and told them in no uncertain terms that this is part and parcel of Brechtian theatre and Brecht is not just talking about Puntila, he is talking about actual social contradictions, social injustice; that we're a teaching department and that it's our responsibility to adapt and to relate whatever we're teaching to the actualities of the moment, especially if it's a playwright like Brecht, and therefore we're not going to apologize to anybody and we can tell the Chief of Police what to do with his protest. So they had to contend with all of that plus the symposia, student movements and so on, the statements—because the papers carry a lot of the statements we make, as much as possible, in fact they seize the chance. We also ran a workshop for which I used Femi Osofisan's text *Who's Afraid of Solarin*, which in itself is an adaptation of Gogol's *The Government Inspector*. I chose that deliberately because Tai Solarin, an educationist, a forcible spokesman, a real fighter against the oppression of the masses, deprivation and exploitation and so on, has been detained for a year and a half. So I imagine there were regular reports of all these activities and that's what led Idiagbon to give a press conference in which he said that people should remember that Decree No. 4 does not affect merely what is published in the newspapers but all subversive lectures and symposia in the universities, which have become the hotbed of sedition and subversion, and that they're going to deal with the universities under this decree. Sure enough, they have moved to stop public symposia in Ibadan. In other instances the university authorities have forced student bodies to cancel lectures and symposia . . . So it's a really fascist situation: all the gloves are off and these people are letting us know just what they are, as if we needed to be instructed, but the struggle continues.

Tell me about your teaching of theatre at Ife. What sort of plays do you put on and teach?

Well, the emphasis is very often on African theatre. Naturally we teach comparative drama, theatre of the world. Three years ago I taught *commedia dell'arte,* which in fact became very cogent for the final year students, as the theme of their long essay. Two years ago it was Russian contemporary drama; three years before that it was Irish theatre; this year it's Nigerian theatre. So we teach all forms of drama: Japanese Noh drama at one time. We make sure that it's a very catholic range. I don't believe in teaching just African theatre exclusively, that's daft, it just limits the horizons of our students.

Do you believe in national or racial categorizing of literature? Do you think African books should be published in a series on their own or alongside writings from other countries in miscellaneous collections?

I look at series like Heinemann's as a kind of time-specific event. The European world, the Western World, suddenly had a hunger for literature coming from this part of the world. The series, of course, was very uneven; quite a large portion of it was total dross, but a fair amount, quite a good amount, was excellent literature. So it fulfilled its purpose. It all depends on the content. If for instance the Heinemann African Series had been more discriminatory, I don't think I'd even have thought twice about the whole question of publishing literature from a continent, a race, in a series of its own. The reason why I have considered it at all is because it occurred to me that the series was adopting a policy of anything goes because it's African and therefore it must be published. If that series had been run by African intellectuals I would suggest that at least one-third of what was published would never have been published and then this question would not have bothered me in the slightest. So it depends entirely; I think it's a very relative question and it doesn't even occur to one if one can dig up any book in a series and find that at the very least it's average, at the very least it matches what is published in any other society and you've not got the feeling that this only got there because there's a large series which can accommodate everything. That's about the clearest explanation I can give of my attitude. But obviously good literature, for me, is very, very important, no matter where it comes from.

You have urged very strongly for the adoption of Kiswahili as a Pan-African language. Would you explain this?

Well, for me—I think this is true of most African writers, most Anglophone writers, not so much the Francophone ones, they went through this assimilation programme, which we never did—for writers like me, there has always been a resentment, an underlying resentment, that I have to express myself and create in another language, especially a language that belongs to the conquerors. I think that is true of anybody: I know the English for a long time resented Latin and French, so it is a very normal phenomenon. Now it is as a result of my recognition of this resentment, that's one. Two, the problem all Nigerians in particular and I think most nationalities in Africa have had to confront: the question, the political question, what should be our national attitude to language, what is going to be the official language? Now, I know that in Nigeria if an attempt is made to impose any of the major languages there will be another Civil War; that is clear. I don't want another Civil War. It's my duty as a writer whose tool is language to think in terms of strategies for creating a national feeling, a national sense of belonging, while making sure that it's not yet another form of cultural colonization.

Then, I had always looked with envy at the kind of homogeneity of Arab culture—*comparative* homogenity, because Arab cultures are also very diverse—and I know that this has been due to two factors: religion, which also has affected the language—and vice versa—for Arabic is considered *the* language of the Koran, and of course the language itself, the Arabic language, this has given to the Arabs a kind of cultural identity which survives no matter how much they are currently bombing one another in Beirut, or how Gaddafi is against—on political grounds—the feudal structures. And I also have always considered the black people as a nation—this includes the black peoples in the Diaspora—I've always had a sense of total solidarity, this sense of belonging. Additonally, I resented the fact that communication with the rest of the Blacks on the continent would have to go through the colonial sieve. We learnt first of all the literature of Europe before we even began to discover the literature of the continent and this communication problem has been due mostly to language. So it is through this that I evolved—through all these various points—quite logically to a position where I think that the black peoples should have a language of their own, quite apart from the fact that I never want to hear anybody say "Why don't you adopt Arabic?"—I don't accept Arabic as a black African language! The Arabs happen to have inhabited a portion of the continent of Africa, but the black people exist, their culture is very specific, all their cultures are very specific, in very concrete terms, *vis-à-vis* let us say Arabic cultures. It seems to me a good idea that, since at various times in our post-colonial or even pre-colonial era we have thought in terms of an African High Command, a Union of African Countries, in addition to the fact that we have a certain contestation in Southern Africa which is very pertinent to us, specifically the black peoples over and beyond anybody else, no matter what messages of solidarity, what ideological affinities we feel for any other parts of the world, the primary struggle in South Africa is the struggle of the black peoples. In other words, culturally, politically, socially, there are *enormous* reasons why the black peoples should have a common form of communication.

I studied the various languages, analytically, that is, I don't speak Kiswahili but I know of the hsitory of Kiswahili, I know a lot of the structure, I know that it's a language very much in formation, I know that it does not belong to any nation as such right now: Eastern African nations have adopted it also, and so why don't we expand from Eastern Africa? It solves the problem of national language in countires like Nigeria where it's a very volatile subject. It's also an act of political will, if we cannot have a union of the African nations, we could at least have a language.

When you say "We could at least have a language," presumably you mean as a means of communicating—a Yoruba would still speak Yoruba?

Absolutely. Nothing touches the indigenous languages. And anybody who likes can continue studying their French, English, Portuguese or Spanish.

So instead of a Shona speaker communicating with a Yoruba speaker through English, he—

He will use Kiswahili. It's a policy that's really so simple, so simple. Think of the useless number of subjects I've learnt at school: I studied Latin at one stage, Greek at another time. If instead of that I had studied Kiswahili, I'd be talking across the continent. I've never understood why, rationally, anybody should oppose it.

Do you see yourself as a Yoruba writer? Abiola Irele speaks of a line of development in Yoruba literature passing from Fagunwa via Tutuola to Soyinka, do you agree with this?

Well, it's obvious that I'm not an Igbo writer! The "Nigerian" writer is a creature in formation. Obviously we're bound to end up as a hybridization. Well I'm not a Hausa writer. There is the Hausa culture, the Tiv culture—we have several cultures in Nigeria—so that makes me primarily a Yoruba writer. There's no question at all about it to my mind, I'm primarily a Yoruba writer, just as you have Occitan writers in France, Welsh writers, Scottish literature, within the same political entity. There is Gaelic literature, literature in Welsh, even when it is written in English, like the works of Powys, for instance.

When did your interest in theatre first arise? What kind of theatre?
I've been interested in theatre since I was a child. I can't come up with any dates. I participated in school plays and graduated from there to writing sketches, when I was in school and then at university.

We know about Wole Soyinka up to about the age of twelve—are we going to know about the next period of his life?
No, I think the veil of discretion must be drawn over the period after the age of innocence!

In *The Man Died* you swiftly repress the memories of a happy childhood that momentarily surface—is that the origin of *Aké?*
No, not at all. There's no way *Aké* wouldn't have come out. It's an ambience that, once you're aware it's passing, once you revisit Aké sometime, you miss certain signs, certain relationships change drastically, that were the norm when you were a child, your own personality has . . . In fact, now that you ask that question, I remember that I'd been trying to find time to write a biography of my uncle. Through that I wanted to catch some of the flavour of that period, what he represented, his times and so on, and I suppose it's from that kind of idea that *Aké* grew since I couldn't do that, but it's still a project that I might still do. It requires going through papers, talking to people. Beere (his wife) is dead now, she died some years ago, but I hope I will still write it one day. You see, it was out of a desire at least to capture something of that period.

Femi Osofisan has said that your use of space is one of the most original aspects of your theatrical activity. Would you like to talk about your use of space in theatre?
Some directors see a *text,* their primary concern is to elucidate the text by action, to propel the innate material of the text, to project it towards the audience. When I'm directing I see myself first of all as creating images in space. The book, the text, is one thing, but the whole business of translating the text onto the stage is that one is moving to a new dimension and I think I have said that the dimension has to be strong, otherwise one might as well read the play. That dimension is more than just the inner interpretation through the actor—that is of course also important—but it's the visual sculpting of that event on stage. That dimension fascinates me a lot, ever since I've been directing.

Are your plays written with this in mind?
Some of them, yes. Not my political sketches, for instance, what I call my shot-gun sketches!

Tell me about them.
That's my favourite form of occupation actually; I build it around individuals I'm working with on stage. We improvise, a lot of things come out, it's never the same, a different thing one day to another . . . Those sketches have a kind of what I'd call a creative joy in that it's constantly being re-created, it's a permanent re-creation and finally of course it's a very direct way of speaking to the people, to my audience, certainly more direct than say denser plays like *Death and the King's Horseman.* I enjoy doing them.

Are they put on in the same places?
No, they move around a lot. The last round of these things—I do them in waves as called for by the circumstances—the last one took us to market places, market spaces, open-air university quadrangles, outside civil service offices—they come out during their coffee break or look through the windows; one took place right in front of the House of Assembly when the big rice scandal was on, when Dikko was fighting for his existence, he was the Chairman of the Presidential Task Force on Rice. That whole rice episode was just a scheme to defraud the nation of billions. I can't think of a greater crime than creating a fictitious scheme which has to do with food or health, two primary needs of humanity and society, a fictitious scheme just to siphon billions into private pockets, no benefit at all to the people who really need it, and that's what the whole rice thing was about. So we did this sketch—it's been one of my favourites—and we did it with a troupe which was not a regular troupe, there were some actor-students among them, but it was a special group that I got together and we performed in all sorts of places and finally went to Lagos outside the House of Assembly. After performing in a quadrangle near by we then piled sacks and sacks—made-up sacks to look like bags of rice—on the entrance of the House of Assembly with a banner "To him who hath more shall be given!" That's been one of my favourites!

Tell me about the film you have just made.
Well, the film was to have been another agit-prop expression, using the medium of film, and it was something that I desperately wanted to do before the elections as pure election propaganda: its material was to have been purely all the crimes of Shagari's government during the civilian stint. When

I started shooting there was a price on my head by Shagari's henchmen and they didn't even disguise it but insinuated it on television and radio, newspapers. They were foaming at the mouth because I denounced the elections on BBC and this had a lot of repercussions in the world press. I predicted that there would be civil war or a military coup, which was all I said: there was no other possible result, no other direction, except a civil war or military coup. So when I returned and we started shooting we had to make sure we were shifting from location to location because these killer squads were really out . . . Many times in fact—we had our own supporters within the police—and the news they used to bring us was really quite chilling, but I was determined to finish that film. And then, halfway through, the coup took place, while we were shooting, and so the whole direction had to change. We could no longer come out with the message, the summons to public insurrection which is what the text originally said, we had now to make it a sort of morality tale of youthful greed and corruption. I should mention, by the way, that I'd planned this film much, much earlier, long before the elections, but just couldn't find any money for it. We knew the Shagari government would do everything in its power to suppress it, but there were at least nine states in opposition at the time, nine out of nineteen states, and we knew this film would go on their television, they would make cassettes of it, it would be shown in cinemas in those states and that would be quite enough. So that was the original idea, but I couldn't get the money and that was when I made the record *Unlimited Liability*. I was just sitting down one day and feeling so frustrated—out of the amount I needed, I think I'd got about 3000 Naira which is about 4000 dollars—and thinking what the hell are we going to do? Then I suddenly thought—we had been doing the sketches, the Guerrilla theatre was already on at the time, but they were so fraught with danger, all the time I was never really very happy at exposing these students and things were getting really wild, really, really, really wild: disappearances, arbitrary arrests—people just locked up for ever and you wouldn't know where they were—murder, daylight executions, people not getting home . . . The outside world had no idea what hell we were going through in that period. None whatsoever. Close to what was happening in El Salvador: abductions, assassinations, before the eyes of families of the opposition leaders; each day was getting more and more dangerous . . . So I was sitting down and thinking, well, I can't make this film, when I said, wait a minute, why don't I put on record a couple of the songs which we're using in these sketches? So we rushed that through. It was marvellous because there was a shortage of all sorts of things in the recording studios, granules for making records were short, there was a long queue of all the various musicians who were waiting to wax their own usual discs and the moment they heard what it was about, all of them gave me their place and that record came out, immediately, in record time, because they all said, "No, this comes first."

So the film itself underwent a number of changes in the course of shooting?

Yes. While we were actually editing, the Dikko event took place. So there was a political statement which the film lent itself to and I re-edited the end so that you could see that the corrupt policeman was the agent of Shagari's government and that he aided the politician-killer in getting out. So we froze a frame when money was being exchanged and inserted a postscript something like: Sometime about July 1984 a clumsy attempt was made to crate one of the guilty politicians etc. etc. and bring him back to the scene of his crime. The nation was manipulated into an orgy of patriotic rage at the failure of this attempt, but they'd forgotten the question of who let him out in the first place, and why.

London, 16 July 1986

Could you tell me how you first started writing poetry, what moved you to write poetry?

Well, that's a bit of a difficult question to answer because I think from school I always scribbled some verses. I do recall that I entered the poetry competitions in the Festival of the Arts in Nigeria—I don't know which—it was conducted nationally at the time. I think I remember taking a bronze medal for a poem on a murderer's last hours. Don't ask my why . . . probably somebody got hanged around that time and I saw it in the newspaper and just pictured what his last hours were like. Now that you asked I suddenly had this flash of this poem which I hope nobody ever uncovers; I'd be horribly embarrassed—I hate all these collectors of so-called juvenilia, the Bernth Lindfors gang! So, as far as I recall I've always scribbled short stories, poems, verses, and as one grows older and more mature and more experienced I suppose one's dimensions widen and deepen.

What poets—African and non-African—do you or have you felt affinity to?

Affinity's the wrong expression. Let's just say that I've always been more fascinated by the . . . Well, I have never really enjoyed what you might call

Tennysonian poetry. I found a close affinity (and I think this is due to the tradition of Yoruba poetry which some people insist is very simple and straight-forward but which for me is very dense, metaphoric, allusive, also witty and mischievous: it's not *solemn*—when I use expressions like dense I don't mean solemn—but sutured with a great deal of play on words), so I do have a great feeling for poets like John Donne and the Metaphysicals . . . poetry which seems to penetrate the surface reality of things, or at least attempt to explore the not so apparent realities which are however very real, especially within my own world-view. At the same time I've enjoyed precise, very concise use of images, the Imagists, for instance, and of course I'm very, very close to Yoruba poetry: *ijala, ewi* and even the poetry of the prose language of writers like D. O. Fagunwa, whose novel I translated. Well, that just about sums it up. It's quite true that I do not find myself challenged, intellectually or even emotionally, by what I call the Tennysonian assonance of poetry.

How about Eliot?

Well, curiously enough I'm not very fond of Eliot. Even as a student I resented having to study him because his poetry doesn't move me in any way. Yes, it's true that I find his *Waste Land* to an extent—it's not difficult even for somebody who is alien to the tragedy which is captured in that poem to empathize with the mood of the poem, the regret, the deep sense of loss—I think in that sense, that's one work to which I responded. I don't share the view of most critics that he thoroughly absorbed or integrated his kind of eclectic range of alien religions. I find the intrusion of the metaphors, religions, an obtrusive kind of exotica inserted in *The Waste Land*. As a student I found myself very detached from that aspect of his poetry.

What poems and literary conventions and forms were most influential for you in your early poetry, or was it a very personal thing?

I don't know, quite frankly. I think most young men and women begin writing poetry out of their personal lives, out of their personal experience, out of their personal emotion. The control of the medium follows, but the initial thing is instinctive response to experience, to encounters, to emotions, to emotional states of mind, correlations which strike one simultaneously as unique and—I use the expression "correlations" deliberately—experiences which seem unique, but at the same time have a reference to one's inner experience, intuitions, and so I cannot really say that one poet or the other, some kind of poetry, influenced me. I mentioned just now the fact that I've

never been impressed by Eliot's use of the oriental religions, but it's significant that when I was in prison, in the poems which came out of prison, I was
drawn towards that particular terrain, so perhaps there had always been that
instinct in me towards particularly the *Bhagavad Gita* which features in *A
Shuttle in the Crypt* and some of the poems there. Maybe I had always sensed
a way in which *I* would want to use it, but somehow Eliot's use was different.
It could be the reason, but it's a purely subjective reaction and one should
always mention that.

**You mentioned Yoruba poetry earlier. Was that something that you
grew up with or that you came to later on?**
Oh no. I grew up with it. The chants of *Ijala* and other poetic genres. I
remember since I was a child we had one Kilanko who was not only a musician but a poet and he used to recite poems when I was at school, in primary
school. No, no, I grew up with it. We had not just raconteurs but poets, epic
recitals featured continuously in our school. On prize-giving day, for instance, students would get up and recite Yoruba poetry. It was part of our
way of life.

And was Fagunwa read at school?
Oh yes, absolutely! He was read at school. Even today, people still take
him in their School Certificate examinations. It's a writer that is constantly
set. I've been reading Fagunwa from early childhood, including pamphlets of
short stories which were always lying around.

**When did you actually start translating his work? At least two epi-
sodes were published in *Black Orpheus* well before the book came out.**
I can't remember. It was certainly a long time ago. I'd always wanted to
translate Fagunwa. I'd always felt this was a novel which should be accessible
to everyone.

**You often use traditional themes, figures and images, developing them
in an original manner and weaving into your verse a multiplicity of cultural allusions. How do the different strands interrelate?**
I should make it quite clear that I don't set out to weave it . . . If something
is part and parcel of your flesh, your skin, it's inevitable. I accept this heritage, I utilize it, I mutilate it, I twist it, distort it. I act complementarily
towards it. We can speak of specific metaphors. We can speak, for instance,
of the figure of Ogun, because all his attributes, his idioms, his language,
metaphors, poetry, all of this I *weave*. So one can talk about *concrete* situa-

tions like this. But when one starts talking about stylistics, for instance, for me that becomes the territory of the critic who's curious enough to find out where the correlations are. I don't set out consciously to set up anything.

There are certain images and themes that recur, under varying forms, throughout your work. Particularly the references to Ogun and to his archetypal journey into the abyss, reappearing elsewhere as a descent into Hades. Then there are your four "archetypes" in *A Shuttle in the Crypt:* **Joseph, Hamlet, Gulliver and Ulysses; why these particular figures?**

Well, they corresponded to certain archetypes, certain experiences, both individual and collective, which were going on in Nigeria at the time. I'm glad that you mentioned the kind of parallel between Ogun's experience and Greek mythology, for instance, because one thing that I like to emphasize, which should not be necessary but which unfortunately is made necessary by what I call the school of purism, is that as anthropologists, social anthropologists, mythologists, ethnologists have found out all over the world—the serious ones—there is a meeting point within human experience, within the collective memory of humanity, within the mythologizing attitude and inclinations of mankind. There are so many meeting points and it's foolish to deny their existence. The story of what is now known as the Oedipal complex, its expression has been tracked down not merely to Greek tradition. It's been found to be a preoccupying aspect of the human psyche in most societies. I was looking at the programme of LIFT just now, and it's interesting that there's a Chinese play which came to London not so long ago which retold the Oedipal myth through Chinese mythology—pre-existing Chinese mythology! And so, coming to Ogun, he's a recognition of a valid aspect, a continuing, a real aspect of the creative and social instinct of my own society. But I have no doubt at all it was reinforced by my discovery as a student of parallel examples in my studies of other societies. In other words, one begins by recognizing certain symbols in one's society, but one's sense of wonder and therefore one's exploitation of materials, one's inclination towards exploitation, one's sense of wonder increases by the recognition of similar . . . even while Ogun, for instance retains his uniqueness, the fact is one's sense of wonder increases by finding parallels in Prometheus, in Gilgamesh, in the other mythologies of other societies, of the Orient, of the West, and so on and so forth. It's not a question of specificity, but of uniqueness and at the same time of complementarity. And I think that basically is why for instance we encounter these four archetypes: there's a Jewish archetype, Joseph; there is Hamlet, whose story is not in any case really English but was borrowed; there is Ulysses, the eternal wanderer (you find Ulysses in Fagunwa: what is Akara-Ogun but a Ulysses?), and so these metaphors came to me quite instinctively, naturally; but at the same time—I feel I have to emphasize this—it was necessary, while I was in prison, to try and distance myself from the immediate environment. That was also a process of sanity, to think in terms of distancing me from the reality, connecting with *other*, larger symbols.

The Ulysses archetype seemed to me to be slightly different from the other three, in the sense that it seemed very closely related to Joyce's *Ulysses*.

Yes, indeed; again, that was deliberate distancing; I did not use Fagunwa's Ulysses, for instance, Akara-Ogun.

Ulysses seems a particularly apt archetype for your work, both in terms of your experiments with time, space and language and of your using myth, like in *Ulysses*, as a kind of order on which to fit the disorder and fragmentariness and problems of contemporary life.

My use of myth . . . I wish you'd phrased that differently, without saying "like in *Ulysses*." Because, take Fagunwa, for instance. In what sense did he use the archetypal explorer, wanderer, seeker, quester? It was in order to organize events that are themselves chaotic and that means the whole experience of search, of quest, and that means of *life*, which tends to be pretty chaotic, to use a framework. It's the same thing with John Bunyan in *Pilgrim's Progress*. Whether it's religion which is the framework or just adventure, or whatever, one constantly uses that framework.

Yes, but to return, despite your objection, to *Ulysses*, there is also a use of myth as a way of contrasting a previous order with a present disorder, to emphasize a sense of degradation.

Yes, but if one looks into it . . . This is why I say one distorts myth anyway. A previous *order*, but . . . just how much order *was* there in the previous myth? It's a "mythic" order: it's winnowed down through the ages, through perception, contemporary perception, and it's useful, just useful.

You have only written two novels. Is there any particular reason for this? How do you see the novel today?

Well, I'm not really a keen novelist. And I don't consider myself a novelist.

The first novel happened purely by accident. In fact I used to refer to it purely as a "happening." I used to write short stories, by the way, which was OK. But the novel for me is a strange territory—it still is—and I turned to it at that particular time because it was not possible for me to function in the theatre. So, for me it was just a happening. Then, again, *Season of Anomy* was written at a period when it was not possible for me to function in the theatre. So I don't consider myself a novelist. And the novel form for me is not a very congenial form. Basically, I don't even like the novel. When I read prose I tend to want to read biographies, generally political biographies, political history, works of philosophy and—this will astonish you—crime, detective stories! The kind of fiction which I really enjoy is good science fiction—and the exceptional detective work like Umberto Eco's *The Name of the Rose*. But general novels and so on, contemporary novels . . . I pick up books, I browse through them very quickly because somebody says "Oh you must read this one, you'll find it fascinating," so I read it, but generally I'm not a great novel man. I should observe that this is a recent development—perhaps no more than fifteen years—maybe less. Before that I was an assiduous devourer of the novel!

You don't espouse the view that the novel is an imported form and therefore extraneous to Africa, I imagine?
    No, no, not at all! But I'll tell you this: there's an exception to what I was saying. When I was a child I *devoured* Dickens. I think there is hardly any volume of Dickens' work that I have not read. There was something that fascinated me about the kind of life he depicted and I remember that in school I read literally all Dickens' novels. I think there was a kind of exotic nature—the transitional life of Victorian England that he captured was to me so exotic. But, generally, the contemporary novel . . . I've read one or two: Rushdie, I've enjoyed, again, exceptionally, Marquez, I love his works: that's another exception. Bessie Head: I found her novels very, very gripping, fascinating, challenging, really intellectually intriguing. Then that black American woman writer, Toni Morrison, the author of *Sula, Song of Solomon:* she's a fascinating writer. Umberto Eco . . . But generally I don't read novels.

    A sense of doom, of endless repetition, despite all attempts to overcome it through individual will-power or through sacrifice, seems to underlie the actions of your characters. Yet there is also a strong sense of a need for change, through what you have described as an evolutionary kink in the circle—the Möbius strip as against the eternal cycle; and you also

speak of the need to break the primal cycle even if it were of good and innocence, if necessary through violence.

Well, some people say I'm pessimistic because I recognize the eternal cycle of evil. All I say is, look at the history of mankind *right up to this moment* and what do you find? All one has to do is open the newspapers *any given day;* listen to the radio any given day, walk through the streets any given day, and you just marvel how in spite of the phenomenal strides man has made in the improvement of the quality of life, technological means, means of communication, the conquest of nature, the harnessing of the forces of nature, man till now has not really solved his perennial problem of mutual slaughter, cannibalism, cruelties, the whole unconquerable evil of power, in all societies, *all* societies, even this one. So for me that is a reality which one cannot escape. Those who want to believe that man is constantly improving, they are free to do so. For me the evidence is overwhelmingly against, but I take the position that it is again a question of struggle. One begins by acknowledging the negative, depressing reality and so one has a choice, either to lie down and die or to fight it. So therein lies what is sometimes referred to as a paradox. But for me it's the most logical, simplistic thing in the world. The very fact that you recognize the unacceptable face of human existence, that very fact means that you either commit suicide—you take your choice—or, if you don't commit suicide, you are bound to resist and to try and devise strategies or contribute towards strategies to enable humanity to make a quantum leap. Because nothing short of a quantum leap can compensate for the centuries of retrogression which human societies all over the world, I don't care where—name it—wherever, even the most so-called progressive societies, the retrogression one constantly finds in terms of the quality of human existence. That is the depressing reality. But, as I said, for me the choice is simple. Either one commits suicide or one struggles against it. And so the quantum leap for me is represented by this sudden kink, this sharp evolutionary kink in an existing, a pre-existing cycle: the Möbius kink, the Eshu kink, it has very many metaphors but it all means exactly the same thing.

Just over ten years have passed since the publication of *Ogun Abibimañ;* would you write a similar poem today?

Well, I was about to say *no* and then I recalled that I have been writing some poetry more or less in the same vein . . . not quite, because this time I merely celebrate the spirit of one human being: I'm more modest. After the betrayal of Nkomati it's highly unlikely I will write another *Ogun Abibimañ.*

By the betrayal of Nkomati I'm not referring merely to the specific accord but for me the betrayal of African countries, even of the front-line states, the betrayal of the black brothers and sisters in Southern Africa, the refusal to become absolutely and unequivocally engaged in the struggle which is going on in South Africa, which is long overdue . . . It's unlikely that I will write another poem celebrating a moment of the acceptance of a challenge. It's not enough, it's no longer enough. It's terrible what has happened. The accord was shattering. But I have been celebrating the spirit of Nelson Mandela and the South African struggle; I suppose because I can't help it. I'm a very celebratory kind of person. I cling to crumbs on the revolutionary field. For me any little affirmative thing literally says "We're still alive" and for me that is always worth celebrating.

Rome, 24 May 1990

There are references throughout your work to the visual and plastic arts and to painters of varying origin, from Skunder Boghossian of Ethiopia to Picasso or Francis Bacon. In fact in your 1985 essay "Climates of Art" you connect Bacon's "scheme of image distortion" with the "aesthetics of movement" expressed by the traditional African mask. Could you discuss the relations between art and writing in your vision?

When people complain of what, when kind, they say is complexity and, when they want to be nasty, they say is obscurantism, deliberate complication and obscuring of one's prose, one's poetry, and demand a very linear, almost transliterating approach to composition, the transliteration of one's thoughts, my favourite answer is just to refer them back to African sculpture, which is by no means simple, which is not always realistic representation but which in fact evokes numinous tensions: tensions between the numinous world and the realistic world, tensions *within* the numinous world, however it is conceived. The tension we find in African sculpture is not linear, it does not evoke a mere uniplane concept of images of the numinous world.

You refer to the example of Francis Bacon. Well of course I use that as a kind of paralleling of the African mask in motion—I refer to the work of Dennis Duerden who very astutely points out that a number of African masks were never even conceived by the artists as the completed physical static order which we see, but that they were actually conceived *in motion,* they were actually designed as a multiple expression in relation to the dance, to the very motions which are created by those masks when they are worn. That is why we do not have what you might call galleries of masks where people go to see "African art" on exhibition. When the festival is over, when the ceremony is over, when the ritual is over, the masks are tossed into the conservatory and are not brought out again until the next event. This alone is an index of the ontology of the masks themselves. They are different from what you might call palace art: the representation of lineages, of kings, consorts, slaves as you have in Benin bronzes, some Ife bronzes, these ones which I call the court art, classical, beautiful . . . They have their definite and distinct aesthetic value and approaches which are very different from the goals in the heads of the carvers of many of these wooden masks, the masks which we seem to be able to admire in the museums, but which are not really the originating and determining concept of those masks in the hands of the carvers. And I just used the analogy of what Francis Bacon tried to do in his painting as being the nearest way I could express the execution of those masks, their overall conception. When they are in motion it's a totally different dynamism from anything you can see in the museums of London and Paris. Now, part of my work as a director involves the fact that in addition, and as an integral part of the interpretation of a play on stage, there is also for me the sensation of carving images on stage. And again this is where my experience and my legacy meet, where the real creative impulse unifies the textual communication and where the means, the method of communication really lies.

The final poem of your latest collection, where the cremation of a worm-eaten caryatid raises the issue of the destruction and survival of art and life in time, is surely also a reflection on the possibilities and limits of art?

That statement is not meant to be a negative one, not a pessimistic one. It indicates where act takes over from art. The artistic form is a perennial representation and reminder of certain imperatives of existence. Whether we like it or not, in terms of effecting change art does have its limitations. And I keep emphasizing that recognition of this limitation is not a negative or pessimistic view of art. For me it is a very positive one. Certain kinds of artistic production in my society are left to rot, deliberately. It's part and parcel of the persona of an art work that it is meant to vanish, to be destroyed in order to be able to reproduce itself. This is the organic nature of art.

I think we have to fasten onto the fact that some societies accept the perishability of art not as a negative thing but as a challenge, a challenge to the regenerative nature of life. The in-built perishability of art in most African societies, especially where wood-carvings are concerned, goes beyond physical perishability—the very action, as I stated earlier, of consigning to the dark rooms of the shrine a mask that has been used for a particular purpose is a recognition of that transitoriness, of the non-dominating essence and value of art. The wooden carving would be left just to perish in many societies—Yoruba societies, Igbo societies—because the next year you would have to renew if for the communal event, for the act of communal re-creation. So when it comes out the following year or two years later or ten years later, the fact that it has disappeared for some time does not—in traditional art appreciation—escalate its material value, unlike the European world where if you succeed in hiding something for a few years, when it comes out then it becomes really astronomically valued. There's some very profound difference here which for me has not been sufficiently explored. So this perambulation is just to emphasize my very deep-seated awareness that—yes—art is for many cultures a perishable commodity which represents the continuum of human productivity. It's not negative. People can look on it as wasteful, that's a problem, but it represents a certain view of art and a very important cultural perspective. It implies also that the art work itself has limitations in relation to the creative act, to the human act, the social act, the communal art which in fact sustains art. It's a complex, but at the same time very simple, logical approach to art and life which it seems to me the Western world has not been able to come to terms with.

"Mandela's Earth" is not only the title of the first section of the collection, but of the whole book. Would you like to go into your choice of this phrase as the general title for your book?

Before I do that, I want to go back to your last question. The poem "Cremation of a Caryatid" is representative of the attitude towards art and life which I was expressing earlier. Yes, there's this work of art, and it is quite possible for little termites to eat into it and destroy it. But those termites cannot, simply cannot, because of the continuum, the philosophy of continuity that is built into both concept and execution, they simply cannot destroy the *creative essence* that produced the work of art. That caryatid *can* be destroyed. It can be destroyed by war, it can be destroyed by civil strife, it can be destroyed, as Achebe expressed it in one of his novels: when a god fails its society, they'll take it out and put it in the middle of the road and set fire to it and a substitute is created. Ultimately the will resides in human beings. It's a sad moment, a sad event that the representative of the mores, the creative essence of society has to be banished, destroyed, sent into oblivion. This process is ritualized, the ritual is yet another dimension of the work, there's a kind of poetic sadness about it, but at the same time it's a *renewing* act, a *renewing* event that there are energies which ensure that this cycle of creativity continues.

Now, this elaboration was triggered off by your question on *Mandela's Earth.* I don't have to tell you I've been obsessed by the whole South African situation and at the centre of it all Mandela's imprisonment, because it took place at a moment when I was defining my political constituency, unconsciously. He was imprisoned at a time when my political energies were being honed towards the struggle for liberation in Southern Africa. Mandela has sort of sat in my brain for donkey years, including when I was attached to the Royal Court Theatre. My play *The Invention* was a very dark satire on the apartheid situation and there were poems I wrote during my student days: Mandela *happened* at that time and probably also assisted in honing my political sensibilities in that particular direction. Up to now I've fluctuated like—I hope—all normal human beings between a positive approach and a despairing, negative feeling generated by the betrayal of the African people by their leadership. The leaders are so suspicious of their own people that they will not mobilize society towards what for me, for three decades at least, has been the destiny of African struggle. In other words I've taken for granted that the meaning of decolonization, independence and so on was the concerted struggle towards the total liberation of black peoples, especially in Southern Africa. So by the time I started putting together the poems of *Mandela's Earth,* mostly triggered off by his refusal to accept a compromised freedom, which for me was an expression of everything I most believed in, there was the sense that whether this symbol, this caryatid, survives his ordeal or not, we cannot permit ourselves to forget the promise of renewal or even the *challenge* of renewal, which is what his incarceration has been all about. It's a lesson not merely for the struggle in South Africa, but for the rest of the African continent under heinous tyrannies beside which the white tyranny is child's play. I've just read in the papers that Mobutu has done it again: some 50 students have been massacred in Zaïre—I heard about that this morning. So this is what we're talking about, this kind of betrayal, this kind of savage treachery by our own kind.

Mandela's Earth was for me a renewal of faith, if you like, just as *Ogun*

Abibimañ was a renewal of faith, a recollection of the enduring symbols of that momentary declaration of intent by Mozambique under Samora Machel. They're just periodic expressions of my refusal to be pessimistic.

Your latest book, *Isara,* is sub-titled *A Voyage Around Essay.* How did you come to write it? And where—or what—is *your* Ashtabula (your father's relation with Ashtabula and the person who introduced him to the place, Wade Cudeback, form the frame to the book itself)?

Oh, for me my Ashtabula is just right where I am at the moment! It's always been right where I've found myself most times. I don't have that kind of enduring Ashtabula beyond my typewriter, what eventually I push out of the roller. *Isara* has always been there in my head, like all works which any writer brings out. But I think one of the not so obviously acknowledged impulses to bringing out *Isara* has to do with the kind of distortion of the history of the development of the modern contemporary African intellectual by what I call the Neo-Tarzanist perspective of modern Africa, denying the existence of contact between modern Africa and the outside world. This contact goes back centuries and all experience is part of the formulation of the intellectual mind of any community. Some of these people write as if it was only when the first student went to study in England that there was any contact at all between the African world—or indeed the Red Indian world or the Papua New Guinean world—and the rest of the entire globe. It's this kind of lie, this kind of deliberate, obvious lie, for what purpose I do not understand. I don't care if the African world and its people never came into contact with anybody, including traders from the outer world. It's of no importance to me. But it happens to be a fact that they did. Why should anyone suggest that, after several centuries of contact, the entire global perception of a continent can only be in the so-called region of "iron snakes and town-criers"? If it were so there'd be no problem. But even the newspapers of the early 1900s and before indicate very clearly that there had been this contact and it had affected both sides of the correspondence. Even the arts of diplomacy have been practised between the kings or monarchs of Africa and the outside world. This goes back quite a few centuries. Therefore today when we talk about the intelligentsia, we're talking about an intelligentsia which is not merely formed of the analytic processes of their own society, but by analytic processes which take as their grist experiences with the outside world. Reading the press snippets, the social documents, the letters of the people involved at the time makes one even angrier that anybody should have the nerve to suggest that there has been a kind of *cordon sanitaire* between the African peoples and the outside world. This is historically false. So perhaps one of the reasons why this book was written at that time, before another book—let's put it that way—has been a kind of "Well, this material has always been there and I would have to use it sooner or later, so why not now, if only to shut the lying mouths of these people who want to regress into a non-existent kind of pristinism." The culture of Africa has never been as "pure" as these people try to make out—and, in any case, pure in what sense? Pure by what simplistic, narrow, uni-dimensional pattern of development, of perception? It's been constantly digesting, analysing and adjusting experiences from wherever these experiences come. So *Isara* is a piece of social history, a filial tribute, and what I hope will place that particular generation which I've known so intimately, which we all know so intimately, in its proper historical perspective and context. And then it's also a personal tribute to these people whom I knew and some of whom died before I could on a very intimate level compare notes with them. It's just something that I had to write.

The figure of the *Abiku*, or child returnee who dies, is born again, dies again and so on, is one of your metaphors for the phenomenon of creativity and it reappears, under different guises, throughout your work. Would you like to talk about it?

Each time I'm asked that question I warn that it depends on what mood I am in when I'm asked the question. Sometimes *Abiku* is a very negative thing to me. I accept and deny all responsibility for any contradiction in what I say about what *Abiku* represents to me. It depends what's been happening to me lately. To appreciate that you have to understand that I grew up with *Abiku,* not just as a metaphor but as a very physical expression of the link between the living, the unborn, the ancestral world and so on. *Abiku* was real, not just a figment of literary analysis. Some of my siblings were *Abiku,* the anxieties involved in their existence, their survival, their illnesses and so on were *Abiku.* And then of course I keep emphasizing the cruelty of the *Abiku* once they realize their own power with their parents, with their elders, how they use and abuse their power, and at the same time the kind of intelligence of the *Abiku* and their loyalty to their own group, almost like children versus the adult world. So it became a metaphor for some of the diversities of experience and society, it became a symbol for cyclic cruelty, cyclic evil, and also an expression for some of the enigma of existence, some of the insoluble aspects of existence. It became a symbol also of unwished cyclic impositions, a symbol for the unwished but recurring. *Abiku* is something you cannot totally kill off. You mark it, you scar it—you know how people scar the child, like the *Ogbanje* with the Igbo: it's a theory people swear to (and it's not just a theory) that, if you scar the *Abiku,* when the next child is born it will have those scars. You're longing for the new child as a symbol of continuity, a guarantee, a reassurance, a consolation. It's the same way as for instance in politics: there's an untenable situation and you're longing for change, you're participating in the process of change, you're looking for a re-born society, but when it eventually emerges it's got the same ugly scars, the same mark of Cain on it as the last one.

Wole Soyinka on "Identity"

Ulli Beier / 1992

From *Wole Soyinka on Identity: A Conversation with Ulli Beier*. Ulli Beier, ed. Bayreuth: Iwalewa-Haus, University of Bayreuth, 1992. Reprinted with permission of Ulli Beier.

Ulli Beier: Recently a famous commentator on African life and literature referred to you as "the man between," and in his article he expounds that eternal cliché of the African intellectual "between two-worlds," between two languages, two cultures. But it seems to me that Europeans worry far more about the "identity problems" of Africans than Africans themselves. I have known you now for over thirty years and you have never struck me as somebody who is constantly aware of oscillating between two worlds. Or have you ever thought of yourself as living in a situation of conflict?

Wole Soyinka: It is a strange but certainly deeply ingrained attitude that certain commentators hold—and of course it is a very Eurocentric thing. It does not occur to me for instance to consider you, Ulli Beier, as a "man between." It does not occur to me that you suffer from a conflict: you come to Nigeria, and you are immediately at home. You can sit in a Shango shrine or follow the Agbegijo masqueraders: you are just at home. And there are some other Europeans like that: Susanne Wenger has stayed in Oshogbo for decades, she has become a priestess of Obatala. It has never occurred to me to consider her a woman between—she is a deeply spiritual person, and an artist, who creates where she has put down her roots.

I look at Gerd Meuer—he is at home one moment here and one moment there. Right now he is in Addis Ababa. It has never occurred to me that there is a problem, or that there is something special about anybody striving towards two or three or four multiple worlds. It is a very Eurocentric thing.

U: It's European, but it is especially German. In this country people still talk about "die Bewältigung der Vergangenheit." They still wrestle with their Nazi past and those who weren't even alive at the time, torture themselves by examining their fathers' role in those years. There is a spate of books on that subject. Very different kinds of books from your own reminiscences of your father.

Germans have a problem with their identity because they are very theoretical people—they don't trust their gut reaction—they have to argue an issue to the end before they know how to react.

W: There is another aspect to this: I think that Europeans still marvel at the ex-colonial—somebody at the lower scale of civilisation as far as they are concerned—being able to respond in a very natural and intelligent way to another civilisation. I think that this, lurching underneath it, is the notion.

U: Of course Europeans have long felt that they have to export their culture in order to lift other peoples to a higher level of civilisation. In the early days of the University of Ibadan there was just this attitude. There was no curiosity about Nigeria at all. The notion that there could be some kind of exchange, some mutual enrichment, was quite foreign to them.

They used a formula to justify any absurdity in the curriculum which they imposed on Nigerian students. If you asked them why they thought it necessary to teach Anglo-Saxon in Nigeria at a time when no African language was taught and when there was not even a second European language, the answer was: "We have to maintain British standards." Africans were only acceptable to Europeans if they could perform on their terms and live up to "British standards."

On the other hand I feel that certain kinds of early African literature have also contributed to this. . . .

W: Indeed, I was going to refer to that. The early African intellectuals accepted this perspective themselves; and—as I wrote somewhere—enjoyed the "angst" which was created for them through the notion of having to transcend one culture and having to link up with a superior one. The early poetry. . . .

U: Well—Senghor. He is certainly somebody who moves very smoothly between the cultures—but on the other hand he talks too much about it, doesn't he?

W: He wanted to intellectualize it. To create "problematique" and then analyse it; and poetise it also because he used both approaches, the creative and the intellectual. Of course, he was a magnificent poet, and therefore his influence was more deleterious than, let us say, Mabel Imoukhuede. You know the kind of poetry we are talking about. But the interesting thing is that Mabel and others soon gave up on that line. There wasn't too much yardage.

U: No, at least in Nigeria such notions were abandoned fairly quickly. But to come back to the European image of Wole Soyinka—"the man between."

There are certain assumptions: your British education, your high achievement in that culture and your exceptional command of the English language, these things now stand—allegedly—between you and your own culture. The English language separates you, so the legend goes, from Yoruba culture. It's like saying you've been converted: he who was a pagan and has now become a Muslim, he who was a Protestant has converted to Catholicism. You have given up one thing to attain another.

W: This is a problem that arises out of analytical attitudes. The very principle of analysers is that an object or a subject is not interesting until you have created many analytical angles and made the subject as complex as possible—never mind whether the various angles are interesting or not. Once you can create multiple approaches towards the understanding of a subject, then of course you can play games with the entire analytical nexus. And that applies very much when the subject is a writer or an intellectual or a creative person. The more complex you can make the subject, the more intriguing—the greater the amount of conversation and discourse you can weave around it. I think that is exactly what happens: whether it is truthful or not—people no longer bother about that. Because it is more interesting to propose, let us say, that because one has had a particular kind of education and because one has had a certain amount of success in operating within other cultural measures, therefore something must have happened to that person.

U: Some twist to his character—some uneasiness in the mind.

W: And yet you have lots of people who leave their society completely and take up residence somewhere else—even in their formative years.

U: Joseph Conrad. . . .

W: Yes, and nobody bothers about this alleged "problem."

U: Nobody asks, what about his Polish soul.

W: That's right, it's only when it gets to this ex-colonial—and unfortunately some of our own intellectuals, they have their own axes to grind. Then they come and say: he is a success only because he had danced to their cultural tune. Some of them are even more overt—cruder—about it. Oh yes, he is completely alienated. They love him, because his opinions coincide with theirs.

U: The Nobel Prize controversy. . . .

W: That's right. You should never get the Nobel Prize, that's the ultimate proof. . . .

U: That you're a traitor to your culture.

W: But some of these people who write these things—they can't stand in their own societies, the way I can go back to my village and be immediately recognised and absorbed . . . they cannot. The contrast would be too shaming for them. So it's a myth that has been created for different kinds of motivations. Then common interest makes them all speak with one voice.

U: Maybe this is cynical of me. But you said that people create complicated arguments for their own sakes, but is it not also a case of people creating an academic career for themselves—creating a "subject"?

W: Of course, that's right.

U: Think of the Professor of English at the University of Ibadan who once said: "Wole Soyinka teaching English literature? Over my dead body. Only an Englishman can teach English literature." And that other gentleman who proclaimed: "If we were to teach the works of Wole Soyinka in the University of Ibadan—who are we going to drop, Milton or Shakespeare?" Now both of them are the big African literature experts!

W: They have to find new angles to replace the original resistance.

U: So they can talk endlessly about the agony of Wole Soyinka standing between two worlds.

W: I've said that many times: there is so much attention being paid to the sociology of the writer—

U: —and not to his writing!

W: Aha! So it is high time we paid some attention to the sociology of the critic. That is important, and when you look into sociology of the critic or analyst, you'll find self-interest, opportunism, often intellectual dishonesty— you will find phantasising over and above the level of a fiction writer. You'll find the polemicist's tendency, which has to be fulfilled, and it does not matter what the subject is. Before you come down to mundane issues like, is he or she married, white or black, or from another race: I mean all those various things that are foisted on the artist, it's about time we directed them at the critics themselves! And I am telling you—the results! I have done it in one or two instances—the results are fascinating. For example, one of those people I call Neo-Tarzanists—digging into his sociology, I found that he had fled Biafra during the war, so he is suffering from that immense guilt complex. He suffers from the adulation I received from his compatriots for the role I played in that war, while he was busy collecting money for the Biafran cause—much of which never arrived in Biafra. Little things like that. So it's about time to examine them and see what they eat, what they drink, what sort of clothes they are wearing, who they move with, whose approbation they seek, what sort of conferences they go to, on what circuit of conferences they are constantly to be found. It's about time we turned this blade around. The results are most fascinating. . . .

U: I think this should be applied on the widest basis. When this research scheme on "Problems of Identity" in Africa first started in Bayreuth a decade ago, I said that "if you think you are entitled to go into any part of Africa to solve their identity problems, at least you should have a parallel scheme of African scholars coming here to solve your identity problems. Because in my mind you have the bigger problem!"

W: The scholars who are into "what makes the African tick," the sociologists and the literary sociologists—they far outnumber and outweigh the creative material that is coming out of Africa today.

U: Easily!

W: So I think it's about time we moved in and studied the identity problems of the European scholars!

U: Another thing is this compartmentalised thinking. When that Professor of English literature said: "Wole Soyinka can't teach English literature," the implication was "he *ought* not to teach English literature." Just as there are still people who feel that someone like Akin Euba ought not to play Mozart. People want to protect their cultural preserves. No African could be sensitive enough to really understand our classical music. And when they say "classical," they take it for granted that they talk about European tradition. No other culture can have produced a classical form of its own.

A famous "ethnomusicologist" in Berlin issued a series of LP's on African and Asian music under the title "Musical Source Material"—as if entire cultures had merely evolved to provide "source material" for his scholarly work. In the same way African literature is merely "source material" for some of the scholars. They may not even enjoy reading it.

W: They're using it for their careers.

U: A related issue concerns the English language. Some commentators, both European and Nigerian, have argued that using English as a vehicle for creative work is a sign of elitism—an argument that has been used especially against you. It's curious, but in a different context, those same people talk about "World Culture" and the "Global Village" and all that—and yet they want you to write in a language that will drastically limit your readership to a very local audience. I suspect when travelling around the world to their different conferences, the same people are quite grateful to find that English is spoken almost everywhere.

W: I know, it is very curious. It's a non-existent debate that falls into two parts. Let's take the language aspect first. You will find that the African critics who are making this complaint are not making it in their own language. One would expect their commitment to be so total that they would turn their back on English and French altogether and write in, say Efik, and say: Anybody who can read me, good! Anybody who can't: let him read Wole Soyinka. For me, that would be the first mark of integrity. If that is missing, it is difficult to take them seriously.

The other thing is this: am I, Yoruba-speaking Wole Soyinka, am I to be cut off from Chinua Achebe? From the works of Taban Lo Lyong, Ngugi Wa Thiong'o, Denis Brutus? If South African writers followed this precept and wrote in their own languages, am I to be cut off from the political struggle in South Africa? It's an argument I have never really understood.

I come now to the second part. I too lament that in Africa, which I regard as my larger community, we don't have a language that binds us all together outside the European languages, the colonial languages. After all, even the European language fragments. I have to study Portuguese to read Dos Santos. I study French to read Senghor.

I'm on record as having seriously promoted the use of Swahili, and in the inaugural congress of the "Union of Writers of the African People" we took the decision that we should set up a cooperative publishing house and undertake the mammoth task of translating all works—all new works to begin with—into Kiswahili. Beginning with all new works. And we encouraged all African writers to reserve their rights to this cooperative publishing cooperation. I haven't seen any practical steps taken by the people who had been screaming their heads off about African languages. For me the two things go side by side. We should all admit that we need a single literature, which makes economic sense. We also asked that all schools should eliminate one useless subject and substitute Kiswahili so that we build up a generation of Kiswahili speakers. The two ideas coincide, I see no problem in this at all. I want to continue writing in English and, more importantly, reading my fellow Nigerians, my fellow Africans, in English and, of course, the literature of the entire English speaking world. I insist on keeping the facility to do this.

Many people oversimplify the word criticism. They don't understand that criticism also means exposition: exposition of the work and the life. They feel they have not engaged in literary criticism if they are not "criticising" . . .

U: In the sense of "finding fault."

W: Precisely. They have to be negative. They make a fetish of it. And ultimately, which is nauseating, they profit from it. And they communicate this in the very language they condemn. How ridiculous can you get? That contradiction never occurs to them.

U: Even Europeans have talked about elitism along the lines of "More people can understand *Death and the King's Horseman* in New York than in Nigeria," which is not true at all. In fact from the reports I read, the people of New York were quite baffled by the play. They couldn't penetrate it at all.

W: Yes. That is true.

U: I don't think that any critic has the right to prescribe a particular language to a writer anymore than he can prescribe the contents of a book or the mood or the intellectual level on which the ideas are to be developed. The irony is that those who constantly nag Wole Soyinka about his elitism, forget that, though you may have written some rather cerebral stuff, you have also operated on a very popular level. I can't think of another African writer who produced anything as popular as the LP, *Unlimited Liability Company.* To communicate on that level you even had to use Pidgin English.

W: I used Pidgin, I used Yoruba, I used mime, I used song, dance. I feel a total—if you like elitist—indifference to those kinds of critics. I consider them quite ignorant. When I read a statement like: "Nobody reads Wole Soyinka outside Nigeria," I ask myself, what do these people talk about. If they said: "This particular work is not read in Nigeria," we could begin to discuss that. But when they make a statement like "In Nigeria Wole Soyinka is far more popular for his political position than for his creative work" I say, I don't know what they are talking about. Unfortunately some of them are Nigerians!

U: Most of them!

W: We do our political sketches, we take them to the market place!

U: *Before the Blackout!*

W: Yes, you remember *Before the Blackout* from the sixties. And again during the last civilian regime, with all the scandals going on. We took the theatre to the museum kitchen at Onikan and from there moved to the street in front of the House of Assembly. We did a series of sketches there and then jumped into the vehicles and ran away before the police could seize our vehicles.

There are various ways of communicating a work to the public. I use all of them, including, as you remarked, a record. We are bringing out a video shortly which has emerged from the latest equivalent of *Before the Blackout.* We call it *Before the Deluge.* They came out of a theatre workshop in Abeokuta and some of the sketches we performed in open places. I reach the public in a way—and I am not being immodest—that few people do. Yet I am the one who gets all this nonsense about "Nobody reads Wole Soyinka in his own country."

U: I remember some very potent poems of yours appearing in Nigerian newspapers. For example the one about the pathetic death of a Yoruba Oba during the 1966 crisis in the West. Everybody would have understood that. Of course, I too may find some of your poems baffling—but few things could be more popular than "Telephone Conversation."

W: Of course there are always works that are more accessible than others.

U: Again this brings up the alleged identity conflict! There are two Wole Soyinkas, so the theory goes: one is the lofty intellectual who despises his readers, the other is the political agitator, the gang leader, who doesn't mind throwing out the occasional doggerel rhyme, another simplification, another variant of the "man between." They don't seem to see that different situations require a different response from the writer.

W: Yes, I believe that the armoury of creativity that is at your disposal is so vast that one would be a fool not to use whatever corresponds to the theme one wishes to use at the moment.

U: I think we have agreed that most Nigerians cope fairly effortlessly with the alleged conflict between their own culture and the Western values that have been imposed on them. They don't worry about it and there is no intellectual equivalent to the *négritude* writers. But at the same time there has been little interaction between the various Nigerian cultures themselves. What attempts have there been made to find common denominators between, say, Igbo, Yoruba, Efik and Angas culture? Do people consider it irrelevant or even undesirable?

Remember what we tried to do in Duro Ladipo's play *Moremi.* Because the play deals with the conflict between the Ifes and aboriginal population, I recruited a group of Agbor dancers for the production: so Duro had two languages, two musical traditions and two dance styles at his disposal. It enriched his play enormously and the final scene was spectacular. The Yoruba dundun drums were playing simultaneously with the Igbo slit gongs and horns. Duro made all the musicians orientate themselves towards a strong simple beat that was played by Rufus Ogundele on a huge Conga drum. It was a very successful piece of "fusion music," even though we did not know the term in those days. I rather hoped it would lead others to develop this idea further, but it wasn't taken up. What a missed opportunity. Imagine a Nigerian orchestra, involving Dundun, Bata, Bembe, slit gongs, xylophones from the Plateau, horns from Ekiti and Igbo country and kakaki trumpets from the North. You could create sounds that would make a European symphony orchestra sound grey.

W: It's interesting you should say that. Just yesterday when we were rehearsing the poetry with Okuta Percussion and Tunji played that Indian gatham, my mind went straight to the Igbo pot drum. And you are right—there has not been that fusion of music. I have felt the need for this myself and, you remember, when I produced *A Dance of the Forests* for Nigerian independence, I brought the Atilogu dancers from the East! And since then, most of my productions have integrated, wherever possible, a wide range of music. My mind goes immediately to whatever is available within my entire cultural milieu.

No, in case of music—you are right. A lot of this is missing. If you have a choir like Stephen Rhodes Voices or say, an Efik-based choir, you'll find that they make a point of including at least some songs from other parts of Nigeria in their repertoire. But it is there on an itemised level, not integrated. When I made my record, *Unlimited Liability Company,* one side and that is acknowledged on the cover. . . .

U: . . . is based on Njemanze!

W: Yes. I have always had this idea of cross fertilisation, but the composers, the real composers, don't seem to use it.

U: There has also been an unfortunate influence, I think. The various state "Art Councils" in Nigeria have promoted a kind of folklore.

W: That's right. You know after the oil boom, there came a time when culture became culture with capital 'C,' and folklore became folklore with a capital 'F' for 'Folklorism.' When there was money for the states to set up individual arts councils and when all these national competitions were organised, each state went its own way with a sense of creative rivalry. This has affected thinking till today. And has impoverished the range of creative possibilities.

U: There was another very negative aspect to those Arts Council competitions. It's an absurdity to have a group of Shango priests, who are performing "Sango Pipe," compete against Alarinjo singing "Iwi" or Babalawos chanting "Odu." What criterion is there to judge it? And usually it involved the humiliation of the performers. Some pompous cultural bureaucrat herding them on stage, then after ten minutes he would get on the stage and say "O.K. that's enough! Obatala priests next please."

W: It's still going on.

U: And then the crude attempts to "choreograph" what to the people concerned is a ritual—not a theatrical performance! I suspect that the unfortunate model for all these developments was Keita Fodeba's "Ballets Africaines."

W: Oh yes, the beginning of Africain folklore, cut to European taste. But at least they moved on from there. Whereas there has been no such evolution here. From the videos I have seen of the Nigerian "National Troupe," I gather that there has been no mandate for it to get a modern choreographer and produce a synthesis. It was a question of getting troupes from different areas and each doing their own thing. There has been, shall I say, a lack of progressive cultural policy. But the answer never lies in government policies. For example: Peter Badejo went to the North, to Ahmadu Bello University, and created a really marvelous form of choreography, utilising material from all over Nigeria with very impressive results. From small beginnings—he went there to take a diploma—he proved himself an imaginative choreographer. Recently he did the choreography for *Death and the King's Horseman* in Manchester. Nigeria is very rich and there are many idioms of creativity which really beg to be welded together. For me it is not a principle: it's just that the material is there. The possibility is there. Why isn't it used!

U: Some Nigerians have come to think that there are incompatible elements in the various Nigerian cultures. This belief has expressed itself in a great deal of political strife, even in violence and civil war. Thirty years after independence—have we come any nearer to any Nigerian identity or have we moved further away from it? Has Nigeria been no more than a colonial conception? What does it mean: being a Nigerian today?

W: That is a question which has been given very high profile in recent times. Consequent on the civil war, consequent on the rise of Islamic assertion, (which has taken its toll in the Nigerian psyche with sudden violent flashes, eating into the university system, with fundamentalists organising themselves and laying down the law for the rest of the university), the question, I am afraid, is on everybody's minds and lips.

It is a very real problem and it demands that a national debate should take place on the national question. Because certain parts of the country feel that other sections are dictating *their* idea of Nigeria, not a national concept— simply their own attempt to impose what they consider the ethics of their locale, whether it's religion, or region or whatever. Certainly it is a very large question. What form it will take, I don't know.

U: The only hope for the country to become a genuinely organic unit is for it to be allowed to grow—isn't it? You cannot prescribe national unity, it can only evolve.

W: Yes, that is correct.

U: Is it not then the creative people who . . .

W: Oh, no, I don't accept any extra burden for creative people. It is as much the responsibility of the politicians, the bureaucrats—because we are talking about quite prosaic things like the resentment of certain states over the apportionment of revenue. That kind of thing is listed as part and parcel of the need to discuss the national identity. It is being suggested that certain areas are being consistently privileged over and above others.

But you see, when the writer comes in and tells the truth about a situation like this, he is then charged with fanning ethnic tensions. In other words, he can add to the problem, while he tries to reduce it. It all depends. There is a joint responsibility. The artists can't be expected to take a leading role in it.

U: Well, of course, if it comes to solving such issues, the artist is only another citizen. But I was in fact referring to something quite different. How does the image of Nigeria evolve? Who defines Nigerian identity? Does it not happen through the kind of creative activity of a Peter Badejo that you have just described?

W: I am afraid it is very idealistic and romantic to think that fifty or hundred Peter Badejos are going to create that national fusion which he achieved on stage.

There was a former student of mine, who was caught in the recent Kano

riots. Jimmy Sodimu, a very marvellous actor. He was one of those who went
independent, who formed their own little troupes. He was in the North doing
a one man show and he had an interpreter. His interpreter was beheaded right
next to him! And he himself received severe matchet cuts. Are you ever going
to persuade *that* person to go on any cultural fusion mission? Ever again in
his life? No way!

U: This happened recently?

W: Recently. This was the very latest riot that was triggered off by that
German evangelist. That riot! There are lots and lots of cases like that. Everybody knows somebody who has been traumatised in that way as a result of
the national question. So people are asking: does it mean that I cannot go
anywhere in this country, on whatever is my mission, my business? There
was somebody driving a delivery truck. He'd done it for donkey's years—
around Bauchi. When the riot started, this man was taken out of his lorry, the
vehicle was set on fire and he was burnt. Just an ordinary worker, a driver.
Just because he was driving a truck load of beer and delivering it to all the
shops. This is no problem for the artist. The artist will create his own work
and fulfill his mission, but it's on a different level. . . .

U: Is it a situation, then, of which we can't know where it is going?

W: No, I cannot. I believe that successive governments have underrated,
have underestimated this question. Even people like myself—we have always
assumed that we have a nation. Or at least, as you rightly said: that if things
were just left, progressively, a nation would evolve. So it's not a question that
we have tackled.

When the whole debate began, I was cornered several times. Let's say, I
give a lecture. Somebody is bound to get up and say: "Excuse me, Professor
Soyinka, what do you say to the national question?" And I would pretend
that I don't know what he is talking about. I know damn well what he is
talking about, and I know that whatever I say can be taken the wrong way.
So I would say something like this: "Listen, I can be in Enugu or in Kano or
in Jos or wherever—as long as I have my typewriter with me, that's where
my nation is at the moment." But I know that's not satisfactory and the
questioner is not satisfied. He wants Wole Soyinka to pronounce, and from
the way he asks the question I know what he wants me to say. And he will
be satisfied with nothing less than what he wants me to say and that would
be misunderstood. The next day there would be twenty headlines and as many
twists in the newspapers. Words would be put in my mouth and I could not

debate it. So I would say: "Listen, if you see me afterwards, we can sit down and talk." I am not going to be drawn into that debate in public because I know what will happen.

U: But beyond this issue of the "national question" there is also that natural sense of obligation that a person like you has towards Africa at large. . . .

W: Precisely. I keep reminding people that I have a very large constituency which extends well beyond the Nigerian borders: I tend to see even Nigerian problems in the context of my vision of Africa. This has been with me for a long time, ever since my student days, when I was so focused on South Africa, that my early play dealt with apartheid.

And even in practical terms: if I get an invitation from Angola or Cape Verde, the passion with which my presence is solicited is much stronger than what I could get from Nigeria, where I am taken for granted. So I make an extra special effort to fulfill those requests whenever I can. This also creates extra problems. If I go away for a couple of weeks, there may have been some new event, something that has outraged public opinion. And they think: Oh yes, Wole Soyinka has stopped speaking. He doesn't comment any more. He doesn't criticise the government. I am supposed to be in Nigeria for 365 days a year giving running commentary on the government's activities. It's an absurd existence, and I ask people: what did you do? What exactly did you do? By the time you have arrived from overseas, this thing is no longer news, it is no longer on the front page. You move to act in a quiet, strong and often successful way. But it doesn't hit the papers. The next thing is you get flak from these lazy, idle, very comfortable armchair critics, whose mission in life is not to participate in nation building, in trying to enforce corrective measures—their mission in life is to point the finger and say: Oh, he's no longer doing anything, he's said nothing.

U: Not unlike those literary critics.

W: Yes, they don't even know what else you've written and how it's been received, but they will say: Yes, he's elitist now, he's removed from the people. It's boring, it's one huge bore! They don't even know that they've said it all before and that they've been proved wrong, it makes no difference.

U: There is a whole level of society that expects you—and maybe Tai Solarin—to take on the burden of pulling the government to heel, of being the consciousness of the nation. Mind you, I remember very well the time of the first real crisis we went through, the time of the massacres that preceded the civil war. Who else was speaking then? The fact is that everybody remained silent, and that was the most frightening aspect of it. There is no country in the world that does not experience violent convulsions. But when everybody is suddenly on the winning side . . .

W: Yes, it was one of the worst periods, the exhibition of collective compromise! Acquiescence! A kind of surrender and therefore moving from surrender to aggressive association with the side that inflicted a very serious wound on the national psyche.

U: Do you think that a lot of politicians still blame colonialism for the country's problems and for their own short-comings?

W: No, not the politicians, but the intellectual commentators. They still do that to some extent, but that has been diminished over the years, as they have seen the capacity for economic deprivation. They finally couldn't close their eyes to internal oppression in their own societies any longer.

U: What about the new debate on compensation for slavery. Isn't that a revival of the argument that colonialism is solely responsible for what's gone wrong in Africa? Of course I am fully aware that colonialism hasn't ceased to exist after independence. On the contrary: the exploitation of Africa by the West is far worse now than it has ever been.

W: Oh yes!

U: But on the other hand, foreign firms could not exploit Nigeria without the cooperation of some Nigerians. That's why we have all those industrial white elephants, those vast factories that produce next to nothing.

W: It's huge! Bottomless-stomached elephants! Yes, they're all over the place! But nevertheless, I found the reparations theme very fascinating. First of all, it's such a wild idea! That I find attractive. Also it could have a concrete result. If for instance the whole industrial world, the former colonial powers, the former slaving powers suddenly say: O.K. we forgive all your debts. That's your reparation. From now on we are entering a new relationship. Now we wipe the past clean: a totally new economic relationship. We are going to be strict. It's going to be quid pro quo: You have, I want, you sell, I pay. It's a curious thing, but a wild idea like this could just . . .

U: Maybe that's the way to finally get rid of these eternally strangulating loans.

W: Thank you. For that reason I don't dismiss it outright. But I agree, it's a debatable notion, a very controversial notion.

U: Well, to begin with, you can't just isolate the slave trade as the one big crime of the West. What about the Aztecs, or the Incas or the Australian Aboriginals. They would have to compensate the whole world! If they tried that—there would be nothing left of the West! That might not even be a bad thing, but it is simply not feasible!

W: And then how to work it out, it's very complex.

U: And in fairness to the West you have to admit that they have had no monopoly on genocide! What about Idi Amin! Bokassa! What about the long catalogue of atrocities carried out by Africans against Africans?

W: O yes! And then we would have to talk about the Arab slave trade which was every bit as atrocious as the European one. I have always said: there must be no double standards! No double standards! If we're going to have reparations, it's very dangerous—a two-edged weapon. But if it can be handled in such a way that the West will get tired of the noise and if they will say: O.K. take your debts, go away, we are all starting all over again, a new relationship—that would be a very interesting development.

U: A utopia!

W: But it's a fascinating exercise!

Wole Soyinka Interviewed

'Biyi Bandele-Thomas / 1993

From *Wole Soyinka: An Appraisal.* Adewala Maja-Pearce, ed. London: Heinemann, 1994, 142–60. Reprinted with permission of 'Biyi Bandele-Thomas.

'Biyi Bandele-Thomas: Earlier this year you were accosted at Murtala Muhammed International Airport in Lagos and delayed by men from the State Security Service (SSS). What happened?

Wole Soyinka: This was in January. I was on my way to Paris. Ironically, it was a trip in which the Nigerian government was participating and arranged by the Franco-Nigerian Association. A book of photographs for which I'd written captions was to be launched, and the pictures were to be exhibited; it was to be a travelling exhibition, showing Nigeria in a very positive light apart from the usual things people hear about. This was the idea. The Nigerian Ambassador to France was to be present, there was to be a symposium lasting an entire week; it was to be opened by the mayor of one of the Paris *arrondissements.* It was a high-level official engagement. Anyway, I got to the airport and—there's always an SSS man in the immigration booth—as soon as I arrived and presented my passport, the man said, "Oh, could you come with us please." So I followed them. I'd checked in, of course. They asked me to go and retrieve my luggage, which was by this time sitting on the tarmac for the security identification before the passengers board. As soon as that happened, I said to him, "Listen, if you people mess around with me, I will not travel, I want you to understand that." He said, "We won't keep you long." So I went along, picked up my luggage, and followed the officers to their room. We got in there and they began taking my luggage to pieces, shook out all my files, picked up my trousers, felt along the hems. It was quite thorough. They went through everything. This lasted about an hour. There was a television on in the room, there was a wrestling event going on, so I sat with my eyes glued to the television. And they said, "Oh, Professor Soyinka, you have to watch us inspecting these things." I said, "You can stuff anything you like in there. I haven't got the slightest interest. Just hurry

Excerpts from his interview appeared in *Index on Censorship,* volume 22, September–October, 1993.

up with what you're doing, find whatever you want to find, because I'm going home." Let's say the plane was due to leave at 11:35. At 11:32 they completed their search. In the meantime, somebody was standing there, holding a telephone conversation with somebody else somewhere. I presume that orders were given that, OK, you can let him go now. So they then packed my things back, gave me my passport, and said I was free to travel. I said, "You're crazy. You think I came to the airport to start chasing aeroplanes on the tarmac?" They said, "No, no, no, we'll take you to the tarmac." I said, "No way, I'm going back home." And that's exactly what I did.

BB-T: You've had several confrontations with this government in the past. But this is a new development in your relationship with them.

WS: It's an escalation. I've had veiled threats, I've had reports—they have their own SSS, I have my own SSS. They have several grades, watch grades, either on A or B or C. And I've been moving from A to B to C, back to A. In other words, one means: report his movements; another means: ask one or two questions, find out what he is doing, who he's seeing. Another grade—even higher—means: see if you can furtively search his papers. And then of course you get to the grade where you are absolutely persecuted; and, finally, there's the topmost grade where, after searching you and so forth, you're *not* allowed to travel. One of these grades, the subtle one, was applied to Obasanjo[1] himself not so long ago. He travels on a diplomatic passport, or rather, he did. I haven't checked the story with him directly, but someone who is close to him told me. And they successfully *lost* his passport at the airport and he couldn't travel. Somehow, his passport just vanished. For two hours the plane was held up for him. For two hours he could not travel . . . I've been on the receiving end of various levels of attention but this was the first time it really flared up into the open. My wife also was harassed. This was in June. She was flying to the U.S. to join me in Harvard where I was to receive a doctorate. At the airport, the moment they saw the name, they said, "Madam, come this way." They took her to the same interrogation room, asked her all sorts of stupid questions: "Where's your husband?" "Why are you not travelling with him?" "You say you're a journalist on your passport but on the form you wrote something different." She said, "Look, I'm not a practising journalist right now, but I *am* a journalist." You know, real idiotic, moronic questions like that. Just to delay her and try to get her to miss the plane, or whatever. Anyway, just before the plane left they released her.

---

1. Retired General Olusegun Obasanjo, Nigeria's Head-of-State 1976–79.

BB-T: In 1960, when *A Dance of the Forests* was produced to mark Nigeria's Independence celebrations, did you look into the future and see us not only leading from the rear but being also the most politically and economically abused entity in what you've described somewhere as "a benighted continent, now mangled beyond hope"?

WS: Let me tell you what happened to me during my studies in England. My focus was very much on South Africa. I took Independence very much for granted. I was not overly excited about Independence movements for the simple reason that it seemed so obvious to me that when people are on top of you, you're going to throw them off. I took it for granted that that had to happen. In some cases, I saw that it was already happening. In Kenya, unfortunately, I saw that this would be a bloody process. In West Africa, I didn't see it as being a bloody process. There were already these various movements including . . . I mean, there were occupational hazards, people like Enahoro were going to jail for alleged sedition against the colonial government. But, for me, this was part of the excitement of de-colonisation, of Independence. So my attention was focused very much on South Africa. I was really obsessed with the Apartheid situation at the time, and of course with Kenya, where the Mau-Mau struggle was just commencing. It took me a while—and I know exactly how it happened—to begin to focus on the kind of philosophy which would replace the colonial relationship with the Africans. It was a single moment at one of the earliest stages of our semi-Independence when the first ministers arrived in England. I remember that a group of us went to meet them wanting to discuss issues. We were all excited that we were going to come home to an independent country, full of creative excitement, we already saw visions of an African paradise showing these bloody colonial people what energy they'd been suppressing. And we came and met these ministers. Within five minutes, I knew that we were in serious trouble. It was clear that they were more concerned with the mechanisms for stepping into the shoes of the departing colonial masters, enjoying the same privileges, inserting themselves in that axial position towards the rest of the community. I saw the most naked and brutal signs of alienation of the ruler from the ruled, from the very first crop. There were one or two exceptions, of course. And then I realised that the enemy within was going to be far more problematic than the external, easily recognisable enemy. And that was when I began to write *A Dance of the Forests*. It was then I began to recollect, to say to myself: well, what's so surprising about that? Why should we expect it to be different? After all, we participated in certain crimes against ourselves, we participated in enslaving our own kind. So, why shouldn't it happen all over again? That's when I began to pay very serious attention to what I saw as a budding dictatorial mentality. These new leaders were alienated, that was the main theme of *A Dance of the Forests.*

BB-T: Three decades on, your misgivings have been confirmed?

WS: Brutally so, brutally so. I wish they weren't, I wish I'd been proved wrong. But, unfortunately, all across the continent they've been confirmed.

BB-T: Let's move to the present: what are your reactions to the cancellation of the 1993 elections in Nigeria?

WS: Well, for me this has been one of the greatest blows to the development of Nigeria as a nation. It has nothing to do with the whole transition programme, which was flawed from the very beginning, including the creation of both the parties by the military. But as I've said in the past, this was something that one could live with as long as the progressive movement within the country could co-ordinate its energies and seize the structure of one of the parties then there might be hope. But of course when the government then proceeded to write the manifestos for both parties, then the whole thing was over. But even so, Nigerians made up their minds that even a mouldy loaf of bread was better than nothing. And that the immediate target, the short term goal for the Nigerian polity, was to get rid of the military. So, everybody mobilised, including those in the political class as well as those who were normally politically comatose, if this was one way of getting rid of the government. Now, eventually, something interesting developed, after all the cancellations, the changes, the banning and unbanning; all the tortuous, contradictory motions of Babangida's regime. Finally, two candidates emerged for the presidential elections. And the results—leaving aside personalities—were such that they created a certain kind of optimism for what has been the goal of Nigerians—at least, thinking and de-tribalised, de-sectionalised Nigerians—just to have a candidate who could command support across the country. And if you examine Abiola's results there's no question at all that he succeeded in doing this. From Kano to Lagos, to Ondo, Kwara, even Bauchi, he gained 44 per cent of the votes cast. And this, for me, was one silver lining in the horrendously dark clouds which had been cast over the nation by Babangida's tricks and wiles and mismanagement of the country and the sinister designs which he seemed to have on the country. And to have those elections cancelled went beyond even the denial of the democratic expression of the people. It went beyond it. The results were halfway announced. . . . But obviously the calculations of the Babangida regime had gone wrong. This regime clearly did not expect Abiola to do so well, so they began to improvise at the expense of the nation. And by expense I mean both monetary expense as well as the psychological and political investment. This single man, with a small cutlery, decided to defy the will of Nigerians. It's a huge set-back for the entire democratic process.

BB-T: In an article which appeared both in the *Guardian* and the *New York Times* you use a proverb to illustrate what you've described as Babangida's bias in these elections. You wrote "Whose cause will the housefly promote if not that of the leg riddled with sores?"

WS: Well, it's this way: the military regime, Babangida's regime, obviously favoured Tofa, and the reason is not far to seek. Tofa was the person who first flew the kite of the Babangida-Must-Stay campaign. He was the one who wrote an article two years ago saying that Babangida should stay until the year 2000. He was totally unknown. Tofa *Who?* That was the question on everybody's lips: Tofa *Who?* I know that this article was not written by Tofa. It was written by the *éminence grise* in the Security Services whom I will not name for the moment but who has been masterminding the entire prolongation programme of the regime. It was written for Tofa by this individual to begin the process of persuading Babangida to stay. The whole thing has been stage-managed from the word go. This regime wanted somebody it could continue to manipulate and Tofa fitted the bill. In addition to that, there were other scenarios waiting to be played. Now it turns out that there are affidavits against Tofa suggesting that he's not fit to be president on moral grounds. So this card was also in the hands of this regime to play. Where the calculation went wrong was the victory of Abiola. And so they had to go to the extent of not merely annulling the elections, but creating new rules to ensure that the two candidates could not compete. Of course, they had to be even-handed; they had to disqualify Tofa also. So what do you do? You cancel the elections and then you create rules which make sure that the finalists cannot re-enter the race, then you proceed to unban those whom you had banned before! This is toying with the nation, this is a diabolical game being played with the destiny of at least 90 million people by the small caucus—fifteen at most— who meet and decide these things. We know most of them. They sit down and cook up this witches' broth with which they poison the entire nation. It's the most callous disregard of law, of equity, of justice, of common-sense, and it's a mark of contempt for a nation which is so full of human and material potential. I've never heard the like of this before. We must search the history books, we must search the whole history of elections and see if any country can come up with something of this nature. It offends any kind of juridical process.

BB-T: What implications do you foresee as a result of the cancellation?

WS: The scenario is not very pleasant. First of all, there will be a successful boycott which will make nonsense of the next electoral process if it does take place. Now what happens then: the only justification for the boycott is that a choice has already been made, and that a fair number of Nigerians recognise one president. So, Babangida goes ahead and holds this other election and some kind of president emerges. So you have a Zairean situation in which there are two prime ministers. But the Nigerian situation is far more serious because we have an electoral process and the people have made their choice. Worse yet, we have a situation where the army has shown obvious signs of disaffection with Babangida's manipulations. So you have a divided army, you have a divided nation, and all because of the—I can't even call it megalomania—of the quirks, of the irrationality of one individual and his tiny junta. It's not a pleasant prospect, I'm afraid, for Nigeria. The only rational and patriotic course is for Babangida, who created this mess, to respect the wishes expressed by the people *under* the rules which he himself set. This is the most painful part of it. This man laid out the rules, people reluctantly accepted these rules, and now he's been defeated by his own rules. And yet he insists that he wants to start all over again. It's too preposterous.

BB-T: There have been rumours that Abiola has been placed under house arrest. Any fears for his safety?

WS: I've been away a week. I've been on the phone and nobody has been able to confirm that. One solution for the other side is just to eliminate him. You eliminate him, part of the problem is solved: there's no more reason to boycott elections, you can't insist on him being president, that's it. So Abiola's security is paramount right now. Ironically, when I was trying to persuade him, I didn't realise that I should be bothering about my own security. It was a few days later that the helicopters came, circled my house, and took off back to Lagos. Their mission was to tell me that they were around, that Big Brother had eyes everywhere.

BB-T: In your article in the *Independent,* you equate these events to a murder; you describe the killing of Nigeria, and you say that "the pall-bearers

are the ethnic manipulators and arms dealers, self-styled latter-day patriots."
One of those to whom you refer is Arthur Nzeribe,[2] who is known to be
incredibly wealthy, albeit through arms-dealing. What has he to gain by con-
triving to have the military in power in perpetuity?

WS: Well, I don't know if you've read Arthur Nzeribe's book.[3] It gives a
very interesting insight into the mind of the man. This is a man who desperately needs to be relevant. He needs to be *knowing,* to be inside the action.
It's a compulsion. If he's not centre-stage politically, he likes it to be known
that he's backstage. He has to have had a hand in every political pie, whether
military or civilian. He exaggerates his role in many things. It's a very revealing book, and of course *this* has given him an opportunity actually to be *seen,*
actually to act out some of the fantasies which are already expressed in that
book. So, there is a kind of schoolboy immaturity in Arthur Nzeribe. It
doesn't matter what role he's playing as long as he's playing it and he's being
seen to play it. He is a psychological study, and this is why he's been able to
team up with our Grey Eminence in the Security. Now, *he,* the nameless one,
he set up the Third Eye Movement, a pro-government thing which now runs
its own newspaper.

BB-T: What's that called?

WS: *The Third Eye.* There's no question at all that the two came together
for a common purpose, and that some of the finance came from the Security
Services. Nzeribe became the culmination of these various moves including,
for instance, the insertion of editorials in the government-owned newspapers,
the *Daily Times* and the *New Nigerian.* All these were either instigated by
this man or even partly written by him. You must have read about the resigna-
tion of Abdulazeez, editor of the *New Nigerian,* which just confirmed what
we'd been saying all along, that many of these editorials came from the
presidency. Either from the Secret Service or, latterly, from the pen of Mr.
Chukwumerijie, *Comrade* Chukwumerijie, the Secretary for Information.
Abdulazeez alleged that Chukwumerijie faxed an editorial from Abuja which
they used in *New Nigerian* which said, in effect, that there is a third party—
which was Nzeribe's, the Party of Twenty-Five Million Signatories—and that
Nigerians have to realise that there is a third party. It's an editorial which, of
course, was calling for the cancellation of the elections. Saying that since
such a large proportion of people boycotted it, blablabla. . . .

---

2. Leader of the Association for a Better Nigeria, which attempted to prevent the 12
June elections through the courts.

3. *Nigeria: Another Hope Betrayed.*

BB-T: Did some people boycott the elections?

WS: No, it's a lie, it's a lie. When they say some people did not hear about the announcement that the elections would take place eventually, the question in my mind is, how did they hear about the original court injunction? If communication was so bad, if the people in the rural areas couldn't hear Nwosu[4] say that they should go and vote, how come they heard about the court injunction? These people are liars, they don't even deserve to be taken seriously. That's the whole story of the Babangida-Must-Stay story. It's complete orchestration from the Security Service.

BB-T: Chinua Achebe wrote last year in an article in the *Guardian,* "I found it difficult to forgive Nigeria and my countrymen and women for the nonchalance and cruelty that unleashed upon us these terrible events which set us back a whole generation and robbed us of the chance to be a medium rank developed nation in the 20th century." Do you share these sentiments? Is it not true that "those terrible events" were possibly partly because of what you yourself have described as the abdication of the role of *thinker* by intellectuals, by the intelligentsia?

WS: We have missed many chances. You know my position about the Civil War, of course. I believe that the war should never have been fought. And I blame, equally, both the so-called Nigerian side and the so-called Biafran side. And when we say blame, we are talking about the leadership at crucial moments. But we are also talking about leadership even during non-crucial moments. During the period of possible recovery, for instance, Gowon wasted many years of development. Then we, the populace, wasted chances by failing to choose the right leadership when we had the chance. Shagari[5] was a disaster. Not even those who praise his character, his personality, tolerance, whatever that means . . . not even his greatest admirers would deny that he was a disaster for the nation in terms of policy decisions implementation. His reign was a zero, a minus.

BB-T: But Shagari was allegedly "installed" by Obasanjo.

WS: Well, I was in the thick of the '83 election. I was not so much in the thick of the '79 elections, although I was involved in some serious monitoring. In fact, I was a polling agent for Bola Ige in one or two places, and I was certainly at the nerve centre of some of the monitoring of that. I remember

---

4. Henry Nwosu, Chairman, National Electoral Commission.
5. Alhaji Shehu Shagari, President, 1979–83.

phoning Bisi Onabanjo[6] and reporting certain events which were taking place in Kaduna with the connivance of the military. I for one do not accept Obasanjo's denial of having had a hand in the installation of Shagari. And of course the whole business of the two-third formula, the appointment of a Chief Justice just before the elections, the revelations about Shagari, even before he became president, of being involved in the choice of this Chief Justice who was later to adjudicate when Shagari's presidency was contested in court. . . . These allegations have to be answered very concretely before I can accept the professed innocence of Obasanjo about handing over the country to Shagari. Quite apart from the electoral malpractices, *serious* electoral malpractices which were actually carried out by soldiers who were taking orders from Lagos.

We the intellectuals, the creative people, what is our own culpability in all of this? Well, depending on what mood I'm in, I've been inclined sometimes to excoriate the entire tribe of intellectuals. But when I look, comparatively, at what really our capability has been, what capacity we *have* in the profession we've chosen in that aspect of our relationship to the rest of society, we're not really a potent lot. We're basically an impotent lot. All we can do is intervene with ideas, and I know that those who've been governing us have never really been short of ideas proffered to them by very serious and dedicated intellectuals. At the same time, of course, there have been the intellectuals of the Establishment, whether in the economic field or in the political field, but ultimately the responsibility is leadership. Those who either seize leadership or have leadership conferred on them. They make the choice. They make the choice between the different sets of intellectuals. And they must live with it, they must bear the ultimate responsibility. The intellectuals are *not* in power. So, I would like to limit our level of culpability to the fact that we are divided; that we have too many sycophants among us.

BB-T: Now, to this question of being Nigerian. Is the statement "I am a Nigerian" not, at best, an acknowledgement of the fact that I have to carry a passport which bears that description, and, at worst, an abstract and absolutely meaningless statement? Would it not be more honest to say, I am Hausa, or I'm Ibibio, or I'm Yoruba . . . isn't there a very strong argument for a confederacy within this geopolitical entity known as Nigeria?

WS: It's a very troubling question. During the Civil War, I'm on record as

---

6. Bisi Onabanjo, State Governor during the last civilian government.

having said that I'd rather Biafra broke away and created its own entity than have Nigeria stay together at the price that it must pay—especially the future consequences of that price, because that kind of price, you don't pay it once and for all. The ramifications carry on for quite a long time. I described the secession of Biafra as being *morally justified but politically erroneous.* I used that very expression. I distinguished between them because I felt that a moral situation had been created which justified any decision of Biafra to seek to be a separate entity. But I felt that it was a political error because of the circumstances of the world, and the circumstances of Nigeria within the African situation. There was also a political error in the fact that when Biafra seceded it failed to recognise the rights of its own minorities to choose where they wanted to be. Whether to be on their own or to be with Nigeria. I've given that background to underscore the fact that I understand that feeling, that question which all but political demagogues must be able to tackle honestly.

Do I want Nigeria to remain one? Do I prefer it to remain a Nigeria as presently defined, or do I prefer something else? I'm going to leave that aside, for now. I'm talking about a kind of demagogic position which says there's an entity called Nigeria and that entity is sacrosanct. I find that a most ridiculous statement. When did Nigeria as a nation come into being? And how did it come into being? Nigeria was an artificial creation, and it was a creation which did not take into consideration either the wishes or the will *or* the interests of the people who were enclosed within that boundary. They were lumped together. So, the genesis of Nigeria, as with many African countries, is very flawed, to start with. In fact, I remember that when the OAU adopted as one of its canons the notion of the sacrosanctity of the colonially inherited territorial boundaries, I said, "Oh my God." My statement then was that I would have thought that the sensible thing would be for the OAU to sit down with square rule and compass and *re-draw* the boundaries.

BB-T: Do you think that is feasible?

WS: No, no, no, it's no longer feasible. But at that time, before independent economic units *congealed* and became difficult to break, it was—for me—not only politically right but economically and psychologically viable to re-define our destiny. We want, in effect, to be re-born along the decisions of our political will. It would have been an act of enormous political strength and determination. If the Europeans can come and do that for us, why could we not have seized our chance to do it for ourselves? So, in principle, I recognise and accept the kind of statement which says just what is Nigeria, anyway? I don't understand it, I know that I am a Yoruba, I know that I am a Hausa, I know I am an Efik . . . I understand that statement. On the other hand, unrolling of historical events, the sharing of certain experiences, political fortunes, economic arrangements, cultural relations, cultural interaction, can itself create a feeling of oneness within even the most artificial of boundaries, and so over a few generations it is possible, I think, for one to begin to feel proud of the cultural riches of Kaduna or Maiduguri even though one is from Aba or Ife.

BB-T: I was born in the north, in Kafanchan, and raised in Kaduna, Bauchi, Jos, Kano . . . all over the north, for the first eighteen years of my life. My parents are Yoruba, and when I went to my father's home town for the first time I was a teenager. I felt like a total stranger and spoke with an accent. Hausa was, basically, my first language. As far as I was concerned (and this applied to my sisters and brothers as well), I was born in the north. I'm Hausa. And then I finished secondary school, got very good results and tried to get a place at Bayero University, Kano. I was turned down, I later found out, because of my name. That, for me, was a revelation. I was being told; go back to where your parents are from. Not in so many words, but. . . .

WS: I'm very glad you mentioned that experience because such experiences, which affect hundreds of thousands of Nigerians in a very visceral way, militate against that sense of oneness which one is talking about. Let me support that with an incident which I know very well. I once attacked publicly the former Minister of Education, Jubril Aminu, who one day, when he was Minister of Education, just repatriated all southern principals from northern schools. One of them was my landlady. She was in the north somewhere, and she'd been there for years, she'd made friends, she was very much at home. In fact, she used to joke that she was so close to the local chief that they used to call her his girlfriend. That's how integrated she was. Now, how do you expect people to respond to that? They've been told, "You're not part of this section of the country," which means Nigeria is being *differently* defined from what they had always believed.

BB-T: A few years ago, a prominent Nigerian politician, Sam Mbakwe, called for the return of the British. Earlier this year, an American academic writing in the *New York Times*—I believe—also made a strong argument for a return to the days of Empire. "Let's face it," he wrote, "some countries are just not fit to govern themselves."

WS: My answer to that is that what Europe is discovering these days is that they too have never been fit to govern themselves. And they only survived because they had ruthless tyrants. In other words, all these years, all these decades, these countries have never really governed themselves. They've succeeded in staying together and progressing in one way or the other—and even that progress is questionable these days—only because they were being governed by an alien, what I call Alienated Power: Ceauşescu, Hoxha of Albania, Stalin and his successors in the Soviet Union. In other words, these people have never governed themselves. And the moment they had the chance to govern themselves, see what's been happening. This relates also of course to the sense of nationality. It throws into question the whole sense of homogeneity—

BB-T: I was going to ask also what you think we have to learn, if there is anything to learn, from what's happened in former Yugoslavia.

WS: It's back to my old position—what is happening in former Yugoslavia is, for me, too heavy a price to pay for the abstract concept of national unity. And, Nigeria should learn that some sacred notions, when confronted by not-so-sacred reality, should be re-examined. If the cost to Nigeria is the price being paid by Yugoslavia or Somalia, then I think we had all better sit round the table and re-examine that concept. It's not just Yugoslavia—we tend to forget scenarios like the brutal civil war which has been going on in Sudan for over twenty years. Now, I think that statement, the statement of a twenty-year-old civil war, is clear and unambiguous. I am most impressed by John Garang's group who, at the last meeting, said, "Look, we're not asking for the dismemberment of Sudan; we're not saying that we want to secede; we are just saying that we do not want to be governed by the Sharia Laws, and that if that obstacle is removed, we're quite willing to be integrated in a particular relationship with the rest of the country." To me, that's a very generous statement, because the *statement* of a twenty-year-old civil war is so unambiguous: it says we don't belong together. That's all.

BB-T: Do you think that a confederacy would be a solution?

WS: I think that would be a solution for Sudan.

BB-T: And for Nigeria?

WS: Well, if the worst-case scenario—which is very possible in the present Nigerian circumstances—starts to unfold, I certainly would not be averse to a confederacy. It's, for me, not the ideal, but if that worst-case scenario is what may result from this situation in which we have a divided army that is allied with those atavistic, tribalistic forces which will not accept leadership except *from* their own section, then I don't see why the innocent people in Nigeria should pay the penalty for the short-sightedness of a small group of people. And we know that the blunder of one individual in this kind of situation can mean tragedy for hundreds of thousands of people.

BB-T: Some commentators have said—and maybe it's a simplistic theory—that if Nigeria's relatively sizeable number of very wealthy people were to come together and invest in Nigeria as they would in a business enterprise, that not only would Nigeria be able to pay off its foreign debts but it might also become a viable entity.

WS: I'm not in possession of facts and figures but I'm inclined to accept that statement. This may be one of the losses which Nigeria will sustain by not having somebody like Abiola at the helm of affairs. Abiola is a very capable businessman. Some people say he acquired his wealth crookedly and that he is in league with multinational corporations and so on and so forth, but all I can say is give me a competent crook rather than an incompetent, inept angel. Especially when you are dealing with a vast and complex country like Nigeria, which has enormous resources, for heaven's sake. It hurts, each time I travel out, to see how much these people here have succeeded where we have failed. If we didn't have the resources it wouldn't hurt, but we *know* these resources are there, and we know that we can transform that country within ten years. And by transform I mean physically transform so people will not know it, in terms of health services, infrastructure, public services like functioning telephones.

BB-T: That brings us to the question of corruption.

WS: Yes, I was going to come to that. There's a philosophy of cannibalism in Nigeria at the moment, a ruthlessness towards each other. Market people—the moment there's a whisper there's going to be an increase in petrol price, even *before* it becomes a reality, they are already increasing the price of food. Even before the rumour is established! We are speaking here—the expression moral rearmament is so ugly because of its connotations with the past—but something is certainly required, call it ethical rearmament, call it human rearmament, we certainly need some kind of rearmament. And it can only begin with an improvement in the quality of life of people, with an evident commencement of transformation of the physical environment, and of course a reduction of corruption. Corruption has become even an *exhibitionist* fact.

There is a level of exhibitionism in corruption which is unprecedented in Nigeria. Not even under Shagari—a totally corrupt government—has the level of corruption reached such heights. Not even in Shagari's era.

BB-T: Where does Africa stand in what has been called the New World Order?

WS: There will be no New World Order until the United Nations has been democratised. I believe very much that it's about time that the system is overhauled. The idea of giving some countries a permanent veto should go out with the New World Order. If the permanent veto is removed, it means that rationality can enter even the process of lobbying. In other words, issues will come more to the fore. Hopefully, the righteousness or the unrighteousness of issues will come more to the fore. Then the kind of muscle which is at present being displayed by permanent membership of the Security Council will not have a place. A New World Order should also include a New Economic World Order. And this is where the issue of reparations becomes relevant. My position here tends to be rather ambiguous: I don't believe in aggressive beggary; I believe very passionately in the principle of paying one's debts. I just believe that the debts need to be examined very, very closely. If you are aiding a country to the tune of one million dollars, and three quarters of that million dollars goes towards servicing your own staff under the term "expertise," then the word "debt" should have a new definition. While I find the issue of reparations rather problematic, there is a ring to it which ties up with a New World Order. When you create a New World Order, you're acknowledging certain impurities, certain flaws in the past relationship and you're saying, having acknowledged that, let us build a new relationship. If, for instance, we say the Old World Order was so tainted, we want to obliterate it and then we say we'll forget the past, *we* will annul the past, and *you* annul our so-called debts, and we'll call this the century of annulment and we move into the twenty-first century on a New World Order—which is not burdened by a deleterious economic past. We give ourselves, globally, a new chance. I believe in that kind of approach to a New World Order, not one that is dictated by the police actions of one superpower called the United States or China or whatever. It must also include a revitalisation of the de-colonisation process, because colonialism is not dead. You have even so-called Third World countries like Indonesia colonising in East Timor and getting away with it. Brutalising the people there, committing massacres. . . . When the United Nations is reformed that way, and there are no more double standards, then it will be possible to tackle issues like that and in effect even give ultimatums saying, look, if you want to participate in this New World Order which gives you an equal voice in the concert of nations, there are certain universal principles, such as a surrender of colonial possessions, which you must embrace and which you must execute, so it's not just the big powers alone I'm talking about. I'm talking about various pockets of re-colonisations, inhumanity. The incontestible universal areas— and there are many—of human rights have got to be acceded to. We cannot have this theory of relativity which some countries were trying to push at the last Vienna conference. You don't run tanks over sleeping students and come and tell me that human rights are relative. It's just impossible. And the same way Third World countries don't say, unless you help us we cannot develop, we cannot guarantee human rights. It's an obscene language. That's what I call the language of aggressive beggars.

BB-T: The term "ethnic cleansing" is one of this decade's contributions to language. Unfortunate as it is, it has been adopted sometimes unquestioningly even by liberal western press. There's all over Europe a resurgence of Fascism and Nazism. What are the implications for us all who are invariably the targets of these philosophies of hate?

WS: I pity the European press their embarrassment. They find it difficult to accept that what happened in Nazi Germany is what is happening right now in certain parts of the world. Like Yugoslavia, for instance, and the former Soviet Union. And left to Saddam, I think he would have done some heavy "ethnic cleansing" in northern Iraq by now. The whole world is a real mess, so many examples of "ethnic cleansing" going on. It's a lesson for Europe and a lesson for us that these monsters are constantly with us and somehow have got to be exorcised. Both by state policies and by moral resolve among peoples. The resurgence of neo-Nazism does not surprise me in the slightest. It's always been lurking there. It exists in this country [U.K.], there are people in this country, even so-called intellectuals who would collaborate if there were to be some kind of fascist overturn in the government. Germany is the most naked, of course. Now Greece and Albania are at each other's throats, they're both performing their own form of "ethnic cleansing." And, let me use this chance to recall also that even in Nigeria, we have to a certain extent been guilty of a version of "cleansing." I refer to the Maroko episode, where three-quarters of a million people in Lagos were suddenly turned into non-people. Their dwellings, their entire habitation where they've lived for generations, were suddenly bulldozed in one fell swoop. I call that "class sanitation." It's another version of ethnic cleansing. It's a crime against humanity. These various forms of de-humanisation are anomalies which have to be corrected before we can talk of any kind of New World Order.

BB-T: Finally: who killed Dele Giwa?[7]

WS: Who killed Dele Giwa? I'll tell you how Who Killed Dele Giwa will be exposed. It would be by the convening of the international jury which I've been working on. I've been taking advantage of my international contacts to try to set this up. In fact, we should have done it early this year but we had some problems. We have gathered the facts together. We will not say who killed Dele Giwa. We will leave the jury to decide whether the evidence we produce points definitely and unambiguously in one direction. If it fails, people will be able to decide whether or not the obvious suspects are guilty. It's no use naming anybody right now. Certain witnesses have fled the country. We know where they are, we know where some are, and they say they will come and give evidence when it's time. We intend to hold it in Nigeria; my present goal is on this year's anniversary of Dele Giwa's assassination. And the guilty parties know very well that all these enquiries have been taking place and are doing all they can to destroy evidence, but it's not going to help them. I resolved, when Dele Giwa was killed, that I would devote quite a large part of my time and resources to unearthing that crime, and it is my belief that we have done so.

---

7. Editor of *Newswatch* magazine, murdered by a parcel bomb delivered at his house in October, 1986.

Soyinka Tells His Exile Story

Bayo Onanuga and Others / 1998

From *The News,* a Lagos, Nigeria news weekly.

In 1994, when the late head of state, General Sani Abacha, had become irretrievably murderous, Professor Wole Soyinka was the first person to publicly give a correct diagnosis of the military ruler's ailment. The dictator, according to Soyinka, was a psychopath who suffered from inferiority complex. It was a stinging criticism that Abacha never forgot, and never forgave.

By early November of that year, the process to eliminate Soyinka was already finalised. The disgraced security adviser to Abacha, Alhaji Ismaila Gwarzo, set his security operatives at work: the Abeokuta office of Africa's first Nobel Laureate in Literature, was put under surveillance.

It was not a laughing matter, even though Soyinka, in a satirical piece he wrote for this magazine, made a joke out of the surveillance of his residence by a helicopter. He warned that if those responsible for the harassment did not stop, he could cause the helicopter to crash-land. When Soyinka wrote that piece, his international passport had been seized, his United Nations' travel documents, confiscated. He had actually been asked to report at 15 Awolowo Road, Ikoyi, Lagos, the headquarters of the State Security Service, where he would have been detained.

But unknown to those who were in his hot pursuit, Soyinka had been adequately informed of their plans. Although he gave them the impression that he would report as ordered, his arrangement to escape through the borders was in top form. Aso Rock only knew he was out of Nigeria when he gave the British Broadcasting Corporation (BBC) an interview in London! That marvellous exit rattled Abacha and his evil men. The psychopathic general was to regret that escape throughout his reign of terror.

Prof. Wole Soyinka, who believes that justice is the first condition of humanity, mounted a global campaign against the regime of Sani Abacha. He was everywhere that mattered. And the world listened to him as he became the most outspoken critic of the Abacha tyranny. In the heat of that campaign, his home in Abeokuta was vandalised. What were the dogs of war looking for? The transmitters of Radio Freedom, which was to become Radio Kudirat, named after the activist wife of Basorun M. K. O. Abiola who was murdered in Lagos by armed men suspected to be the agents of General Sani Abacha. The radio is still ruling the airwaves. And Soyinka has promised it won't die. He once told Chief Gani Fawehinmi that he would return home whenever he finished his assignment. What assignment? To provide an enabling environment for democracy in his homeland. This task has not been accomplished, but Soyinka thinks there are prospects for democracy now. He is quick to add though that vigilance must be our watchword. The battle has not been easy, but the fighter is not tired.

Last week, Soyinka staged a triumphal return to Nigeria, after four years in exile. The crowd that received him was unprecedented. The welcome party itself became a cultural event befitting no doubt the persona of this African literary giant and its first Nobel Laureate in English literature. Less than fifteen hours after he touched down, Soyinka consented to a two-hour marathon interview with *The News* team of Bayo Onanuga, Kunle Ajibade, Odia Ofeimun, and Osita Nwajah, on his experience in exile, his third since Biafra.

Q: When you arrived at the airport, there were two receptions waiting for you. One was by an overwhelming enthusiastic crowd. The other one was inside, by the security men. Would you please tell us what they were like?

A: No, no, no, there was no reception by the security people, at all. The plane arrived early and I was taken to the VIP room. And it wasn't just by the security people, but by a security group of our own organisation. They organised where they could pick me right from the plane. It was together that we went to the VIP room. It was there I was told that Pa Adesanya and the others would be coming and since the plane had arrived early, I thought we should wait for them. So that's what led to the long wait. Then one gentleman came around to tell me that they were trying to position the vehicle.

Eventually, some people came in and you could read panic on their faces. They said "Prof., we don't know what to do with the crowd out there," which was becoming quite uncontrollable. And that the crowd felt I was being held against my will and somebody out there was in fact threatening fire and brimstone if I didn't show up. So, I said let's go out and that's when we got out together. With Bola Ige and the others.

Q: So the issue of your passport didn't crop up?

A: The issue of my passport cropped up. Somebody came, somebody acting in a very routine way. You know I was with my son; the officer came to ask for the luggage tag and also ask for the passports. So, he took my son's passport then he turned to me and I just did that (makes a gesture of well, search me) and immediately, he fled. I think when I did that, he remembered that my passport was somewhere in their own custody. So, it was only when I was leaving that I turned around to all the security people with their long Kaftans and I said, "which of you, has my passport?" And they all collapsed, laughing, and the tension was broken.

Q: Is there any arrangement underway to return the passport?

A: I fully expect to have the passport back before I leave here. It didn't mean I didn't have a passport when I arrived; I had passports from friendly countries and of course, my UN passport was in place. But there was no intention, absolutely no intention of my entering this country with anything but my Nigerian passport. And, when I leave here, I expect to leave with my Nigerian passport. Otherwise, I will leave the same way as I left the last time.

Q: How did you find the reception outside?

A: Overwhelming. In fact, I became frightened for the crowd. The pressure was on, so I had to calm everybody down. I am very glad I came at night. I shudder to think of what would have happened if it had been a holiday or a weekend.

Q: 1994 was not the first time you went in exile. Can you compare the last experience with the others?

A: The first exile after my imprisonment under Gowon was an exile of despair. The Nigerian civil war had just ended, but I said the war had not ended. I wrote, before we all plunged into that war, that it was a war which will not end. The Biafrans will never give up. People did not understand. War ended on the field of battle but we all know that the Biafran war is still being fought till today. When I got back to the university, I found myself in despair at the complacency, the smugness of my environment. It was like, "Oh, yes, we've kept the nation one" you know, that stupid slogan, "to keep the nation one is a task that must be done." To keep the nation one in what aspect ideologically, economically, in terms of the inter-relationship of the parts, in terms of the structure of the parts? What is keeping the nation one? And the jingle was at such a level that it used to hammer through my brain. And I knew that we were in serious trouble.

So, I needed to get away from that atmosphere. It was like something which you are convinced that you know, but with others around, after a while, you begin to feel as if you are a mad man. So, I decided, for my own sanity, that I needed a break from Nigeria. I went to France, I remember. That's where I went to purge myself of my prison experience by writing *The Man Died*. I remember taking an isolated spot—it was a farm lent to me by a writer's critic, right in the heart of a very barren place. I had total isolation. In fact, my companions were some giant rats who ate my soap. Because there was nothing to eat, they ate my soap. And then having written *The Man Died*, I felt I had exorcised something from deep within. Then, I could face the world again.

However, that period of exile lengthened after the publication of *The Man Died*, a very popular book with some parts of the government. Of course, you know, I came back after some time. I'd moved from Paris to Cambridge and then I left there and went to edit the magazine *Transition* in Accra, Ghana and teach at the same time at Legon University. After the coup (against Gen. Gowon) I studied (General) Murtala Mohammed's programme and felt that under that particular regime, I could come back. I didn't ask anybody to negotiate anything, unlike many people thought, that there were discussions between me and the regime.

The second round was involuntary. At that time, there was a price on my head not advertised but the Inspector-General of Police and his cohorts in the NPN (National Party of Nigeria) had put a price on my head. How did we know it? Some of the police themselves came and told us. And it was life or death. So, we kept moving from place to place. One day, I got a message from Bola Ige that he wanted to see me urgently. So I went there. When I got there, he was addressing a crowd. So, I had to wait on the periphery and this policeman comes over to tell me, "We've been looking for you. You must leave the country immediately." He gave the information which we knew already, and said that sooner or later, someone was going to do it. He said, "Don't even go home. Just let's take you straight to the airport." The very people, some of those among the hit squad, were the ones who actually bundled me to the airport and virtually bundled me into a plane, because they were determined I should leave. They said, "If we don't do this, now, others will do it (the hit job)."

Q: That was in 1983?

A: Yes, it was 1983 under President Shehu Shagari and Inspector-General Sunday Adewusi's regime. And I had to keep moving London, Germany, Paris, etc., etc. and I've met, incidentally, members of the military who put an end to that squad.

Q: What was your offence at that time?

A: Oh, simply because I was denouncing the rigging of the election. I was very active in trying to get the people to reject the Shagari regime. I preached popular insurrection against that regime, that results of the election should never be accepted, otherwise we would be enslaved by this bunch of murderers. And that's what they were. Anyway, that round was a very reluctant one, very reluctant. I didn't go willingly. You remember at that time, we were recording *Blues for a Prodigal* and we couldn't even shoot at the right locations. We kept on shifting each time; we couldn't do it as it ought to be done.

This one now, again, was a reluctant one. I had been receiving warnings. In fact, he (indicating Kunle Ajibade) used to come to my office and sit down there, looking at me and then he would ask me, "When are they coming for you? Prof, why, why haven't they picked you up yet?" And I would ask him, "Kunle, what happened to my article, you said it would appear on such and such a date?" And he would say, "My editor, he decided that, 'this one, is too much,' if we publish this one, you're gone." So, I decided I'd leave.

In fact, it happened fast. You remember, the launching of my book was prevented, first time, second time, and then when the association of journalists in the Ogun State Chapel wanted me to have a little chat with myself— this is the kind of interesting story that you want, anyway more of that in another place—the police called the journalists and told them, this thing will not take place. I was being turned into a no-person.

And finally, the very hard news, that I was to be given the Su Kyi (Burmese opposition leader and Nobel Prize winner) treatment. They would begin with that, put me under house arrest and then from there, make me disappear while they pretended I was under house arrest, and (they would) take me somewhere else. We had the details of how this thing was planned. And so, I decided it was time to move, to go and establish the outposts of the resistance and let the world know exactly what was happening to our people. I didn't leave by plane this time (laughs). It was one of my best journeys, though.

And the difference this time, of course, is that I was kept very busy. I never really felt like I was in exile. Virtually, twenty-four hours everyday, fighting for the cause. Seeking support for those inside, setting up Radio Kudirat, linking up with some of our people, arranging meetings with the external opposition and the internal. It was a very busy, really, really intense period. So, I had no time to feel I was in exile, no time to resent being in exile.

Q: After you left, some embassies and some of your friends were accused of having helped you to escape and were given some kind of rough handling. How guilty were they?

A: Not at all, not at all. All I can tell you is that after I arrived in a neighbouring country, I went to an embassy where I knew that the country was friendly, and they gave me travelling papers. I can assure you that no embassy had a hand in my departure. I can say it boldly. What might be true was that I told a couple of embassies that I might be obliged to leave the country. But they were the last to be notified when I phoned them from the other side to let them know I had already done it. I did my best as in such matters to involve as few as possible who had any kind of profile. Those who assisted were people from within the heart of our organisation who were not known. And the lies which were told to get people in trouble were pure concoctions of those who had scores to settle. It was a very vicious campaign. The report they sent to Abacha, we learnt, was concocted for no other reason than to settle scores with Dr. Olu Agunloye, who was Director of the Federal Road Safety Commission (FRSC).

The person who did it was of course that thief, Major Salawu. He was the one who sent a totally false report. He went so far as to forge—I want Nigerians to know how far he could go in concocting incriminating "evidence." He went so far as to forge a note which I sent Dr. Agunloye, at the beginning of the creation of the FRSC, seven years before. Agunloye was to meet me with a vehicle, at the airport, here, in Nigeria. He painted out the date and made it seem that that note was newly written and that Agunloye was to send three cars—he changed words—it was such a crude forgery that only an imbecile or someone just waiting for an excuse to act in a very vicious manner could believe it. And Agunloye was up for the jump. I think it was Diya who went to Abacha, when he heard about the thing, to tell him that the whole thing was a forgery.

In addition to removing Agunloye from the office, they were prosecuting him on many levels. They really wanted to frame him. I understand that what Abacha said was, Kai! Hmnn, it's a good thing we didn't go any further. The involvement of Dr. Agunloye was that I went and grabbed one of his vehicles, which we did all the time. If I was going hunting and he had a spare jeep, I just go and pick it and drive to the bush. Which was not a crime. They wanted to destroy that man's life, simply because of his hatred the criminal, Major Salawu, had for him. Maybe I'd like to know what happened to Major Salawu, who was due to be sentenced for about 30-something charges of conspiracy, stealing and so on and so forth (when he was initially employed, at the inception of the FRSC). Suddenly, we didn't hear anything about the case, and that criminal was brought back to serve in the FRSC from which he had been thrown out. So that was the kind of regime . . .

Q: Did you use a Federal Road Safety Commission jeep to cross the border?

A: No, this was a personal vehicle. In any case, I didn't cross the border in the vehicle, I assure you. I just used it to travel up to a point and then sent the driver back. That's all.

Q: How did you get out?

A: Aaah! I'll tell the story some other time. That's a saga in itself, which I will narrate at the appropriate time.

Q: While in exile, how close were you to danger from Abacha's goons?

A: Ooh, that became quite serious. There were intelligence reports which were written by various countries. There was an incident in Italy once, when I was given very tall police escorts. In the United States also, there were a couple of incidents which were very definitely related to Abacha's hit men. I know that there were three people, suspected to be Abacha's hit men, sent back at the airport. There was a kind of North Korean link, somewhere, from the reports they had.

And we had information about Major Mustapha's killer squad. Our network had exposed its existence. We knew where they were being camped in Abuja. I gave the name of Mustapha in the reports we made available to the U.S. state department. I told them, "this is where to look for those who would be coming after us." That was at least two and half years ago. The FBI came to see me when I was in Harvard; at Emory University, my Vice Chancellor became personally concerned. The university police were put on alert anytime I had a public event. They always saw me to the airport and were there for me anytime I was coming in.

Q: What really happened in Italy?

A: Well, they picked some kind of information. The result was that I was put under police escort. You know, I'm not cut out for that kind of thing. I will wake up in the morning and find six security people outside the door (laughs). So, I had to go out in Italy under some kinds of disguise.

Q: You did that quite often in the last four years?

A: Aaah, yes, quite a lot. Most of the time, I found a way of getting around any encumbrance.

Q: How did you look?

A: Aaah! You want me to start revealing to you, some of my. . . . No, no, no (general laughter).

Q: There was this report, sometime, that some people tried to break into your hotel room?

A: Yes, that did happen. It did happen. I was in the hotel, but I went out. When I came back, I was told that three men had come to look for me. Now, nobody but one or two people knew I was there. I didn't expect anybody. I was staying there under an assumed name. Fortunately, the bar where they were asked to wait for me did not open into the lobby.

Q: Which hotel was this?

A: It is in Washington, D.C. So, since I wasn't expecting anyone, I didn't go to see them. When I got to my room, I found that it had been broken into. So without any further ado, I packed my bag and sneaked out of the hotel. Then I called the bar to go and look for those men in the bar and find out who they were. I think that is where the fracas came, because when the gunmen saw the challenge, moving towards them, they fled and the hotel management called the hotel security.

Q: While you are talking about the dangers you faced under Gen. Abacha, tell us, did he not also try to make peace with you?

A: Yes, yes, he sent two emissaries, one through our foreign office, through an official there. The other was through a retired military officer, who is a friend of mine. He sent them to tell me each time, that I should pick representatives and he would send his people to meet us anywhere, anywhere in the world. And I said, "It's very simple, I'm willing to talk to the devil as long as I receive some token of sincerity and the only token which I require is the immediate release of all hostages. That's all. Release all the illegal prisoners and so on and so forth, then, I know that you really want to discuss ways and means of terminating this murderous crisis." In fact, the fellow who came from the foreign ministry—we talked quite a while, we met more than once—said, "Prof, look, why don't you meet with them and say when you get there, they meet your first condition. The important thing is to start." I said "Look, you don't know this character. He's not serious, he's a jiver and he's just trying to persuade the international community that he's made overtures." In fact, one of the West African heads of states was involved in this initiative. He just wants to lie, that "look-o, I've made these efforts and they're not responding."

So, I said try this experiment. Go back to him and say that we will meet him with no preconditions. But when we get there, we will set out the agenda. And first on the agenda: the release of all prisoners. So, I said, "go and tell him." Of course, (laughs), there was nothing at all.

The other line, this individual eventually became his extraordinary ambassador. It is he who called me one day and said, "I told him not to waste my time anymore. The man is not serious. He's planning his self-perpetuation and I've told him to forget it, I've told him I'm not carrying his messages anymore."

Q: Could that be Maj.-Gen. Joe Garba?

A: No, I'm not going to tell you who he is. No, I've no objection . . . I've not seen him. If he says I can mention his name, I will tell you.

Q: There are structures set up by the exiles, so why did you not ally with a body like NADECO?

A: Well, to say we didn't ally with NADECO is not totally correct. We were all working towards the same goal, but you have to understand that we were all coming from different directions. You know my temperament and it's not one which works very well, very handily, with certain sets of mind. So, it is better to interact with people like that on specific projects than be within that single organisation. And it was very effective. The important thing is to get the results. You know, the structure for me is secondary. At the beginning, there were suspicions I don't want to go into that now, so we lost a lot of time owing to suspicion. Me, I was always happy if someone else did what he was supposed to do. It frees my hands to do other things. But some of them, with the kind of minds they have, they were brought into the picture of what you were doing but you didn't come fully in with them, they felt you know, you were . . . I don't understand. It's a very strange thing. The result was that we left certain areas uncovered. My attitude was always, "look, if you want to cover that, please go ahead, the more the merrier."

So, at the beginning, there were problems, quite frankly. But after a while, they discovered that we could work together, we can divide up the labour, divide up in zones of operation, go on the offensive in different ways. So we ended up working very harmoniously together. But at the beginning, it was very difficult.

Q: What do you consider the greatest problem of the campaigns by Nigerians against dictatorship from outside Nigeria?

A: The greatest problem . . . there are two. Let me speak of the external one. The first word in the dictionary of the outside world is business. They want to get back as fast as possible. Human beings don't matter. There are exceptions of course, thank goodness, but for the majority, it's business. "How soon we can get back into business?" Governments are mostly controlled by business lobby. "We're not there, the other people are there, living off all the profit and we are standing on ideals."

So, governments start making excuses for quick accommodation. They exaggerate small, contemptible gestures of accommodation by repressive governments. They blow it up—"Ah good! See, we said we could trust him, see, he's just done this." And I ask myself, "Oh my God, what kind of humanity really controls the destinies of people?"

And then, when I'm about to despair, you know, when I'm about to give up, and I did give up on many countries: "You people, go ahead and keep talking to those ones, me, no more, but maybe something will come out eventually." But, when I tended to judge them harshly, I would look at some of our own people inside. If you remember some of my broadcasts on Radio Kudirat, I was addressing those compromisers. I used to run into some of them at the airport. They come "Prof, we understand what you're doing. But you know, actually, it's not as bad as you think. If you see the roads, they're being tarred, they're being mended. And he's dealing with the failed banks too you know." I felt . . . I felt like slapping . . . I mean, I wanted to be violent. I felt more violence against such people than I should have against Abacha. "You're talking to me about roads being mended, when your brothers and sisters are rotting in jail, when people are being killed in the streets, you're telling me that the electricity has been restored in your village?" You know, these are supposed to be intelligent people. Now, how can one then blame external governments when your own people are exuding that kind of slave language, being grateful to have been whipped on the back of the hand rather than on their genitals. It's very, very interesting. So, each time I felt this government has betrayed us, these ones have backed down, and I look again at our own people.

But, of course, there were those of them who were very solid, throughout, some in the Scandinavian countries, Caribbean countries, New Zealand; we had those who refused to be bamboozled or compromised.

So, that's one of the problems. Then, on the inside, of course, the usual, internal problem of organisation. You know, for instance, we began with NALICON, then we tried to bring others in groups like the UDFN. They nearly destroyed us. NALICON was a very tight organisation, but when we tried to expand in order to maximise all our efforts all over the world, we took on board very, very dangerous elements. We discovered there were two youths who were direct agents of Sani Abacha. We found one of them was an agent and had recruited another. And their conspiracy was to take the organisation to the level which we would not expect.

Later, we found that one of them had even written a script for Abacha, how to turn himself into a Pinochet. I have it and I will show it to you. This is a student.

One of them, his name was a Christian name and a Yoruba name. And he changed his name later on . . . I prefer to ignore them completely. But if they surface and become a threat to any other organisation, then, of course, they'd be named. In fact, I'd give you their names in spite of it, but I don't want them named yet.

One of them, in fact, wrote and tried to give an account that I recruited him to head the military wing of NALICON. This student, he said he was my Chief of Staff in NALICON (laughs). My "Chief of Staff" is the very boy who wrote a script, you know, a proposal, the way and what have you for Abacha to use his machinery to turn himself into a terrorist. They recruited a woman. She didn't know the game. Her only motivation was greed. This girl robbed us of close to $8,000. And she went along with those two who had tried to take over the organisation. Till today, she has not accounted for the money. Because she had already misappropriated our funds, she had nowhere to go, except to join that gang. That way she felt she'd never have to account to NALICON. I feel very sorry for her (laughs). NALICON is going to extract that money from her even if it's the last thing we will do. But we've been too busy with other things. So she think she's got away. She's the daughter of a former classmate of mine, this girl. She's going around to form a new organisation. In fact, she started to infiltrate JACON. And I had to send a message to JACON that "look, you better watch out for this character. This is how she left UDFN. She was thrown out. And till today, she has yet to account for our money."

Q: On account of your struggles against Abacha, you were actually penned down for treasonable felony when bombs were being thrown here and there. How do you respond to that?

A: First of all, the whole thing was part of a package—I have to reveal this to you. Before the charge for treasonable felony came about, Abacha and his

men called a meeting of West African leaders to discuss extradition. Some of
them told Abacha to go to hell. Others said "ah, this is going to be difficult."
Some others like Togo agreed and so we got wind of that and so certain
countries were no-go areas. Shortly after that meeting was the announcement
of the treasonable felony thing. The plan was that we be caught in one of the
West African countries and as a result of the extradition treaty, we will just
be put in mail bags and posted to Aso Rock. That was the whole idea.

In fact, being accused of violent crimes and so on did not even bother me
as much as the kind of assault made on me which was most contemptible,
the assault by publication. I'm talking of magazines like *Conscience International.* When I read the first edition. . . .

Q: Major Salawu contributed extensively to that edition.

A: Oh, yes, he and Abiola Ogundokun. You know, I couldn't finish it. It
took me two days. I would just read a little, go and do other positive things,
just remind myself who I was, then come back and read a couple more pages
until I finally finished reading the journal. This journal was sent all over the
world. It was sent to embassies for distribution. I'd never read such an assault
on an individual. I don't know if some of you have read this racist anti-
semitic publication of the Nazis called *The Protocols of the Elders of Zion,*
in which the Jewish race was denigrated in the most unbelievable ways.
Things were attributed to the Jewish race, that they couldn't make children.
. . . You know, the feeling in my gut was something like that. It was like all
the venom which had been heaped on the head of the reader. A copy was
sent—believe it or not—by the Chief Information Officer in the Nigerian
Mission in New York to the president of my university. His comment was,
"Are they really that desperate to treat their Nobel laureate? So, this is what
they feel is the entitlement of a political dissident who had also been a Nobel
laureate?" He treated it with total contempt and increased the security around
me. That was his reaction. He increased the security people around me. He
called the police department and told them that he wanted them to secure me
because people who are capable of writing this kind of thing may want this
man dead.

In fact, when I met General Abubakar, we had to finish the official part.
Then, as we parted, I said, "let me warn you that I'm going to sue your
mission in New York for dissemination of libel. So, I don't want to hear
tomorrow, "Oh, we spoke, it was a friendly discussion and all that, why is
the man suing us?" I'm giving you warning that I'm going to sue." And I'm

going to sue, because when we went to Edinburgh Commonwealth Summit, I had to refer to that journal and there was an Indian journalist who said, "Oh, yes, we've seen it, it's in India, it's in India." A glossy journal with my photo on the cover so that people will be interested in it. I never read such filth in all my life. It was just concocted. It just disgusted me. I just felt, what sort of a country is capable of such a thing, what manner of desperation actually leads to this kind of publication, to even take the judgement of a court and trust it? The lawyer who represented Salawu was interviewed. He lied about it. For me, that man should be de-barred. For me, this is an act of contempt of the court and you trust everything. You somersault, you attach the crime of your client to the character of a plaintiff. Anyway, there will also be a court case here. It will be the grandfather of all libel cases, now we have the time to attend to a little personal business. Before, there is no time even to think of. . . . You know, if I felt violated personally, all I had to do was to think of people like Kunle Ajibade, undergoing worse things. Now we have a little time, we have a little time, we are going to see some interesting libel suits.

Q: When this struggle started, it was basically to see to the actualisation of the results of the 1993 election. But there are so many phases that occurred thereafter. It became a battle for restoration of democracy and later a battle to make sure Abacha did not hand over to himself. How do you see that latter phase of the struggle?

A: We mustn't strive to slice the struggle into distinct phases. Each one was contingent on the other phases. Fighting to ensure that Abacha did not succeed himself was insisting that there was already an election, that there was a president-elect. And it was a cause for democracy. So, the focus, of course, shifted because here was a man, utilising the resources of the entire nation to dehumanise and enslave that nation. So, this became a very personal battle, because they saw clearly that they were in a dictator's good books today, tomorrow, they might be for the jump.

So, those who supported Abacha because they thought that he was carrying out their agenda realised that they were endangered. So, eventually, some of them took action. Let me tell you, nobody is going to persuade me that Abacha died a natural death. Let me tell that straightaway. It's like you send a dog to bring some meat, and instead of the dog returning to his master with the catch, it would start devouring it. It does it the first time, it does it the second time. Then finally, you see that the dog's gone mad and is now coming at you, so you defend yourself. Now, this to me, is the story of Abacha's death.

Now, the struggle for 12 June was written in the context of democracy. So, the struggle for democracy still goes on. The principals of that struggle have changed—some have died, some have fallen by the way side, some became enemies of the very cause which they set out to fight for, real opportunist enemies of that cause.

The issue of democracy goes beyond the issue of 12 June. When you have a civilian democracy, what it means is that there is a greater flexibility in defining and redefining the very structure and operations of democracy. That's what it means. There are issues to be settled. One of the reasons why I think Abiola's programme was popular was that he had promised to summon a sovereign national conference. This issue has not gone away and it will not go away. We have to—the word is restructure. There is no other word for it. Some people may not like that expression. But we've got to restructure in such a way that it does not matter so much who is at the centre. All these things about power must shift, power must . . . yes, it's right, it's healthy for society, when it is not seen that power is being monopolised by one section of the country. But more importantly what kind of structure is that person at the top presiding over? What are the limitations which are placed on that power? Are we still going to continue to have states going cap-in-hand to the centre to ask for what is rightfully theirs? What is the relationship of the state to the centre; how do you solve the whole problem of boundary between the states, which is being manipulated deliberately and is taking lives and property, almost routinely, from north to south, everywhere? Revenue allocation and so on and so forth. What exactly, what kind of level of autonomy must the states have? Is development going to be absolutely dependent on the centre or can we organise the economic pattern of the nation in such a way that states can decide their own priorities and develop at their own pace? Education for instance, are we going to continue with the situation where a minister of education can just draw a line across the country and say all principals of federal institutions above this line, go back to your places of origin? What sort of country are we running? There has to be a level playing field in order to choose who is going to head the government.

So, the struggle for democracy has not died as a result of the death of Abiola. On the contrary, it's become more intense. Because those who killed Abiola did it simply because they had sworn, and they said it openly. So, it's not putting words into their mouth or imagining their motivation; they will go to any length to ensure that power does not go to certain parts of the country. We cannot pretend that that is not there. We cannot abandon the right of any individual to aspire to the presidency of this nation. That has to be fought, also on its own terms. All I'm saying is that for me, it's far more important, far more crucial, to decide what is going to be the structure of this democracy.

Q: You mentioned that Abacha did not die naturally and that Abiola was killed. Do you want to share some information with us?

A: First of all, I've said elsewhere that I got a note—I received it from one of my listening posts. I was travelling rapidly at that time and the note was just following me, until it eventually caught up with me about three days after Abiola died.

It said, "Desperate! Desperate!" It said everything must be done to get Abiola out of custody immediately, that the cabal had sworn that he would not come out alive, that they didn't care if the country exploded as a result of his death. Abiola must not come out alive.

I immediately contacted our people to see what could be done to put pressure on this regime to get him out of there. Already, it was scandalous that Abiola had stayed in prison that long. There was no reason why he should have been there one day longer. And as I have said before, I hold Abubakar's regime for this death, by neglect, by failing to release Abiola immediately. I also hold a number of international civil servants for accepting the unethical process of going to pressure him in prison to release his mandate—there's absolutely no excuse for it—the Commonwealth, the United Nations, the U.S., European Union, these are all organisations founded on democracy. These are all organisations founded on democracy and the justice of human rights. And yet their representatives were going to Abiola in prison to try to pressurise him to give up his mandate instead of going there to say take this man out, let him consult in liberty.

I used to say to my colleagues, "Listen, if Abiola says he's renouncing the mandate, don't worry, let him come out. And then let him say it. It's only what he says in freedom that is valid." And so for international civil servants to go there and tell him, "Oh, we've been taking legal advice and your mandate has expired," "Oh, if you abandon your mandate, the regime is ready to . . ." For me, these are criminal acts. And if we are to go back to your questions, the longer he stayed there, of course, the surer it was, that whatever was done to him was already taking effect. And don't forget, we now have evidence of various slow-acting poisons you could use against people in prison.

Remember that Yar'Adua, before he died—we carried it on Radio Kudirat—Yar'Adua had told people that he'd been forcibly injected with something. He didn't fall down immediately and die. I'm convinced that Abiola's death had been decided by Abacha. I'm convinced that Abacha was responsible for the murder of Abiola. The process had been set in motion, probably accelerated towards the end so that he could die in the presence of either international witnesses or even maybe this own people, when they go visiting. He collapses and that will be all.

As for Abacha, he died in the hands of his masters, those who were convinced at the beginning that he was carrying out their mandate. Instead of softening up relations for their eventual takeover, while Abiola had begun dying. I'm convinced Abiola had begun dying before Abacha met his end.

Q: What of Abacha himself?

A: I think we know exactly. . . . You see these things, you cannot be 100 per cent certain, but let me tell you that we think we know exactly how Abacha died. We've heard rumours, we've listened to the various versions here. We think there is some grain of truth in certain things but the linkage has not been made with Abacha's murder—sorry, not murder, because that's not murder. He was executed.

Q: You never met Abacha. . . .

A: I met him, I studied him, that's why I knew him. I sized him up very accurately.

Q: What can you say about the system that threw up a man like that to be Nigeria's head of state?

A: It is sad, it is sad. It is not a good reflection of the military itself. The civilians had nothing to do with it. It is the military who created Abacha. They had the opportunity, several times, incidentally, to get rid of him, because they knew him. They knew he was a psychopath. And they had opportunity of getting rid of him. In fact, he was recommended for dismissal a couple of times. But you see, some of them needed him around to do their dirty jobs. And after doing the dirty job for others, the man said, "Why not me, have I got tail behind my legs? Why not me too?"

Q: Do some comparison between Abdulsalami Abubakar and Sani Abacha.

A: Oh, my God! There is no comparison between the two. If one has to compare Abdulsalami with anybody, it would be with Babangida. Which means we have to be very, very careful. He's smooth, he's very personable, he's very likeable. But, as I always say, it's the constituency that matters, it is not so much the personality.

There is no way you can compare Abacha with any human being on earth. Remember, I've said before that I don't even believe he's a Nigerian and I even suspect that he doesn't belong to this world, that he dropped from the outer world, somewhere. There's nothing you can compare Abacha with.

Q: How did you come to meet Abubakar? Did you contact him?

A: No way, no, no, no. He requested to meet us. There'd been indirect contacts from his side. His people phoned me. A friend just called me and said, "If he wants to talk to you, can I give them your phone number?" And I said, "Why not?"

Q: Just by way of a little information. You went straight from the airport to visit the family of Basorun M.K.O. Abiola. And at the graveside of Alhaja Kudirat, you said "Long Live Radio Kudirat." How long do you want to operate this radio?

A: As long as the cause for democracy is still being fought anywhere. We are working very hard to quickly internationalise Radio Kudirat. The struggle for democracy is not over here first, so Radio Kudirat is absolutely essential. Even when the civilian regime comes, we've got to have Radio Kudirat to continue, in or out, to monitor the process. And we want to open it out eventually. This is very, very ambitious to the democratic cause in other societies.

But, of course, my immediate task is the Truth Commission. We will invite people like you, who may want to record your experience, send them to Radio Kudirat—details: names, time, hours, etc.

Abdulsalami says this is not his priority. Alright, that's fine. But the whole essence of democracy is that people must want to do things for themselves, not wait for a central authority. There is no reason why you, you cannot set up a Truth Commission, cannot begin a national conference. Those who want to attend will attend, those who don't want to attend will not attend. If you remember, under Babangida, an attempt was made to organise a conference on the national question. So, we're not waiting. Of course, it's easier if it's backed by authority, if it's backed by resources and so on. But if it's only one naira we have, we have a one-naira Truth Commission. If it's one naira we have, we'll have a one-naira national conference. So, the Truth Commission is starting. It's starting with the evidence, the collaboration of people like you, we're going to talk to officials, we're going to talk to children. "What was it like when they came to take your father, what was it like when they came to take your mother?" We want people to understand. Because we have a short memory in this country. You know, we have a very, very, sadly, criminally short memory and that is why these things happen to us again and again and again. But, if we had an on-going Truth Commission with all these facts, with all the testimony of people and we gather all the evidence. . . . And remember, by the way, we started the Truth Commission long before now. Before the Commonwealth Summit in Edinburgh, we set up a tribunal in London. It sat for two days, took evidence. We had people who came from Nigeria, from their various places of exile, to give testimony about what was happening under Abacha. We called it a preliminary hearing. It was presided over, by the way, by a jurist. We sent the report to the summit to assist them in deciding whether such a country was due or deserved to be called back into the fold of the Commonwealth.

So, what Radio Kudirat is doing now is in the continuation of that tradition that we initiated. And for several minutes we hope to give testimony on it. We have commentary on it. And those who are accused will be given a chance to respond; if they don't respond, that is their business. If you give evidence against Major Mustapha, for instance, we'll tell Major Mustapha, "You have a right to respond. Come and defend yourself." The son of Abacha, who is accused of applying electric prods to people, will be given his chance to come and say what he thought it was, whether it was a toy, whether it was his father who taught him, whether that's how he was brought up, or whether he was accustomed to herding cattle. We want the evidence of Col. Gwadabe, Obasanjo, we want to interview him, let him say exactly what happened to him. Col. Bello Fadile, who gave evidence against him, who was tortured, let him come and say exactly what was done to him. Let people understand what happened in this dark period in the name of the nation.

Q: One of the happiest people today will certainly be General Abdulsalami Abubakar. Are you not bothered that he could use your coming back to Nigeria to justify the claim that things have returned to normal and they are moving towards democracy?

A: If Abubakar wants to profit from my visit here, by all means. But I know what I came to do here, that I've come to assess the situation on the spot myself and consult with the pro-democracy people inside. Honestly, we have a lull, an interlude, if he wants to use it for propaganda, and it was used. Oh, that reminds me, I need to ask for an autographed copy.

Q: There are so many candidates jostling for the presidency now. But what kind of president do you think would be able to take Nigeria through this transition to what would be called a democracy?

A: A kind of president who will be controlled by a democratic structure. In other words, let's concentrate on the structure. This country has shown that even a moron can actually say he is ruling this country. It doesn't mean that he is beloved by anybody. It doesn't mean that he even understands how to run his household. The important thing is to be able to confine power within certain limits and be able to call power to account. That's all.

A president doesn't need to do what he doesn't like to do. Even economic facts can restrain a president. Of course, we want an ideal president. This country is not short of talents. It used to make me mad, when these accommodating foreign governments will say, "Yes, but if he goes, who do you put there next?" It is so insulting. So I say, "Let's analyse your head of state: he did this, he did this, he did this. Is that the ideal head of state? Why haven't you had a military coup here? You are trying to ask me that if this animal goes, what human beings do you have to take his place?" So, I have no doubt at all that we have somebody who will obey the rule of democracy.

Q: Will that person include some of the ex-military men who are trying to stage a come back?

A: I think that it depends on what rank you're talking of. There're some people you don't even know; they were former military officers.

Q: Like Generals-Obasanjo and company?

A: All I can say is that in a democracy anybody can put himself forward as president. It's up to you and I to decide what qualities we want from them, what their background is, whether we think their background is conducive to genuine democratic dispensation. It's up to us. But I will not support the idea of formally, officially banning anyone. No, I will not support it. But I reserve my right to campaign heavily against any individual whom I believe is disqualified by their past history or by their present conduct. That's my right.

Q: For how long are you going to be around?

A: My visit will be six days, so you mustn't take up any more of my time.

Q: The Ogun State Government has offered to renovate your house; are you going to accept that offer?

A: I read about it. And all I have to say is that I appreciate the gesture. But it will be most improper of me to accept any kind of personal rehabilitation. In fact, it is unthinkable that I should be the beneficiary of any project of rehabilitation. There are lots of starving people who plain justice demands should be rehabilitated. Whether they are Ogoni, whether they are journalists or even business people who have been deliberately impoverished by Abacha's dehumanising policies. Let various state governments announce a tested programme of rehabilitation and I will take my place. I'm not too proud. I'll show you, this is not pride. I mean, I can use some rehabilitation myself. But, let a programme be announced; I'll take my place in correct order of necessity. Let the government accept the principle of reparation for all those who have suffered under the previous regime and I'll be the happiest person in the world. When I go to my house and see the damage done to my house, I will sue and I will get the court order to the military to repair the damage they caused.

Q: There was a time Abacha was looking for you. They suspected you had sneaked back into the country. Did you do so?

A: I prefer to leave that question unanswered for now.

Index

5975

AED - 2786